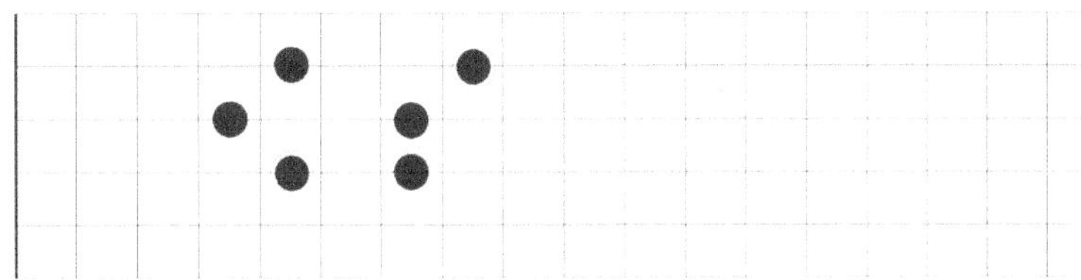

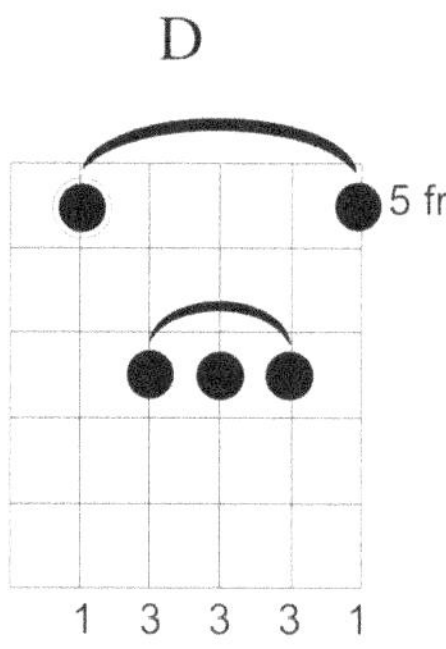

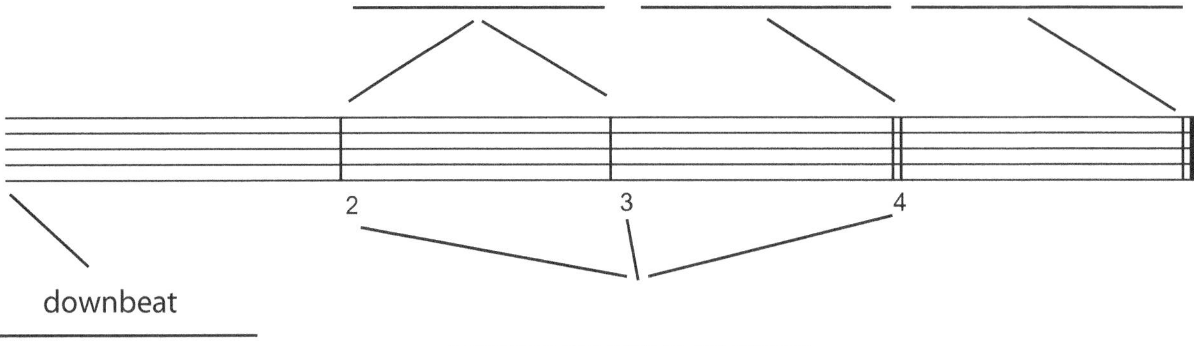


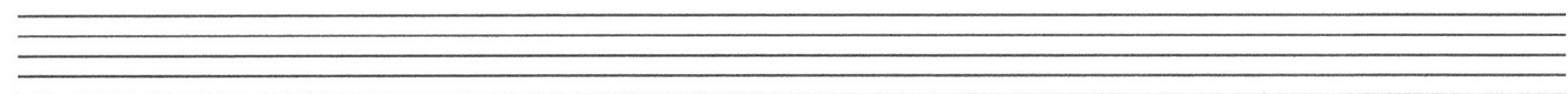

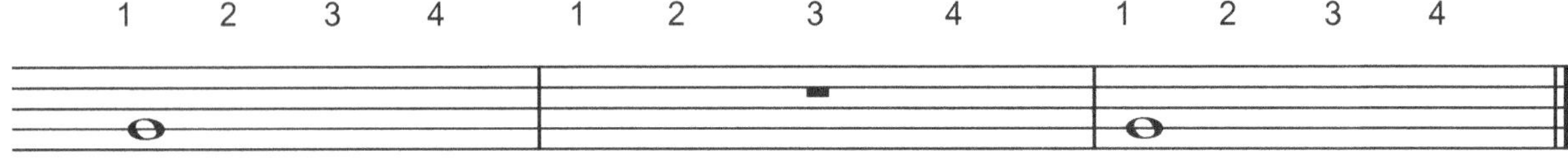


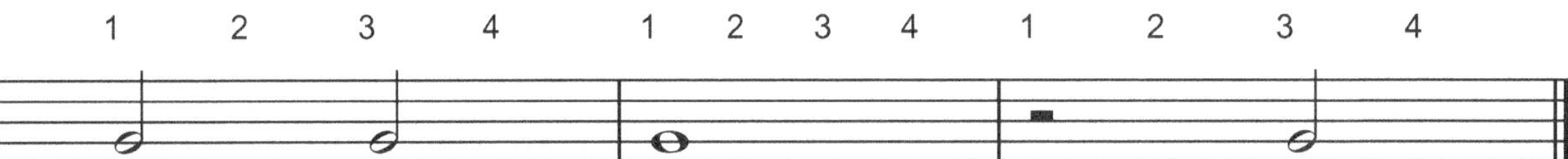

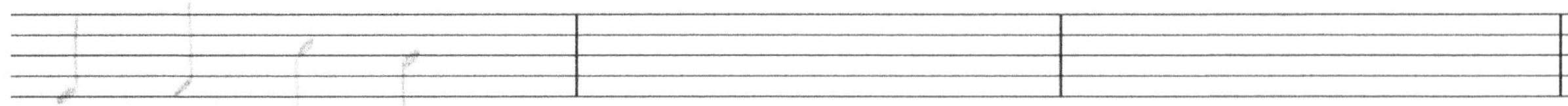

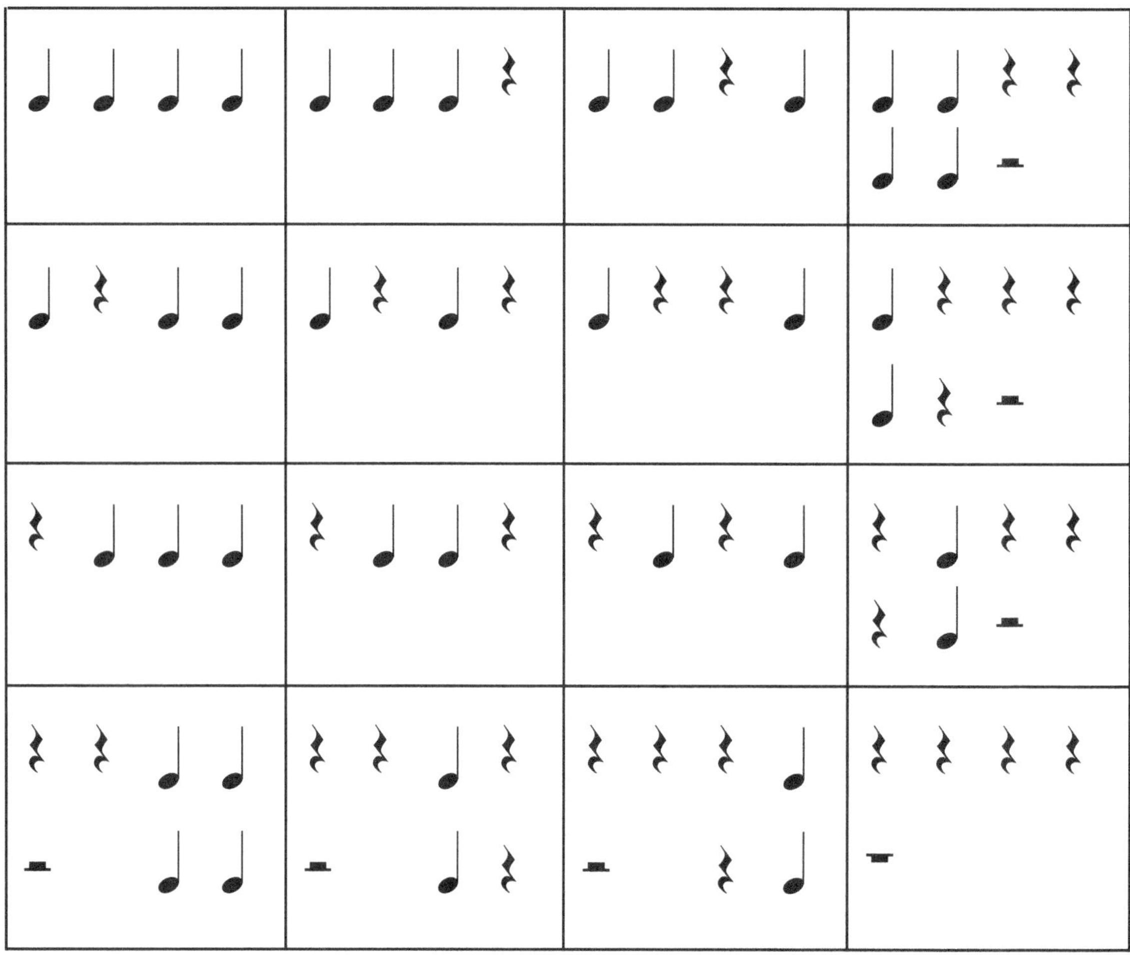

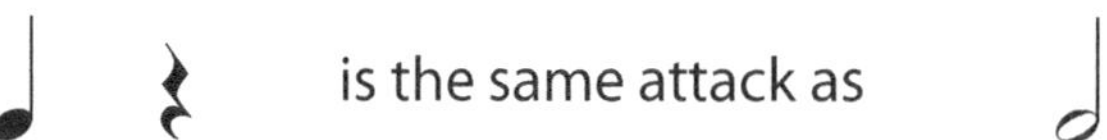

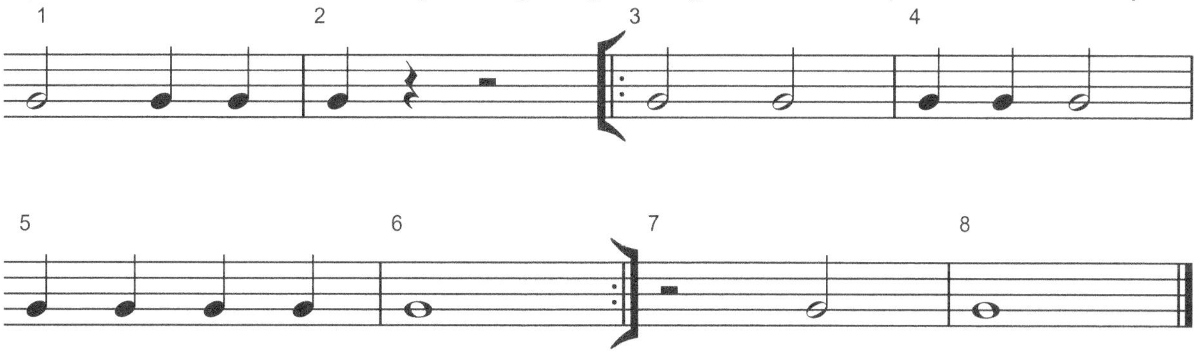

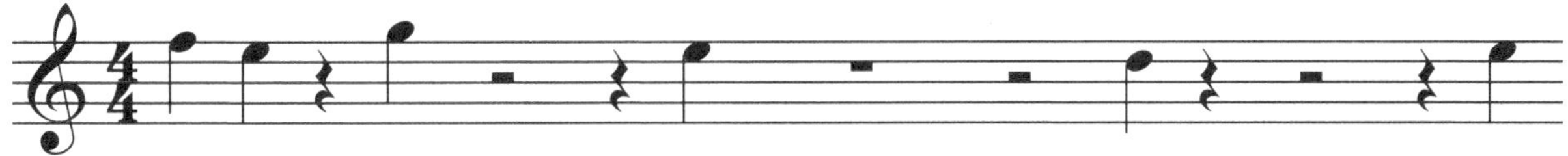

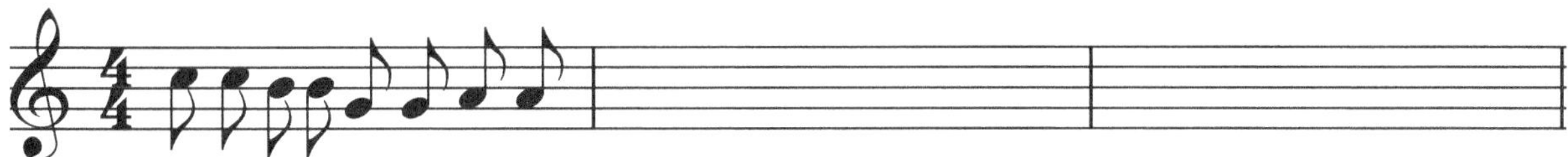

   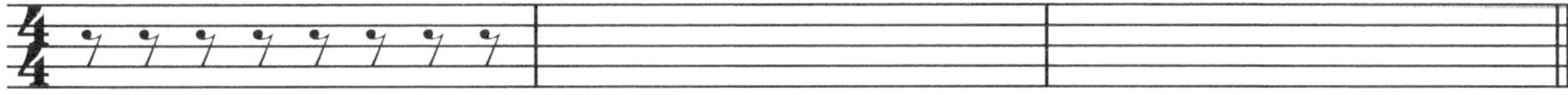

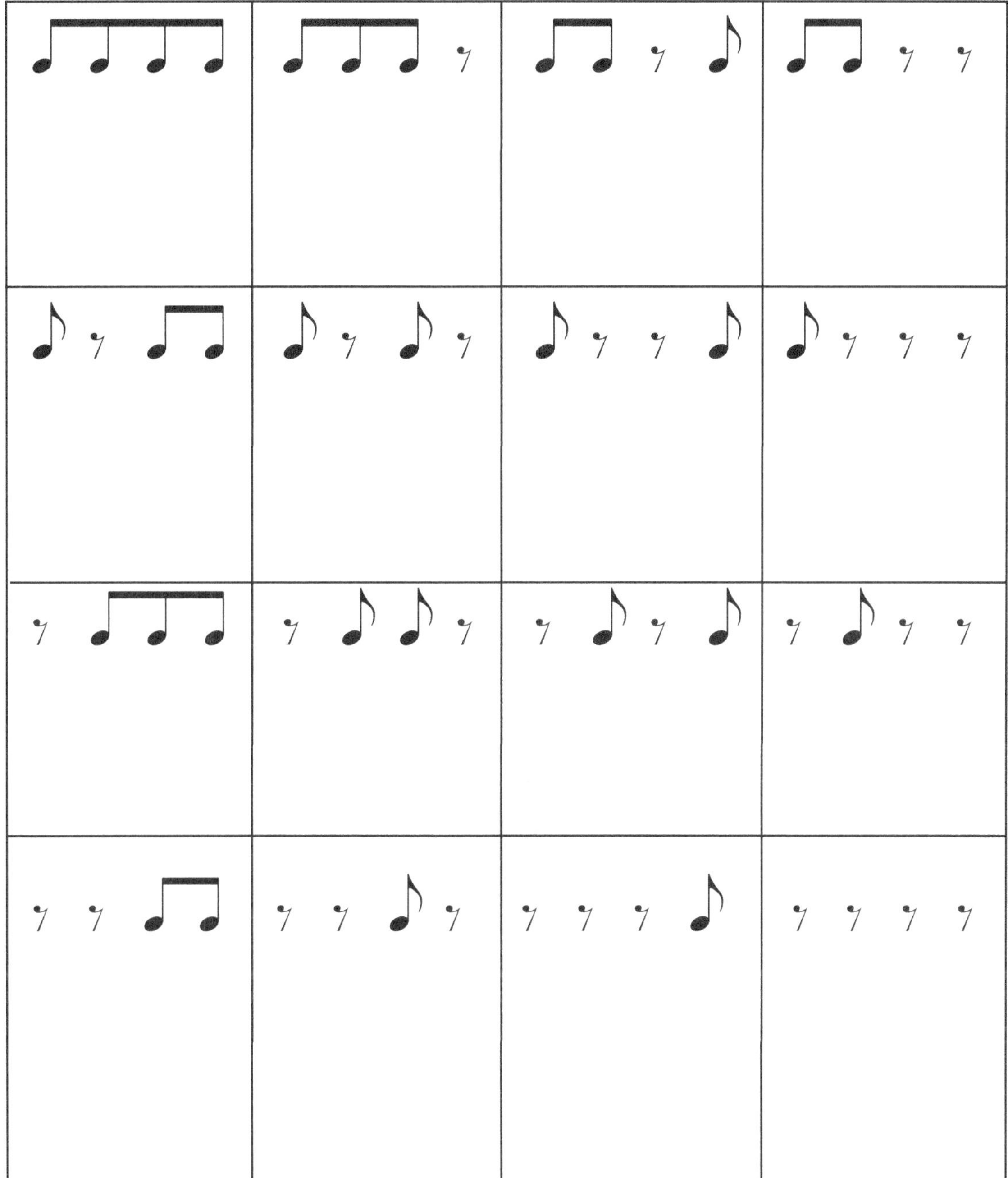

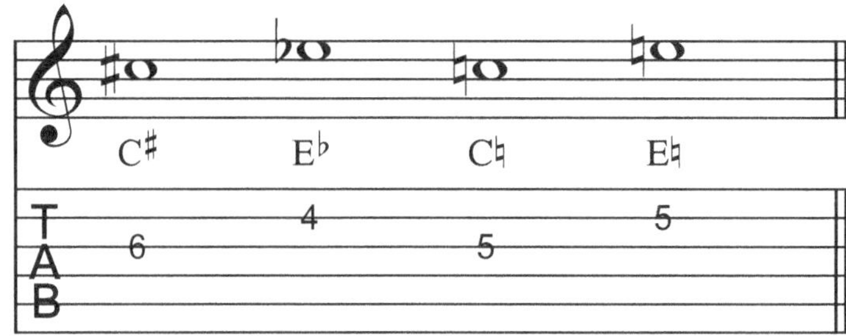


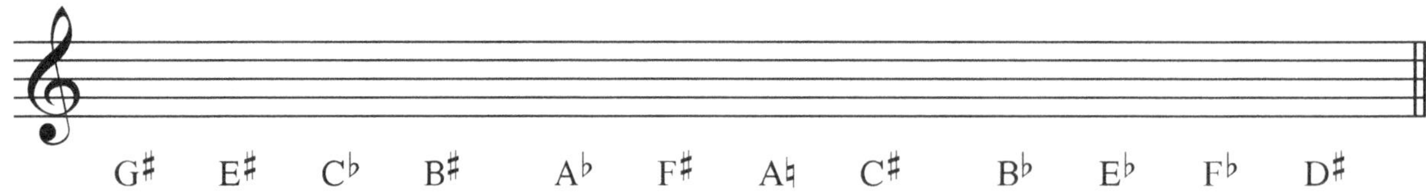

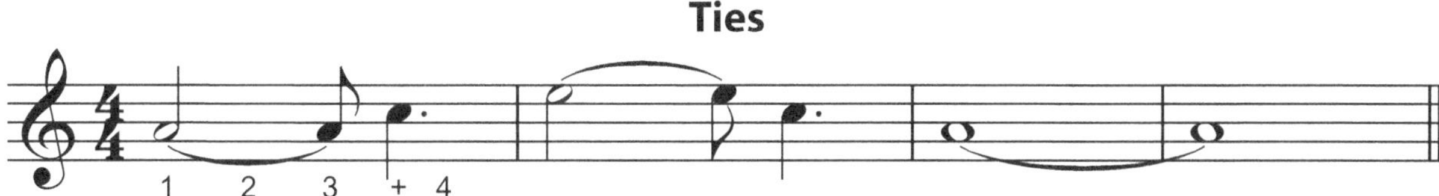

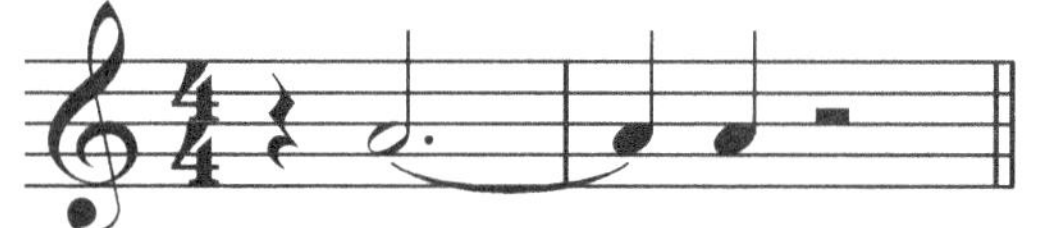

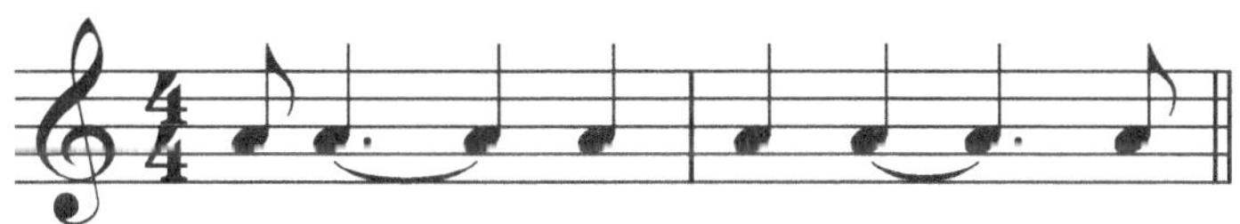

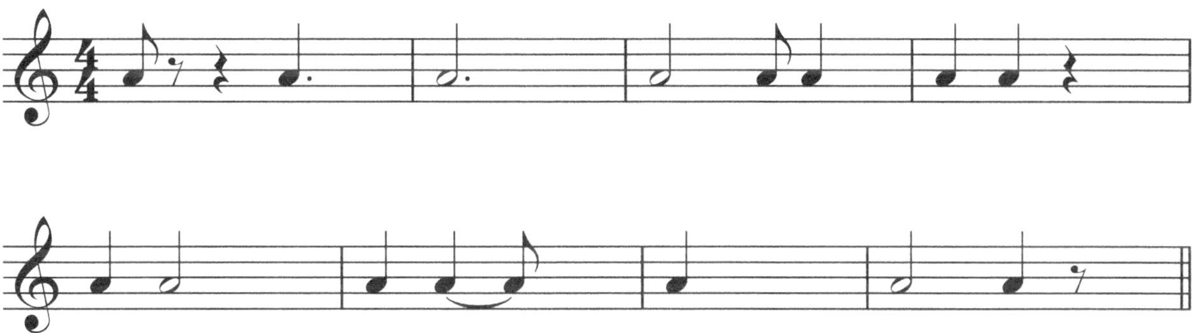

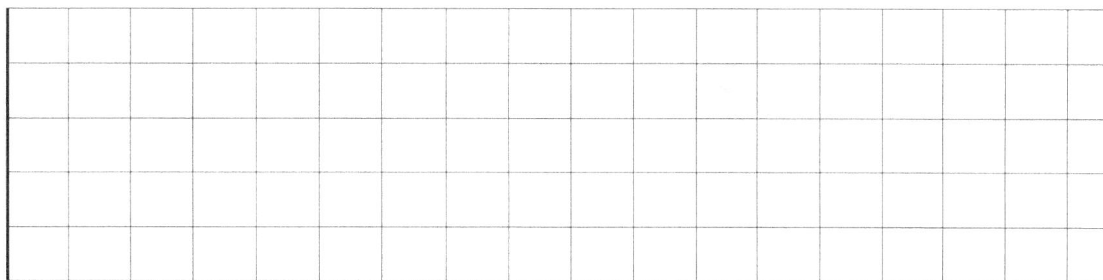

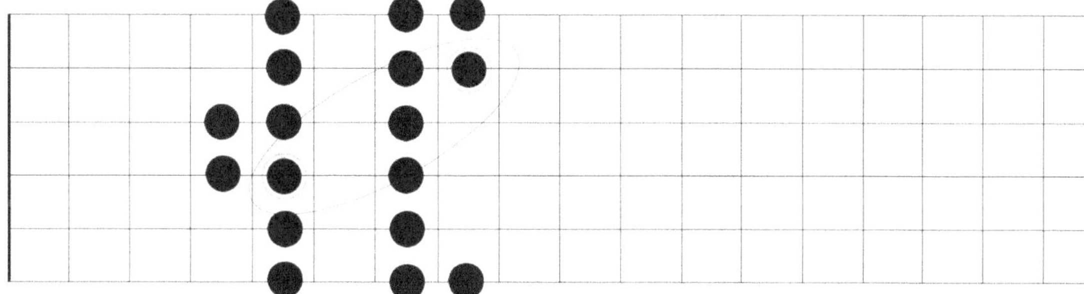

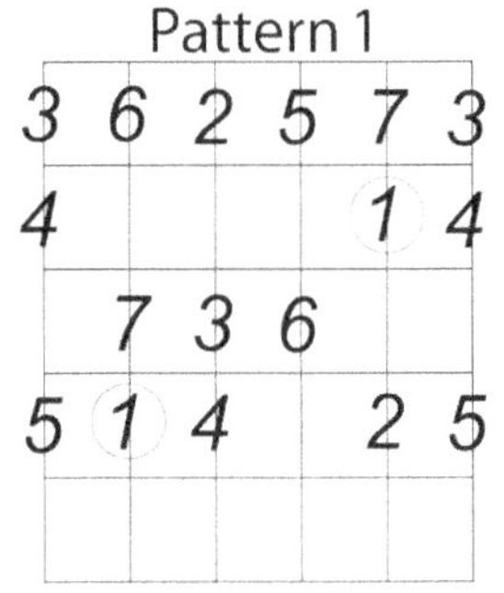

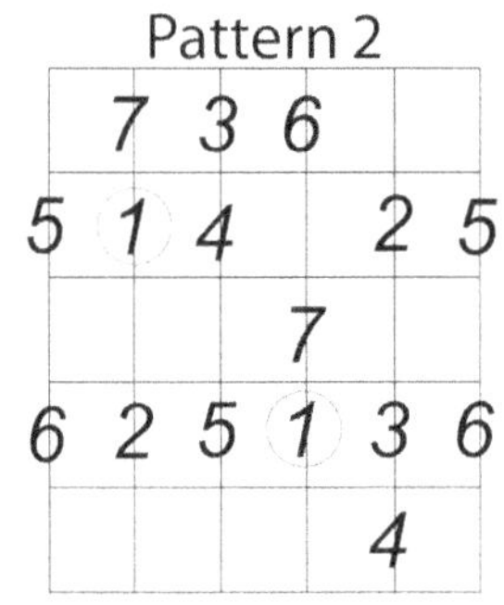

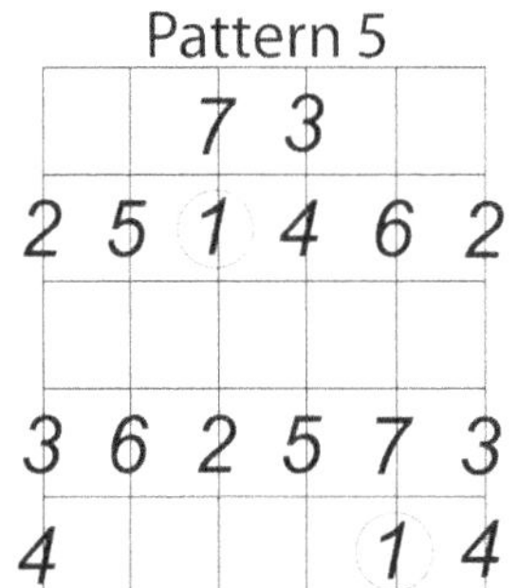

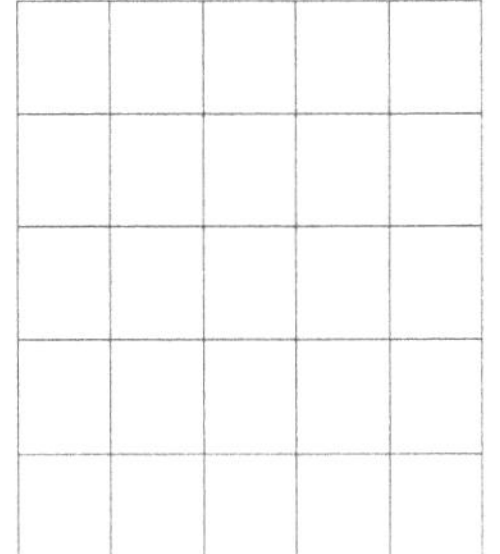

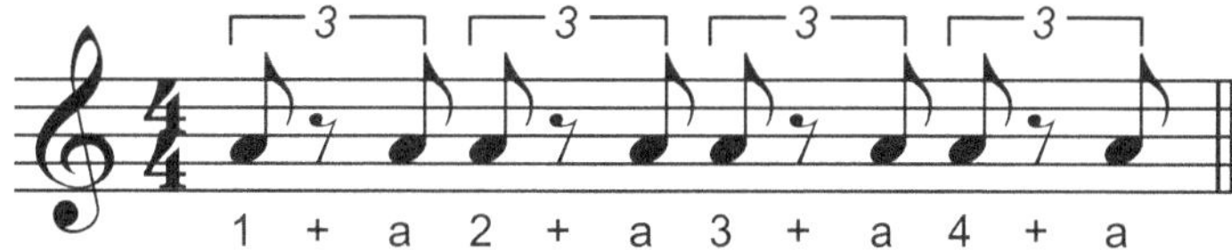


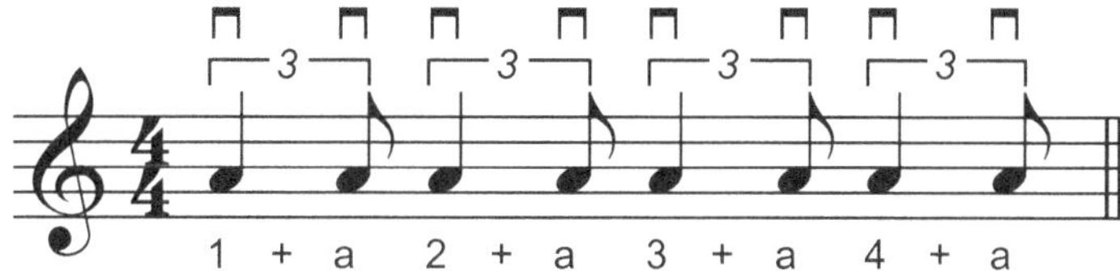

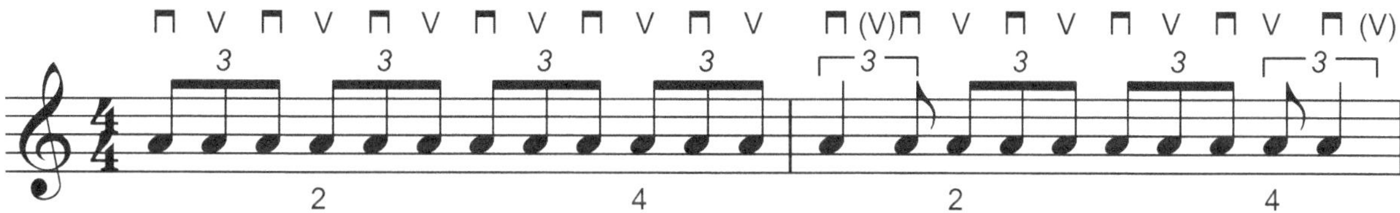

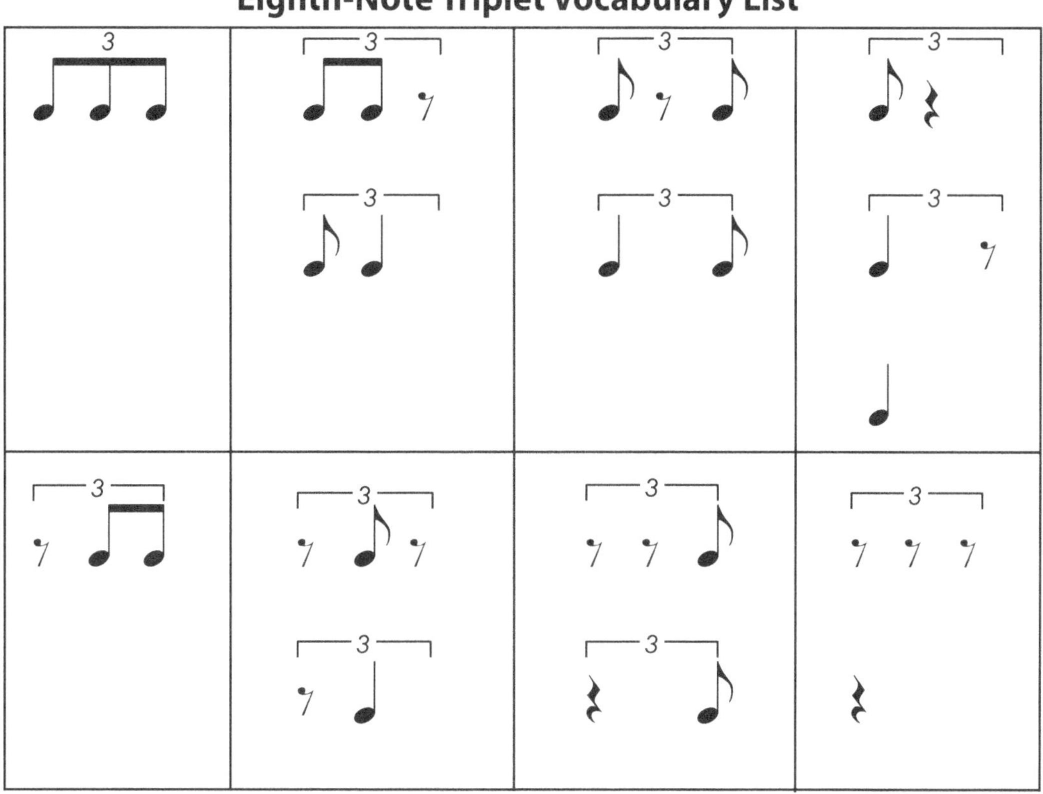

Notice the pattern: all odd-numbered intervals (1, 3, 5, 7) are on like staff positions: two space notes or two line notes. Even-numbered intervals (2, 4, 6, 8) are on different staff positions: a line and a space, or vice versa.

Exercise 66.

Write a series of diatonic 6ths ascending and descending the C major scale.

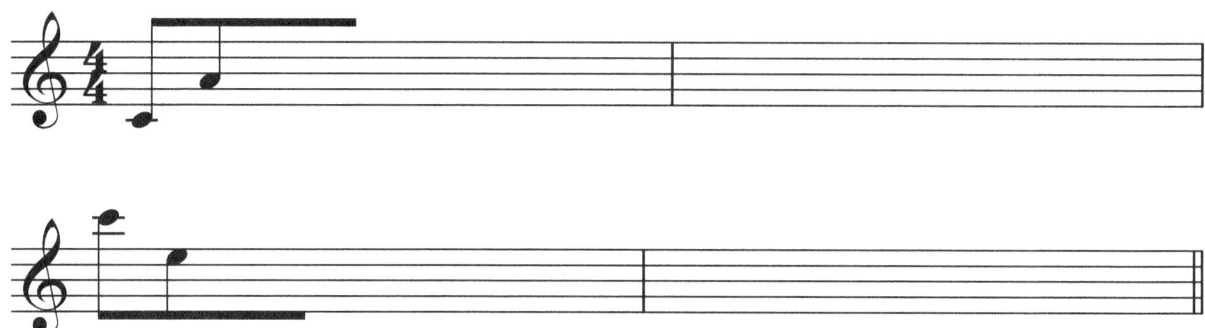

Exercise 67.

After each given note, write a notehead that is higher by the diatonic interval indicated.

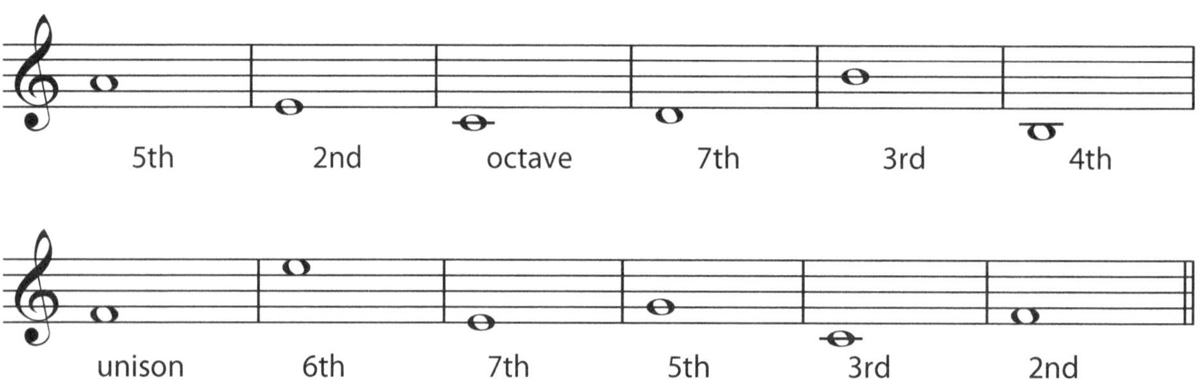



Exercise 68.

After each given note, write a notehead that is lower by the diatonic interval indicated.

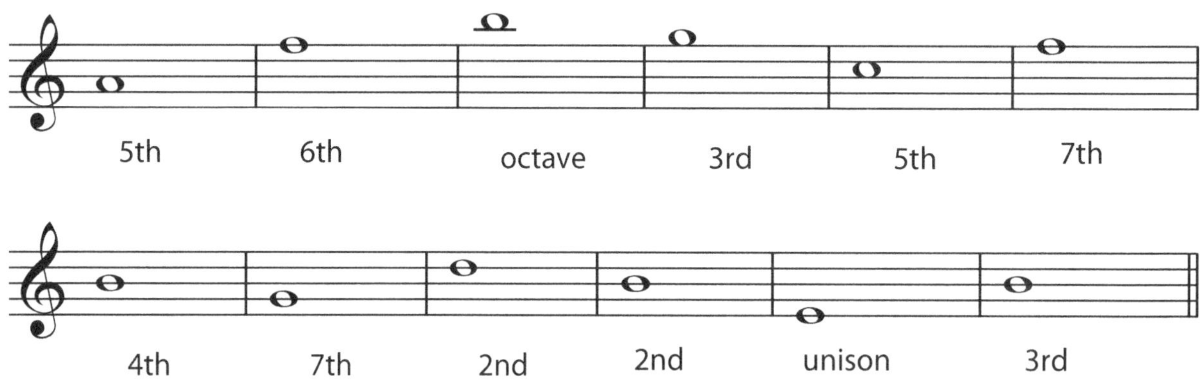

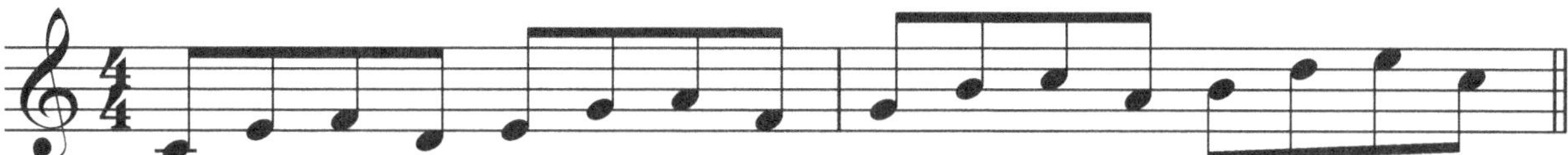

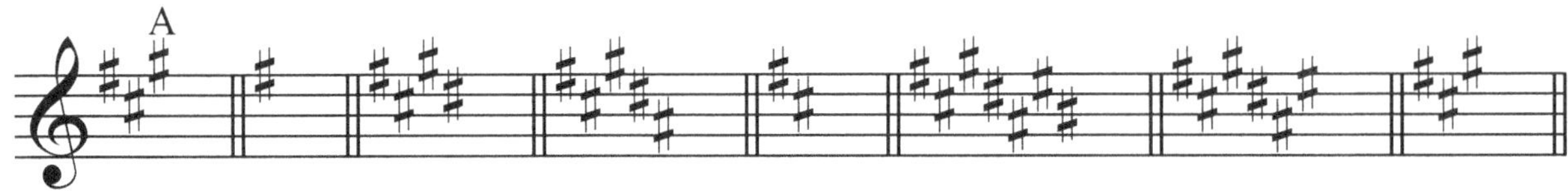


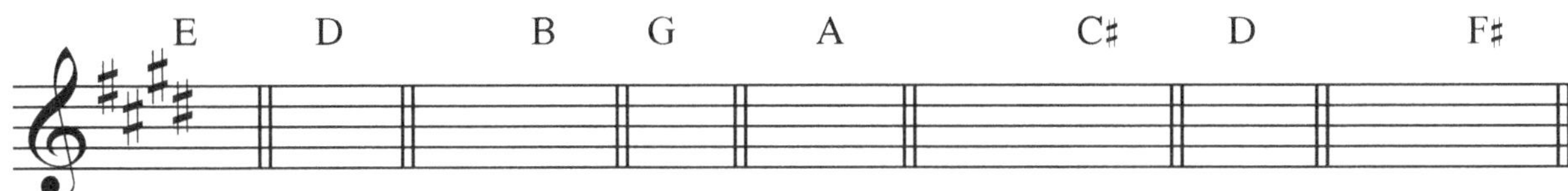

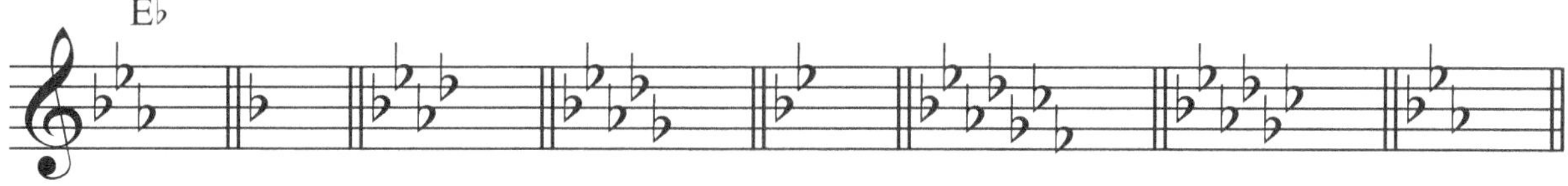


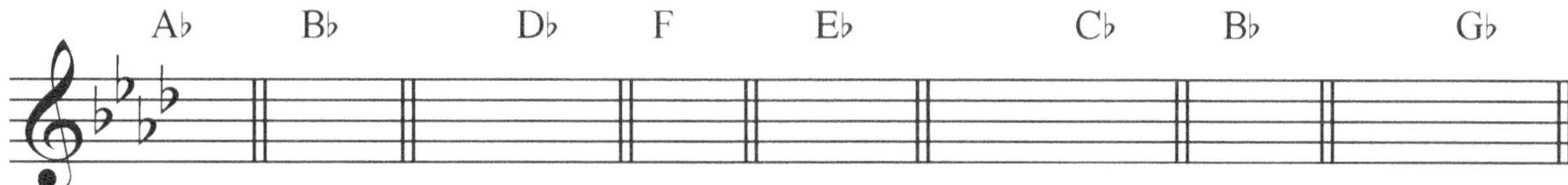

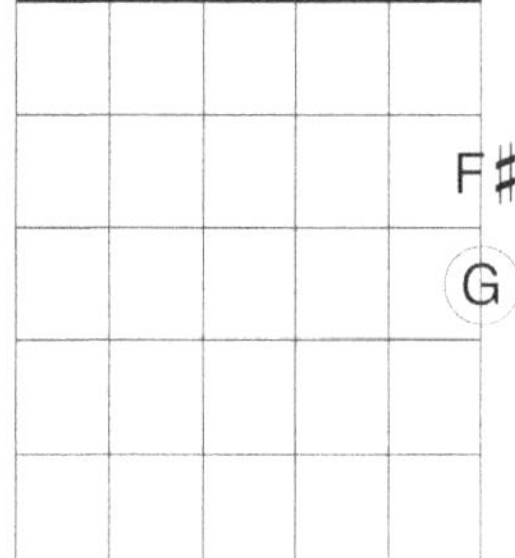

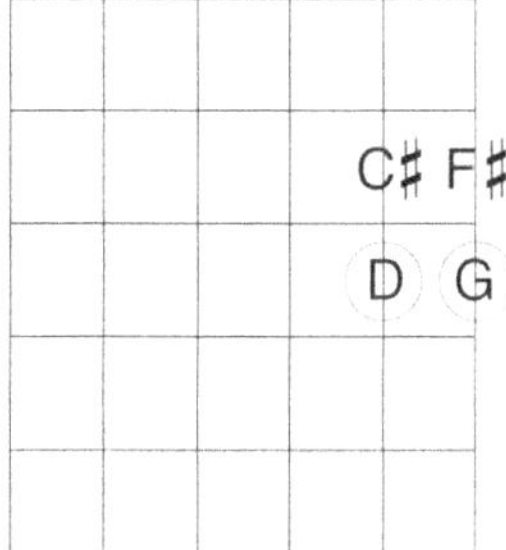

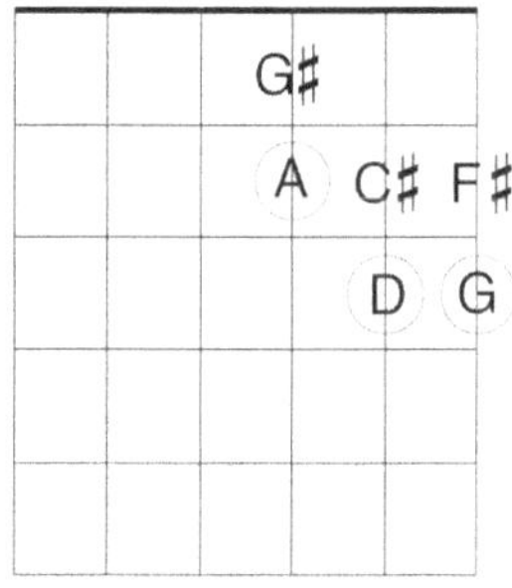

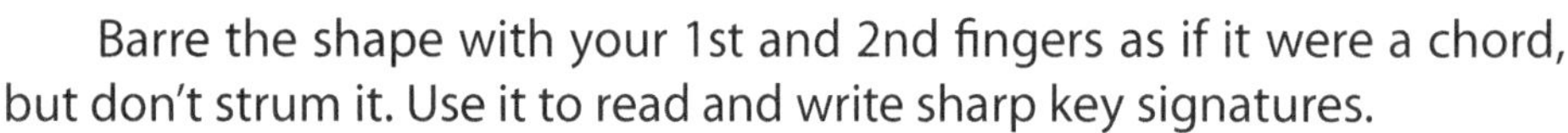


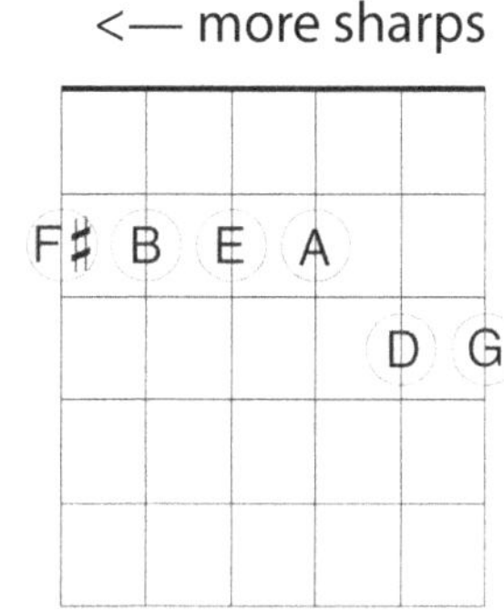

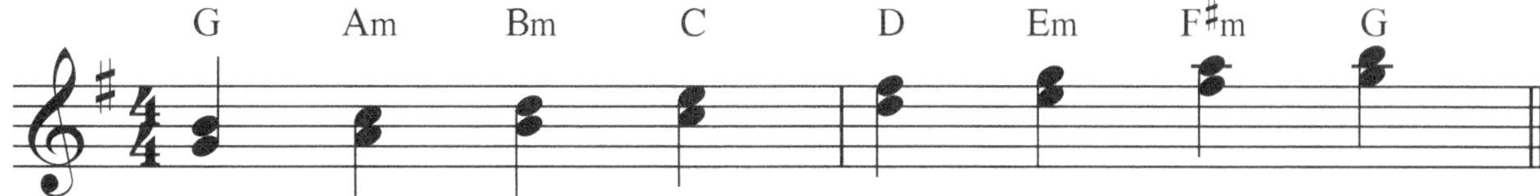


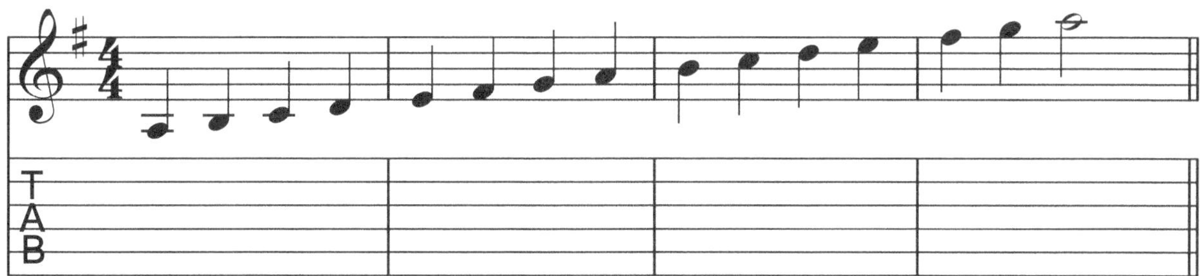

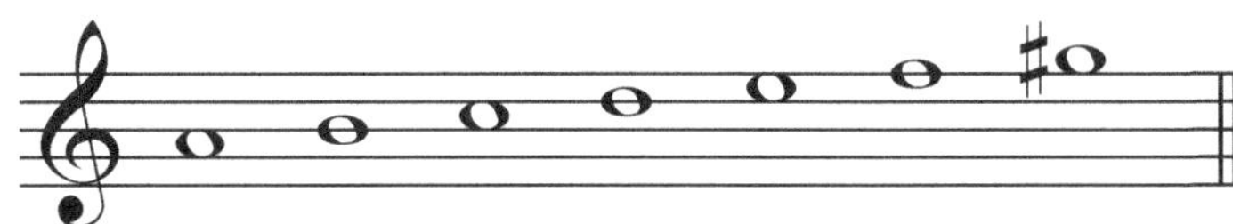

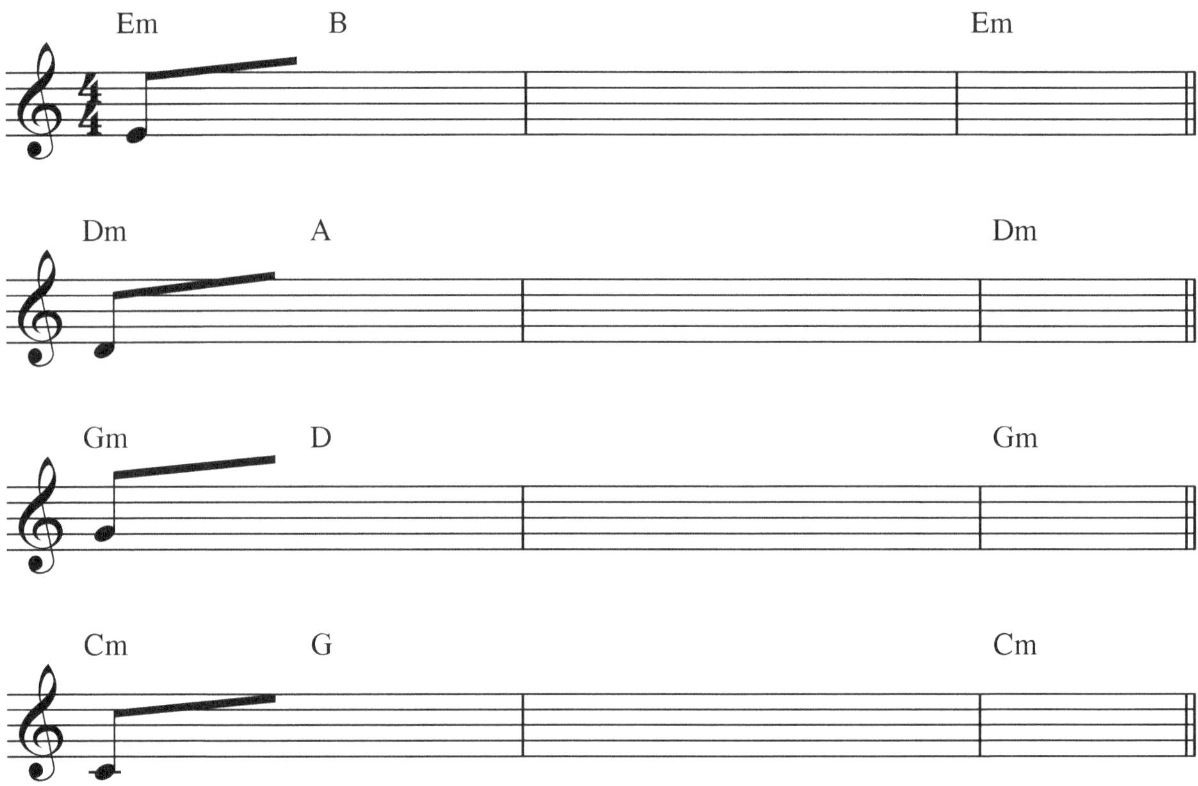

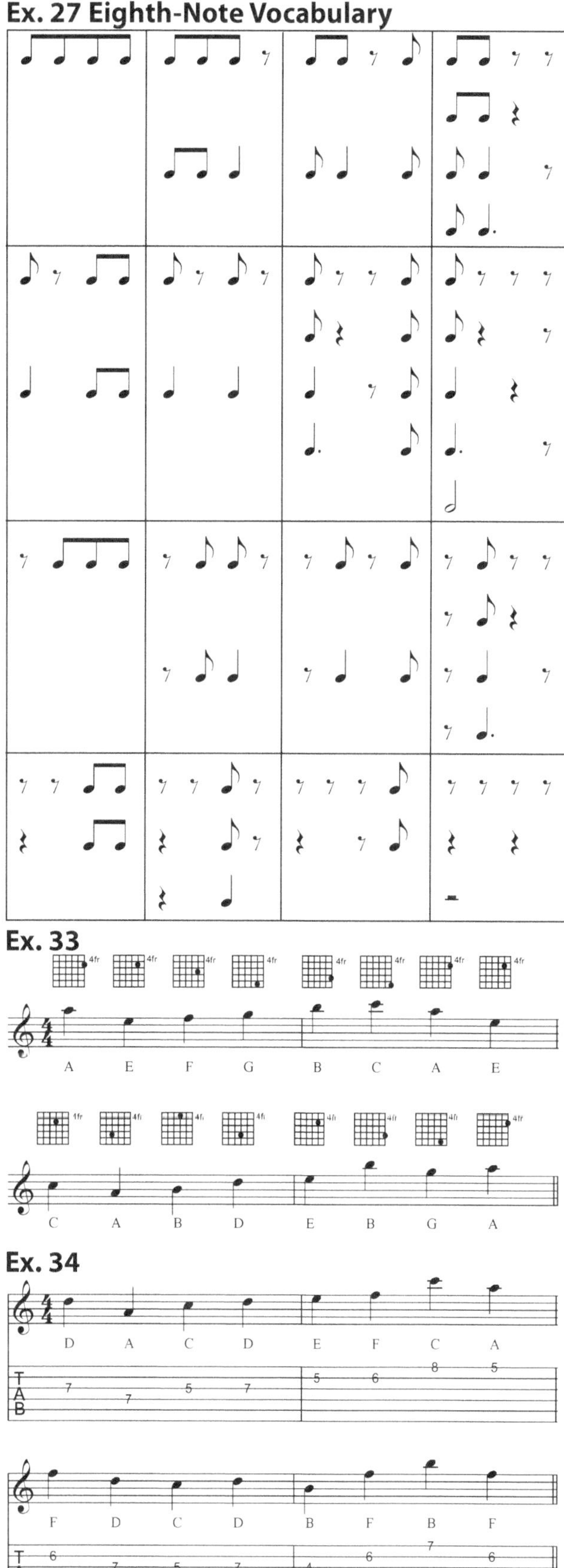

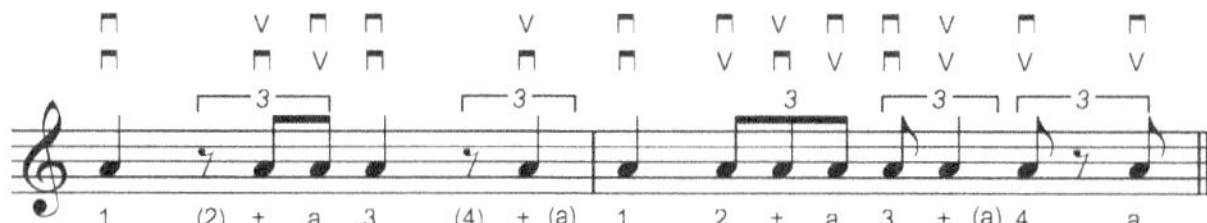

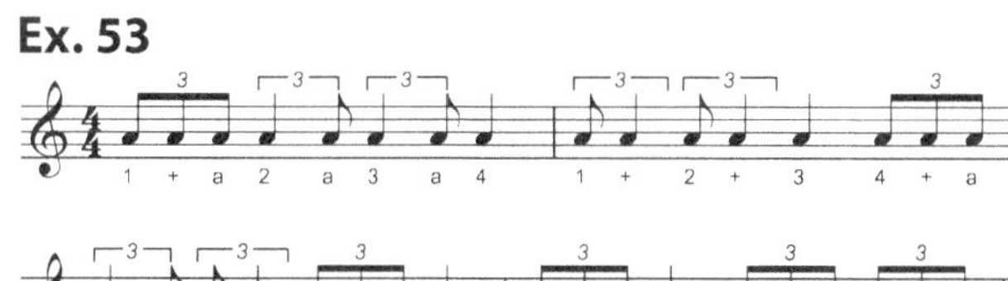

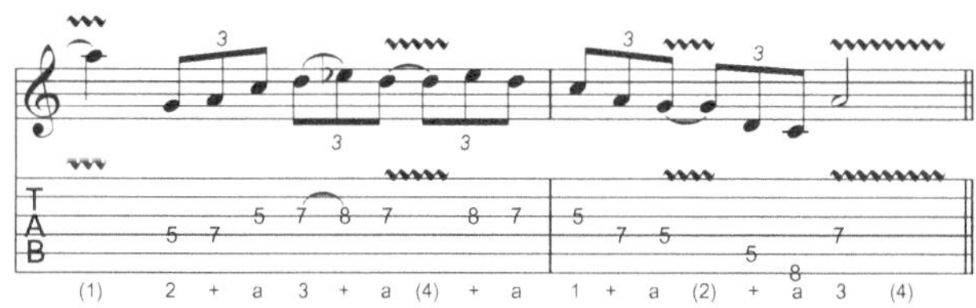

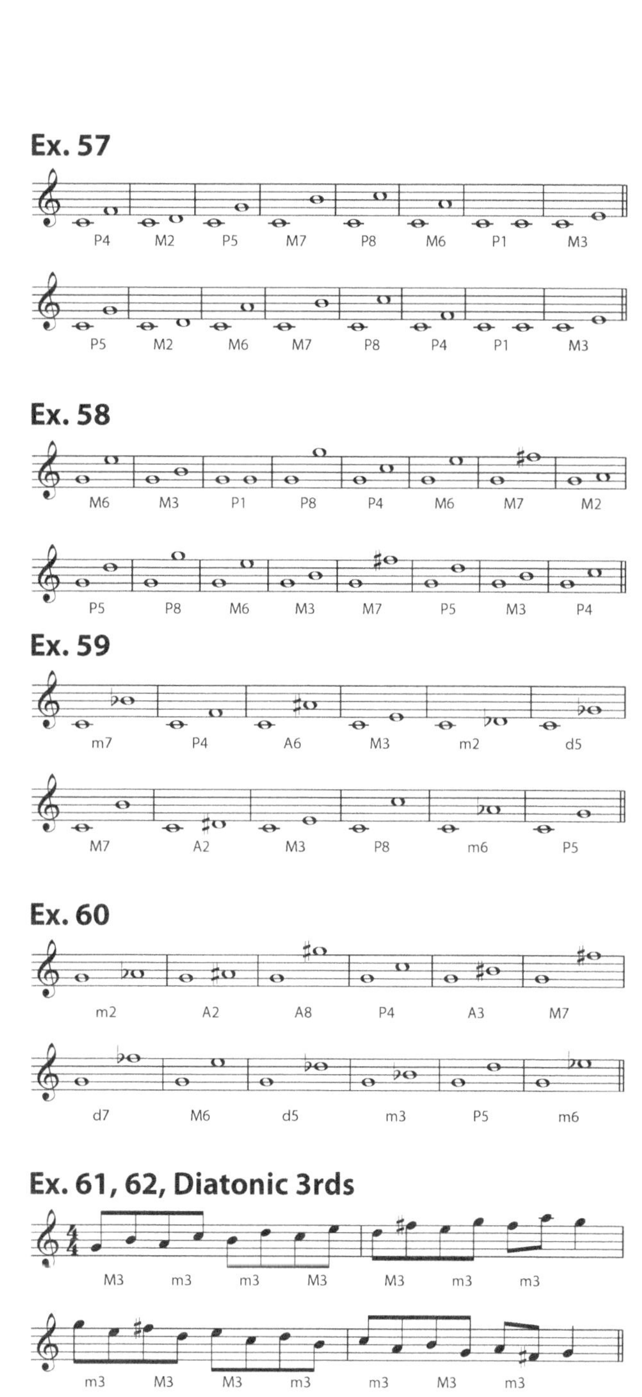

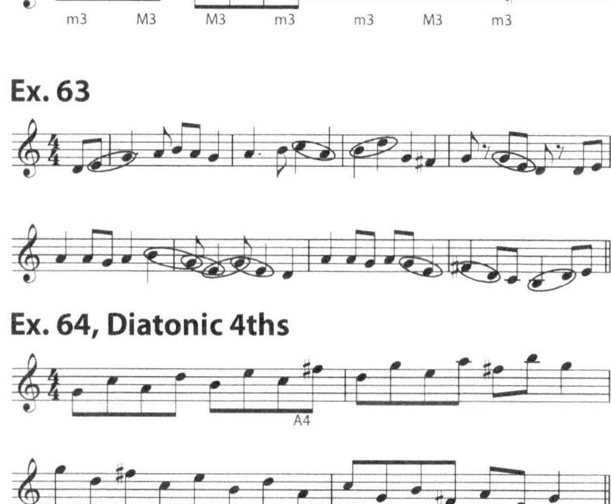

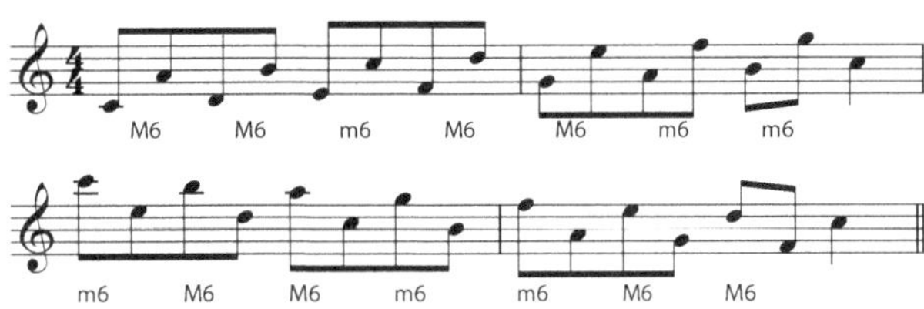


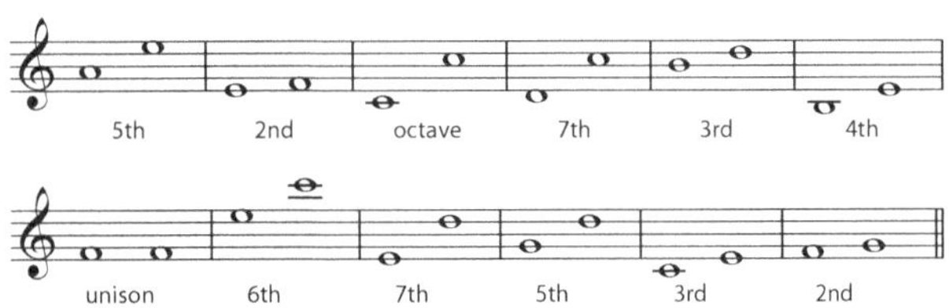


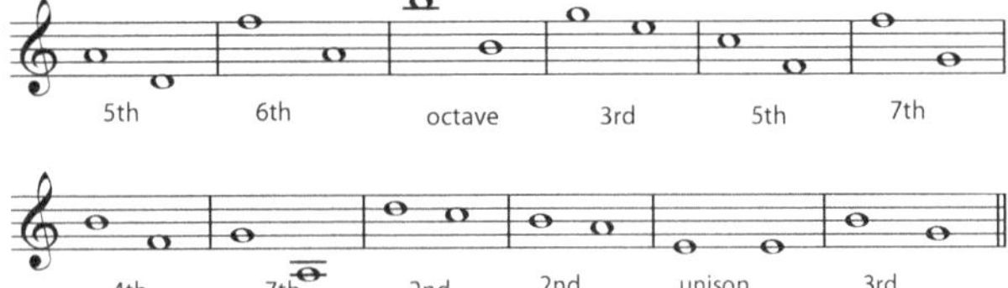

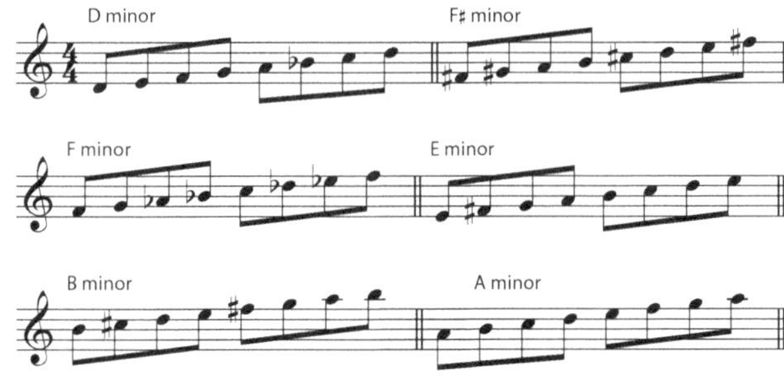


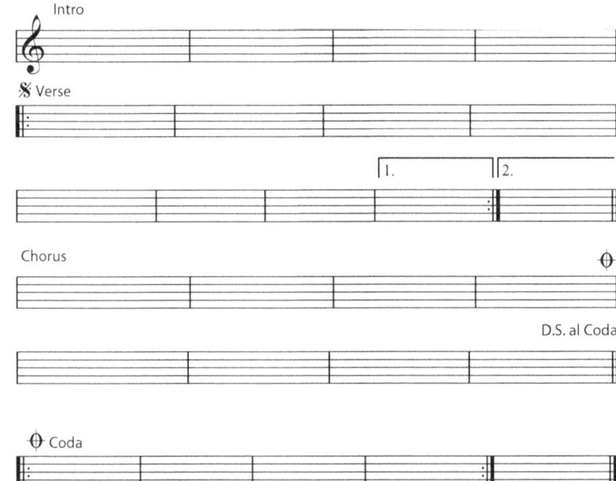


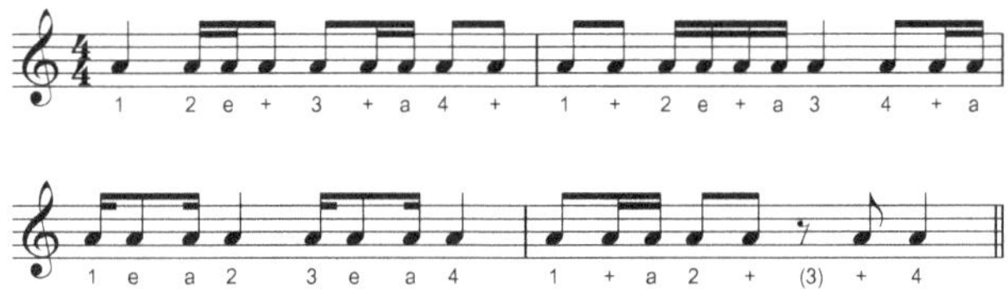

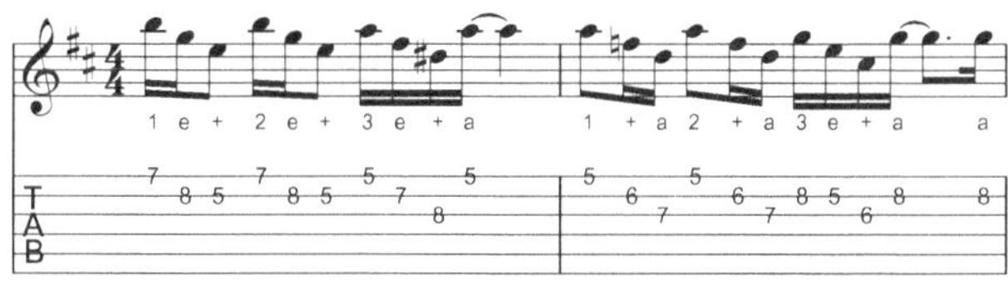

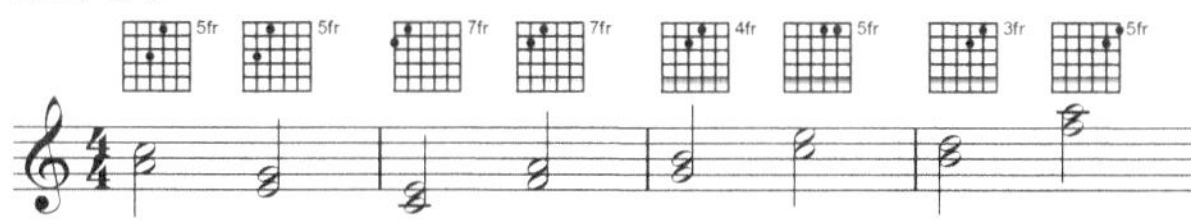

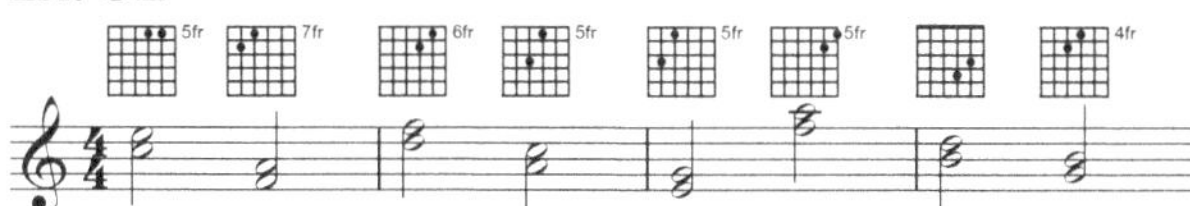

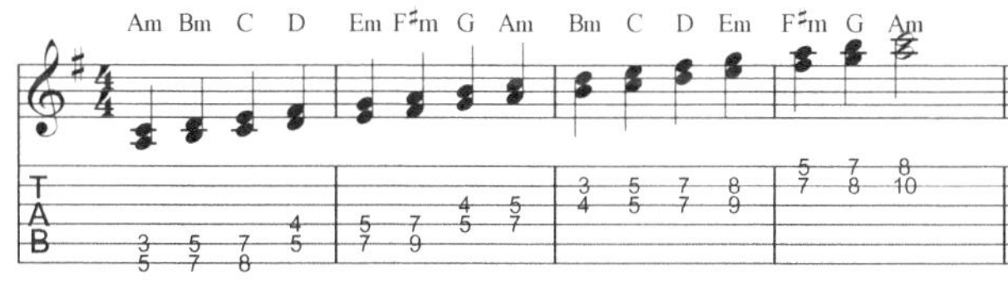

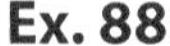

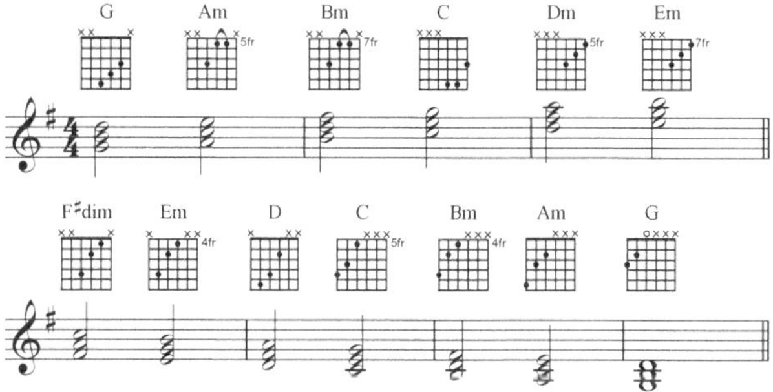

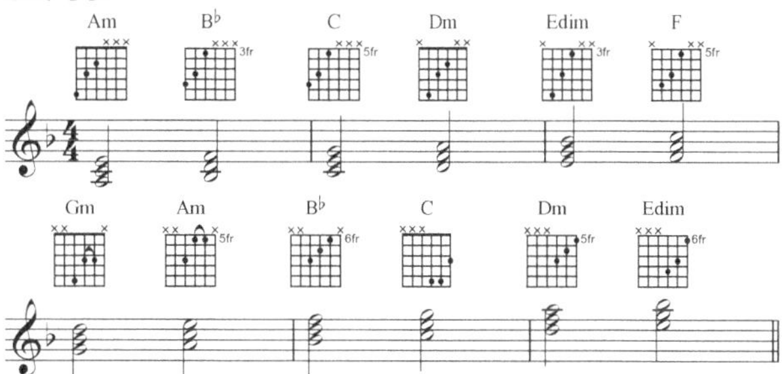

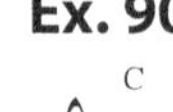

## Ex. 90

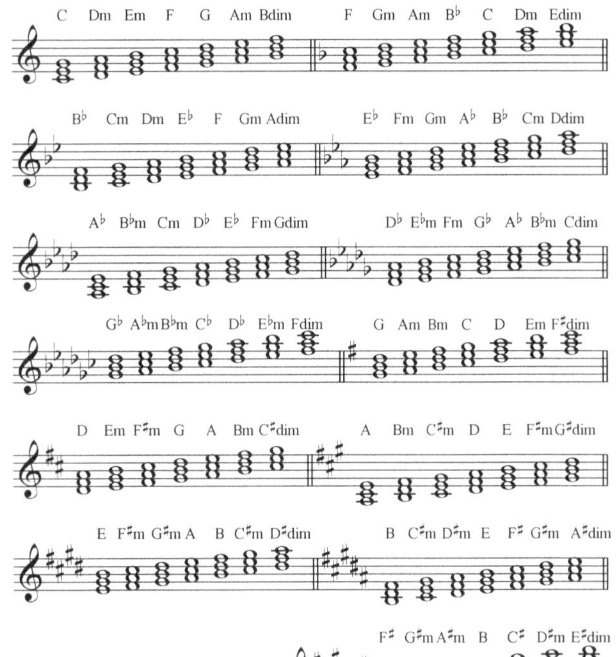

## Ex. 92

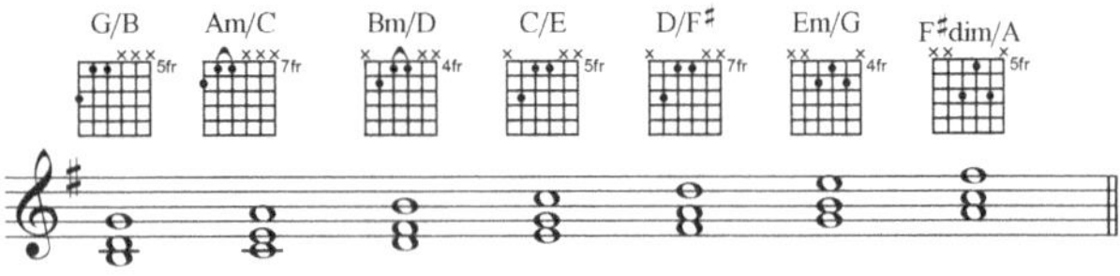

## Ex. 93

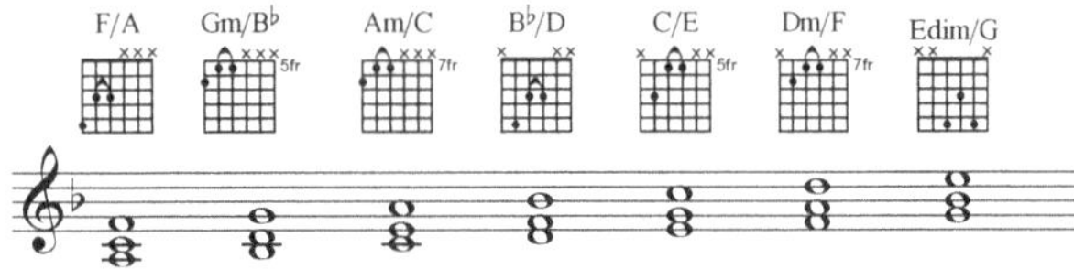

## Ex. 94

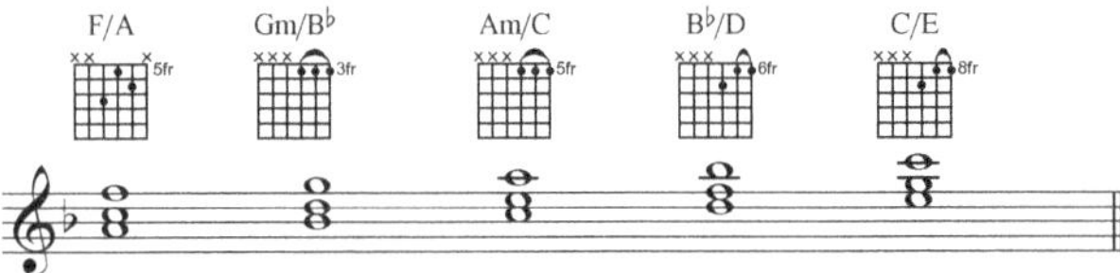

## Ex. 95

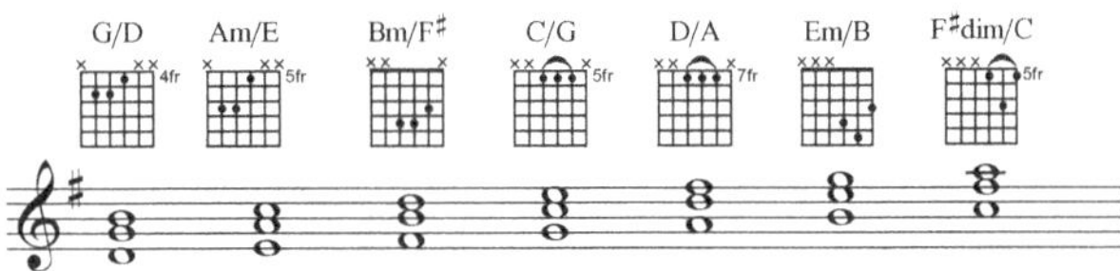

## Ex. 96

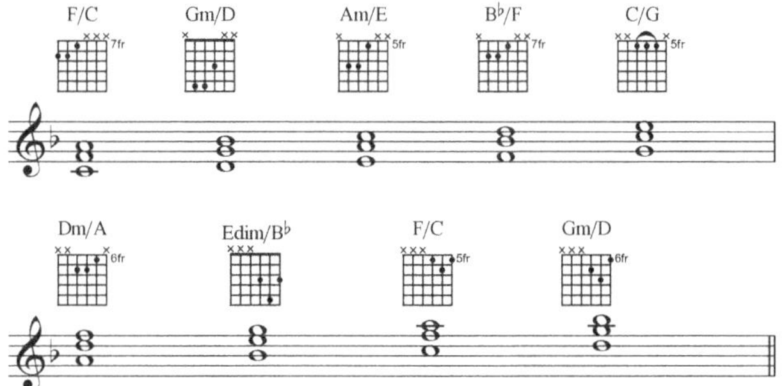

## Ex. 97

## Ex. 98

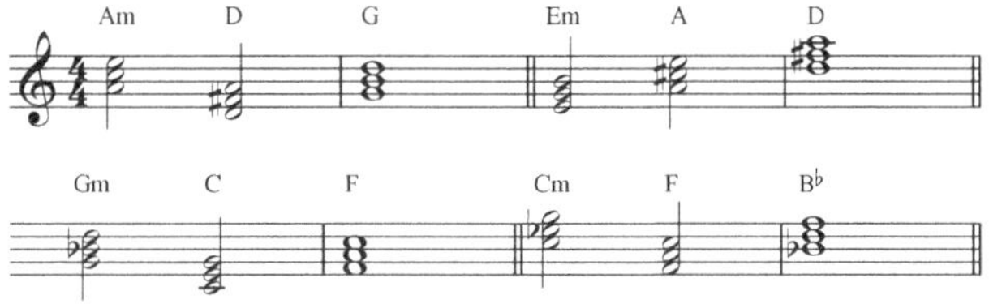

## Ex. 99

## Ex. 100

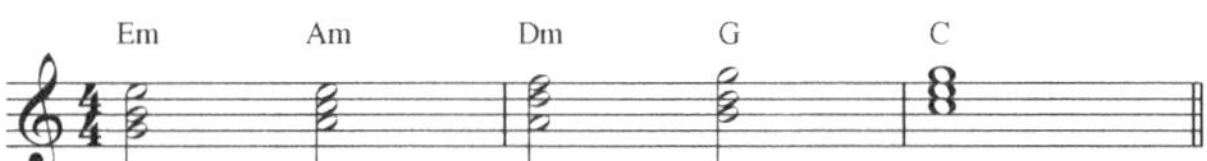

## Ex. 101

## Ex. 102

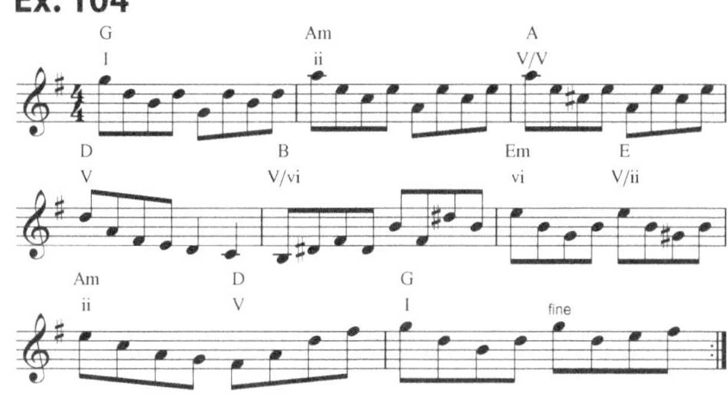

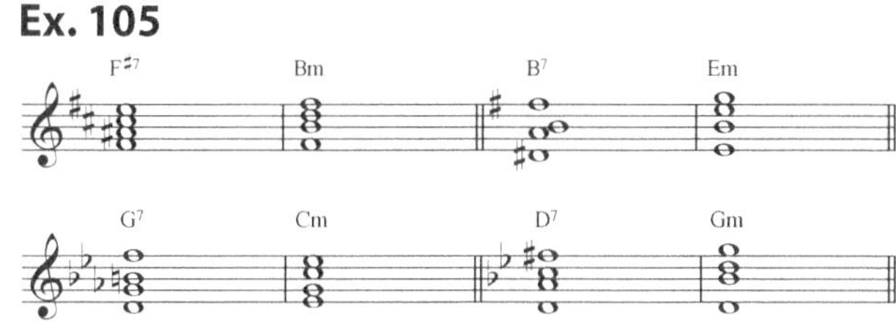

www.ingramcontent.com/pod-product-compliance
Lightning Source LLC
Chambersburg PA
CBHW081421210726
48464CB00020B/1346

# GUITAR
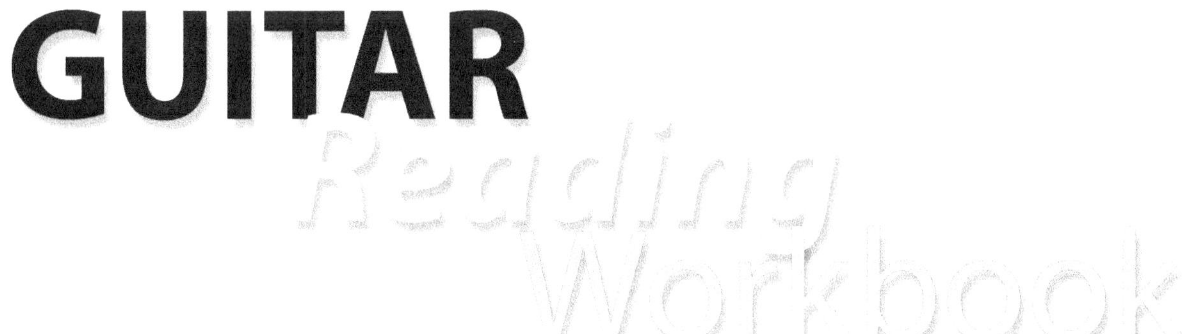

Reading Workbook

A Basic Course in Music Notation for Players of All Levels

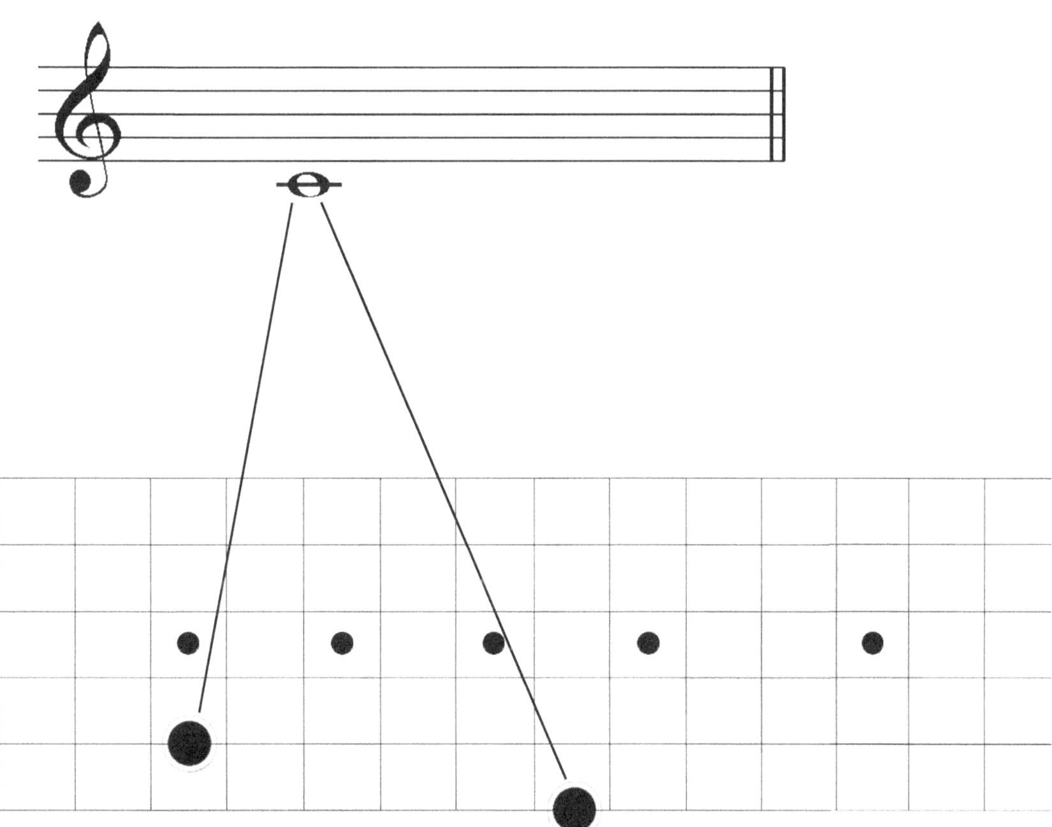

by Barrett Tagliarino

# About the Author

Barrett Tagliarino is a Los Angeles-based guitarist with over 20 years of recording, performing, and teaching experience. He's been an instructor at Musicians Institute in Hollywood since 1987, teaching lead and rhythm guitar styles, ear training, theory, and reading. Barrett contributes columns to magazines such as *Guitar Player*, *Guitar Edge*, and *Guitar One*, is the author of seven music books including *Chord Tone Soloing* and the *Guitar Fretboard Workbook*, and is featured on the *Classic Rock Soloing* DVD.

Barrett's first guitar instrumental CD, *Moe's Art*, showcases his playing and compositional skills in a blend of rock, shred, blues, country, and other styles. To buy it and his latest recorded releases, download free tracks, and read his guitar blog posts, please visit his website, monsterguitars.com.


ISBN-13
978-0-9802353-0-2

ISBN-10
0-9802353-0-8

# Contents

# Introduction

This book is for any guitarist who wants to read music, including beginners who haven't played much, and also those who have some playing ability but now want to start reading. It focuses on musical building blocks like basic rhythms, note names on the fretboard, scales, and chords as they appear on the guitar. If you are unfamiliar with these things, this reading workbook is a good way to start learning about them. You will then be less frustrated when you start to read songs, because you will be reading bits of information that you already know. When you are not frustrated, it is easier to keep up good practice habits.

Except for basic fretting and picking, no prior knowledge of music on your part is assumed. If, however, you already know some notes on the fretboard, and any scales, chords, or arpeggios, you'll find that the exercises will solidify your knowledge and help you become musically literate all that much faster.

**Learning to Read and Write**

Imagine a class of first-grade kids. Their teacher shows them the alphabet, and has them practice writing a new letter every day. They have to repeat aloud the sounds the letters make, and draw pictures or make projects to go with them. A is for apple, B is for ball. Soon they are reading and writing words and easy sentences. Within two years, they can read stories and write a card to Grandma. Nothing astounding, but pretty good for a seven-year-old.

Now suppose the same first-graders were never taught their ABCs, and never practiced writing their letters or naming them aloud. Instead imagine they had to start right in with reading complete stories. They'd have a rough time, wouldn't they? I don't think they'd learn it as fast this way. After a few months, some of them might be ready to give up on the whole idea.

Letters on the page represent sounds that are already familiar to us. Through repetition (and studying the alphabet first), we gradually learn to read ever-larger groups of letters at a glance, recognizing words, phrases, even entire sentences, without stopping to look at the individual symbols. Words are added to our vocabularies when we copy them down on paper, then use them in new sentences. Reading is just one facet of overall literacy, where content is understood as it is read, and our own ideas are conceived and written down without hesitation.

The same applies to reading music. When you become musically literate, you are not a machine that translates notes, one by one in rapid succession, into sounds that come as a surprise when you hear yourself play them. That's not how it works, at least not for me or for most of the musicians I talk to. Just as when reading a book aloud, we recognize and interpret the ideas being communicated.

With the word *interpret* I am not suggesting that any inaccuracy in reading is appropriate, or that some of the written music can be ignored. I'm saying just the opposite. As with written language, you can perform better and even more accurately if you understand what you are reading. You can, for example, correct any errors the composer may have committed in putting it to paper, add to it if it is obviously just a sketch of an idea, or modify it to suit your instrument if it was written with a different one in mind.

Unfortunately many guitarists try to learn to read music without writing any notes on a page (and without counting or singing), and without working on the little vocabulary words like scales, arpeggios, or basic rhythmic units. We're going to fix that. It may seem like a bit of extra work, but the payoff is that you'll know what you're playing as you read it, making it easier to play and remember.

**Practice**

Regular, deliberate practice with a purpose in mind is the only route to expertise in any field. Music is no exception; in fact it's the perfect example. Missing a day here or there will not ruin things, but if your practice is inconsistent or done without concentration, you'll have to keep starting over. Five minutes per day, every day of the week, is better than spending a full hour but only on Sunday. Twenty minutes of serious work is more productive than an hour of messing around.

The best investment you can make for developing your musicality, including your reading, is a **metronome**. It doesn't have to be fancy; just get one. Also get some **single-staff music paper**.

Set aside a place where you can keep your materials at the ready, so there's nothing stopping you from working for just a minute if that's all you have. Stick a pencil in the book at your current place. If possible, get a solid music stand and keep the book on it, ready to go.

Depending on your level, a chapter may take one to three weeks of study. Written exercises drill your understanding of the information presented. They should be done immediately after reading the explanation, then written out again on separate paper throughout the week if needed. Once a written exercise is completed, read and play what you've written. Chapters also include practice lists to help solidify the material.

Early chapters contain easier topics to learn, so you may find yourself blasting through them. That's fine, but don't expect to breeze through the entire book. You're inevitably going to hit a tough spot somewhere. Don't let that bother you. Just slow down, right there. If you don't have a private teacher, you'll have to be your own guide to the pacing of the material. Take your time, but try to keep moving ahead, even if you're only 90% sure of your understanding. You should go back and review earlier chapters from time to time. You'll find things you missed. Though good books and courses are linear, presenting ideas in a carefully-planned order, learning often happens in a non-linear way, where sometimes you have to review the early stuff with a new perspective in order to see the big picture.

Finally, practice with a study partner. It never hurts to ask if someone is willing to read with you. You'll learn faster if you read in as many different situations as possible: with a partner, with a teacher, in a classroom, in front of an audience, etc. You will try harder when you're there, and the pressure of not wanting to sound bad will make you more diligent about practicing on your own.

**Reading Materials**

This book covers the basics in detail, but it does not contain a supply of songs. You'll need some reading materials that are suitable for your level. Bluegrass-type folk music and easy classical studies are a good place to start. Songs and studies that are intended for beginning violin or flute can also be read on guitar. Though they won't sound exactly like the original recordings, there are also easy guitar arrangements in print of popular music that make reading practice more fun. You wouldn't expect a first-grader to read the *New York Times*, so be realistic about your selections if you are just starting out.

# Chapter 1: The Staff

*S*tandard notation depicts *pitch* (high or low sound) and *rhythm* (timing) with symbols all musicians read, regardless of instrument. It uses a *staff* with **five lines** and **four spaces**. *Noteheads* representing pitches are written on the lines and spaces. Lines and spaces on the staff are always numbered from the **bottom up**.

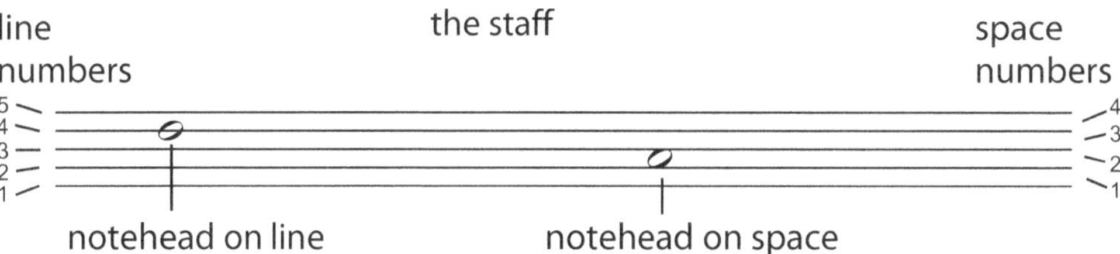



As we progress we'll learn how noteheads are modified to show rhythm with precision.

Exercise 1.

Practice hand-drawing hollow noteheads on each line and space of the staff. When drawing noteheads in a space, do not overlap the line. When drawing notes on a line, make sure you can see the white space on either side. Take pride in your noteheads; make them with quick but careful slanted ovals drawn with a single stroke of a pencil.

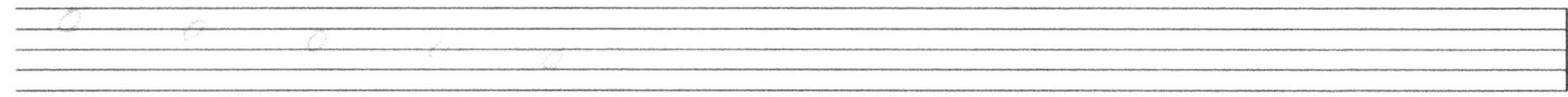

## Tablature

In guitar books and magazines, usually the tablature staff is below the notation. Loosely speaking, the tab staff is unnecessary if there is also a notation staff, because all the music should already be written on the notation staff. Tab has six lines that represent the strings on the guitar. You finger the string at the fret number given.

Unlike on the notation staff, only the lines are used, not the spaces. The strings on the tab staff are numbered from the **top down**, the opposite of the notation staff, following the traditional method for numbering the strings on the guitar: string 6 is the lowest-pitched, fattest string.

Tablature is easier to figure out at first and is great for showing guitar specifics: the exact fret for each note in a difficult lick, songs with non-standard tunings, and parts that are played with a capo. Tab is unreadable to non-guitarists, however. The better teachers will recommend you learn standard notation so you can communicate with other musicians.

Traditional tab has no rhythm, except to show the order notes are played in. The actual rhythm is left up to the reader to guess or copy by ear from a recording. Some magazines address this by combining the rhythmic elements from standard notation with tab to make *rhythm tab*. Learning standard notation will enable you to read rhythm tab.

According to my heroes, no guitar book is any good without some pictures with dots on them to show you where to put your fingers. Let's make sure we're familiar with these from the beginning.

## Fretboard Diagrams

Horizontal fretboard or *neck diagrams* are good for easy visualization of scales and chords, especially when they cover many frets. Similar to tablature, the strings are numbered the same as when you look down at your guitar from a playing position. Circles or dots are used for notes. You can just use circles because they are faster, and easier to make big enough to see. A circle around a dot marks the root of a scale or chord.

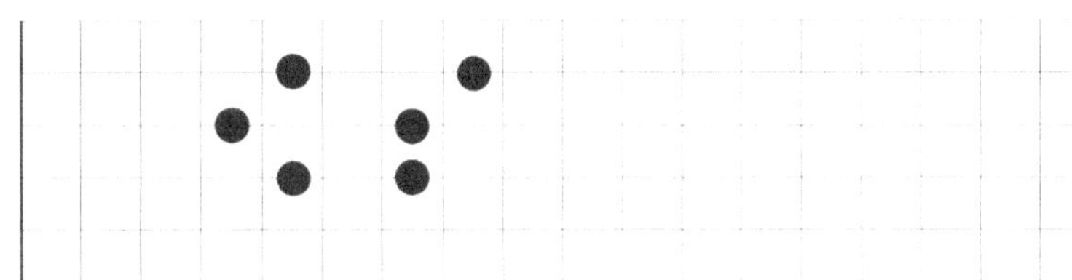

Exercise 2.
Practice fretboard diagramming by jotting down any scale you know. If you don't know any scales, just quickly put two circles on each string at any fret. Make it clear and easy to read.

## Frames

These vertical diagrams are usually called *chord frames* because they're often used for depicting chord shapes. We will use frames to practice drawing chords and scales, and for locating single notes. The vertical lines represent strings 6-1; the horizontal lines represent frets. If you point your guitar up to the sky in an invocation to the demonic gods of metal, it will resemble a chord frame.

In an *open position* frame, the guitar's nut is represented by a thicker line across the top. If this line is missing, there should be a *position mark* showing the placement of the index finger. A dot represents a finger pressed down to play a note. A circle above the diagram represents an open (unfretted) string. If there is no mark on a string at all, assume it is not played.

A curved mark or line connecting two or more notes on the same fret show that they are to be barred with the same finger. Left-hand fingering may be indicated with numerals below the frame.

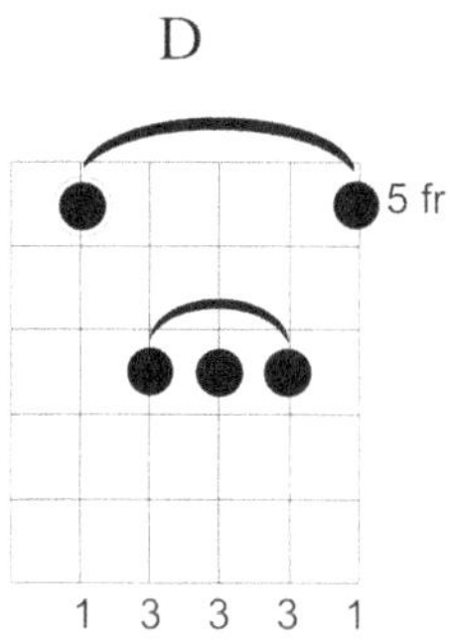



## Exercise 3.

Draw any chord you know on the frame below. If you don't know any chords, copy the C chord used when explaining frames. Make it easy to read, and write the name of the chord above the frame.

## Exercise 4.

Transfer both the neck diagram and the chord frame from the previous exercises into tablature. Spread the fret numerals out across the page for the scale. For the chord, stack the numerals up.

The first exercises are meant to be pretty easy, but please don't skip them if you're a beginner. Make accurate, clear notation. If you are ready, let's move on.

# Chapter 2: Counting

A line (or *system*) of music is divided into *measures* (or *bars*), each of which ends with a *bar line* that goes from the top to the bottom of the staff. In a song, *sections*, such as verses or choruses, are ended by *double bar lines*, and the song itself is ended by a *terminal* (or *final*) *bar line*: one thin bar line followed by a thick one.

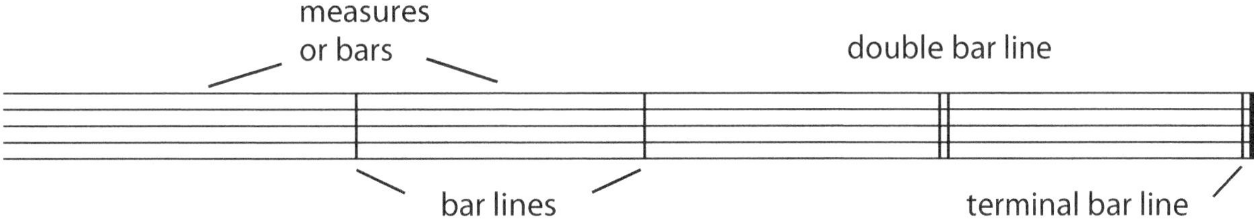


For each measure below, count aloud, while **steadily** tapping the toe end of your foot (not the heel) on the floor. To get ready, count aloud "one, two, three, four," by yourself first **before** the music really starts. This is called a *countoff*, and it allows everyone playing to start together. Beat "one" of the music is called the *downbeat*.

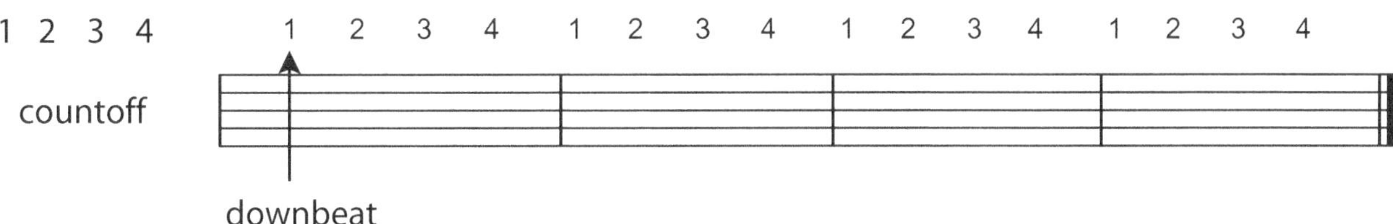


*Measure numbers* are often written above or below the music with arabic numerals. To avoid clutter, sometimes only some measures have the numerals written; for example, the first on each line.

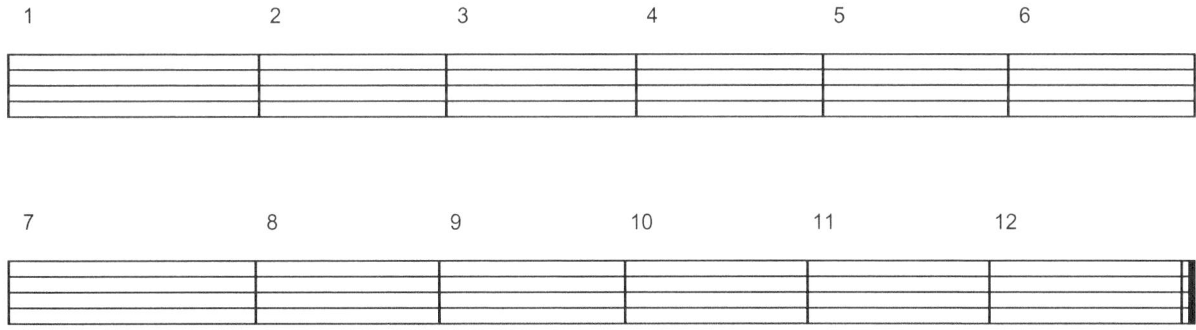


Guitarists need to devote some of their practice time to foot-tapping and counting aloud with the metronome, away from the instrument. Besides counting the beats within each measure ("1-2-3-4, 1-2-3-4," etc.), practice counting groups of 4, 8, 12, and 16 measures **and** their beats aloud. For example: "**1**-2-3-4, **2**-2-3-4, **3**-2-3-4, **4**-2-3-4, **5**-2-3-4, **6**-2-3-4, **7**-2-3-4, **8**-2-3-4," and so on.

The foot needs to be a reliable clock against which you will time your playing. After a few minutes of daily practice for about a month, hanging with that metronome will start to get easier. You want your brain to keep an underlying awareness of which beat in which measure you are on at any given time, while you think of other things. In this way, music is different from written language. You cannot repeat a note or start over if there is a mistake. Start building the habit now: **no stopping** once you've started.

Exercise 5.
Label these parts on the staff.

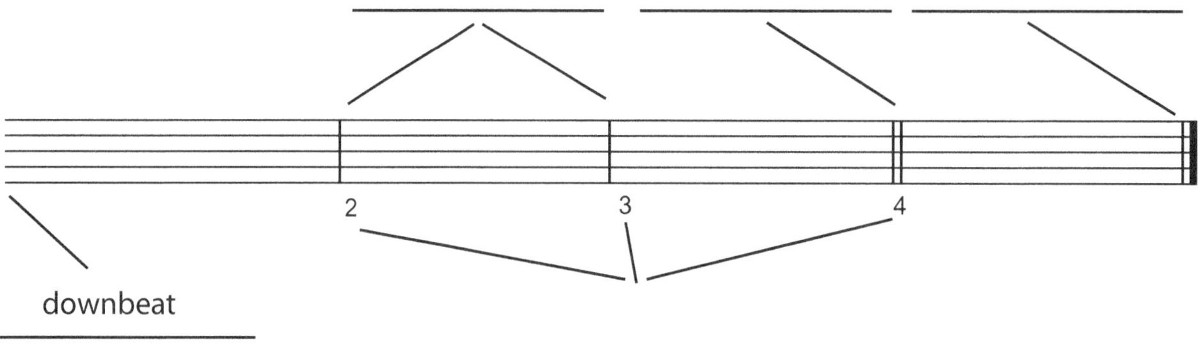


Exercise 6.
Divide one system in half by drawing a bar line in the middle. Divide each side in half again, and put a terminal bar line at the end. Go back and end the second measure with a double bar line. Make your bar lines completely vertical (slanted lines have another meaning).

## Note and Rest Values

A hollow notehead is called a *whole note*. It lasts for four beats. Count off four beats, then play the open G string on the next downbeat and let it ring while continuing to count aloud. Stop the note on "one" in the second measure, but keep counting. The block hanging down from the fourth line is a *whole rest*, which is four beats of silence. Continue counting and play another whole note in bar 3.

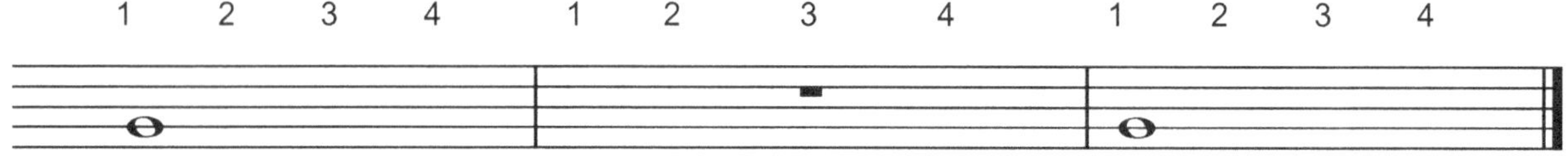


By adding *stems* to hollow noteheads, we get *half notes*. These are two beats long, so two can fit in a measure. The corresponding half rest is shown in the final bar. The half rest sticks up from the third line. Think of it as being lighter than the heavy hanging whole rest.

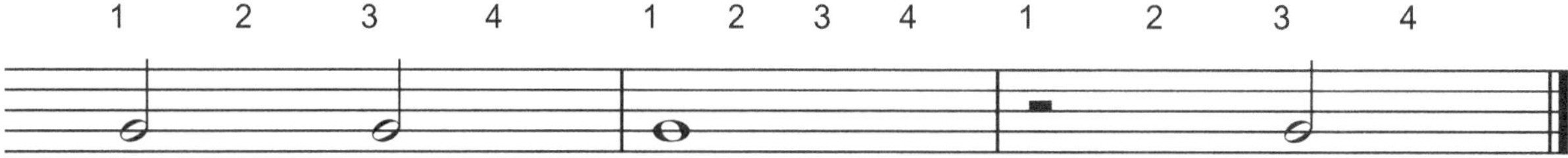


The angle between the head and the stem is (almost) always obtuse, never acute. Your noteheads can be the same tilted oval every time, though an engraved whole note is not slanted toward the stem—because there is no stem.

When a stemmed notehead is below the center line, the stem points up from the right. If the notehead is on or above the center line, the stem hangs down from the left. As in the examples, the stems on your half notes should stick straight up or down by about three and a half lines.

10

Practice drawing half notes on this staff, placing some notes below the center line, and some above. Use the correct stem directions.

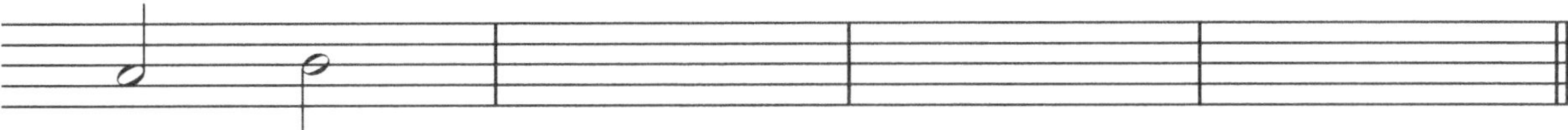

Practice drawing whole **rests** and half rests on this staff.

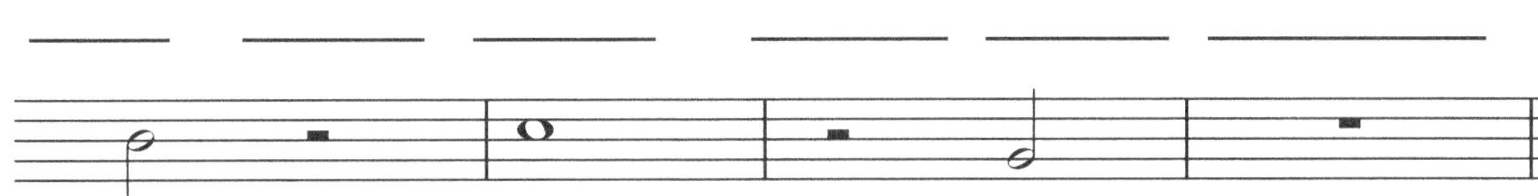

Exercise 7.
Label these symbols on the staff.

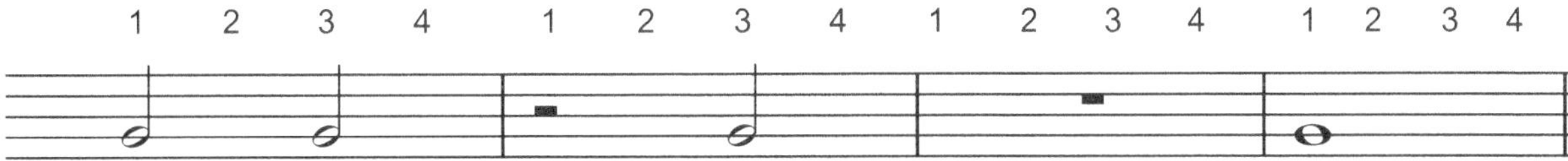

## How Rhythmic Notation Works

Each measure starts with beat "one." Although notes are usually spread out within each measure in a way that reflects their start times, it is not the spacing that tells the reader when to play them. Instead, the duration of the previous notes in the measure dictate the starting times of the later notes. Think of them as bricks lined up end to end. In measure 1 below, the first note is a half note, two beats long. It causes the second note to start on beat 3. The same goes for the half rest in the second measure. Its duration causes the next note to fall on beat 3. Knowing this, you're on your way to reading all kinds of complex rhythmic notation. A whole rest (measure 3) breaks the visual pattern, hanging in the middle, yet we know it starts on beat 1 because it is the only symbol in the measure.

Exercise 8.
1. In the first measure below, draw two half notes on the second line.
2. In the second measure, draw a whole rest hanging from the fourth line.
3. In the last measure, draw a half rest sticking up from the third line, followed by a half note.

When you've finished writing, count off, then play the entire example on the open G string. Then count off again, but this time, instead of playing, **clap** your hands on the correct attack time for each note as you count aloud and tap your foot.

A *quarter note* has a solid notehead and a stem. It lasts for one beat.

Let's draw some quarter notes by hand. Make a quick but legible solid notehead by making the oval a little tighter than usual, so that one or two more strokes down its middle with the pencil fills it in. Then add the stem. Draw quarter notes on lines and spaces of this staff. Use correct stem directions!

Beat one below shows a *quarter rest* as drawn by a professional music copyist (or by notation software). We'll draw a simple but clear version of the quarter rest like this:

1. Make a backward slash across the middle two spaces.
2. Make a counterclockwise hook at the top.
3. Make a counterclockwise hook at the bottom.

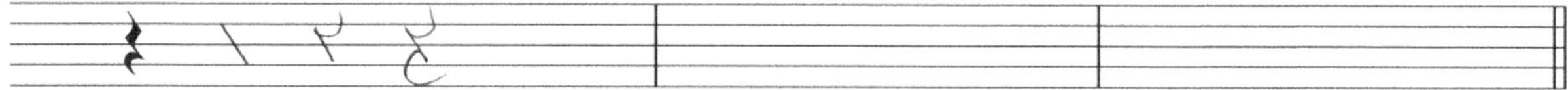

Add eight quarter rests of your own for practice.

I apologize for belaboring the drawing of simple symbols. In years of teaching full-grown adults, and even in playing with professionals, I've found a surprising amount of music is unreadable to the extent that it holds up the show. It's best if notation is written plainly, with no personal flourishes. Make your notes and rests look the same as everyone else's, and let your originality be expressed by the music itself.

These two pyramids show that a whole note (four beats) is equal in duration to two half notes (two beats each), each of which in turn are equal to two quarter notes (one beat each). The same applies to rests.

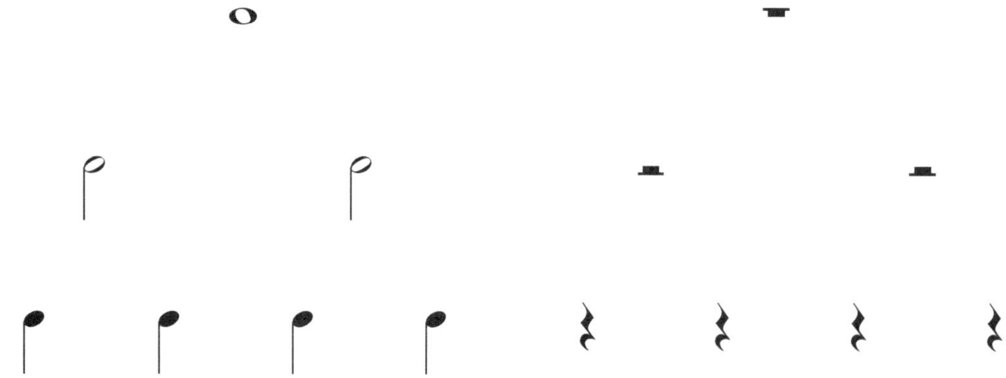

Exercise 9.

In this example, notes are placed on various beats. Write the beat number on which the note should be played. Do not mark the rests.

Exercise 10.

In this exercise, notes and rests are placed on various beats. Add the missing **notes** of the proper size so that each measure contains four beats' worth of duration.

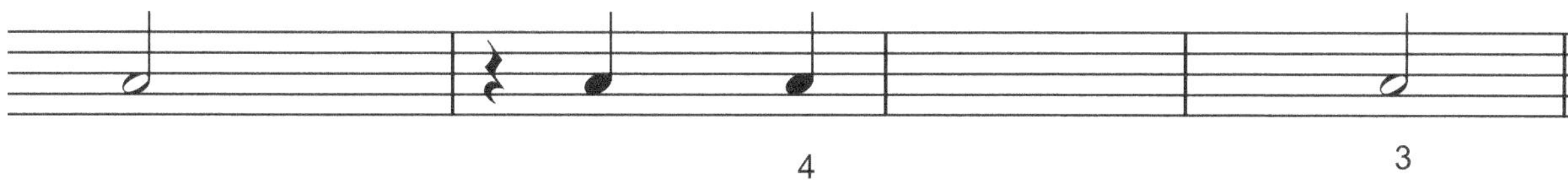

Exercise 11.

Add the minimum number of **rests** needed to take up the beats where nothing is played. Always choose one large rest where possible instead of two small ones. Make sure that all notes fall on the beat numbers indicated **and** that each measure contains four beats' worth of duration.

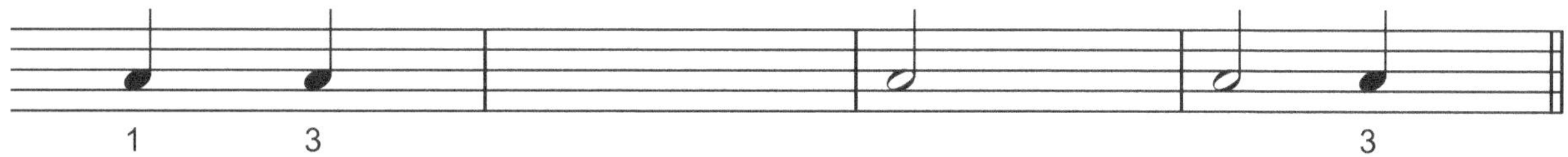

## Quarter-Note Vocabulary

Listed below are all the possible ways we can fill a four-beat measure with quarter notes and rests. Tap your foot and clap the measures, counting aloud with the metronome.

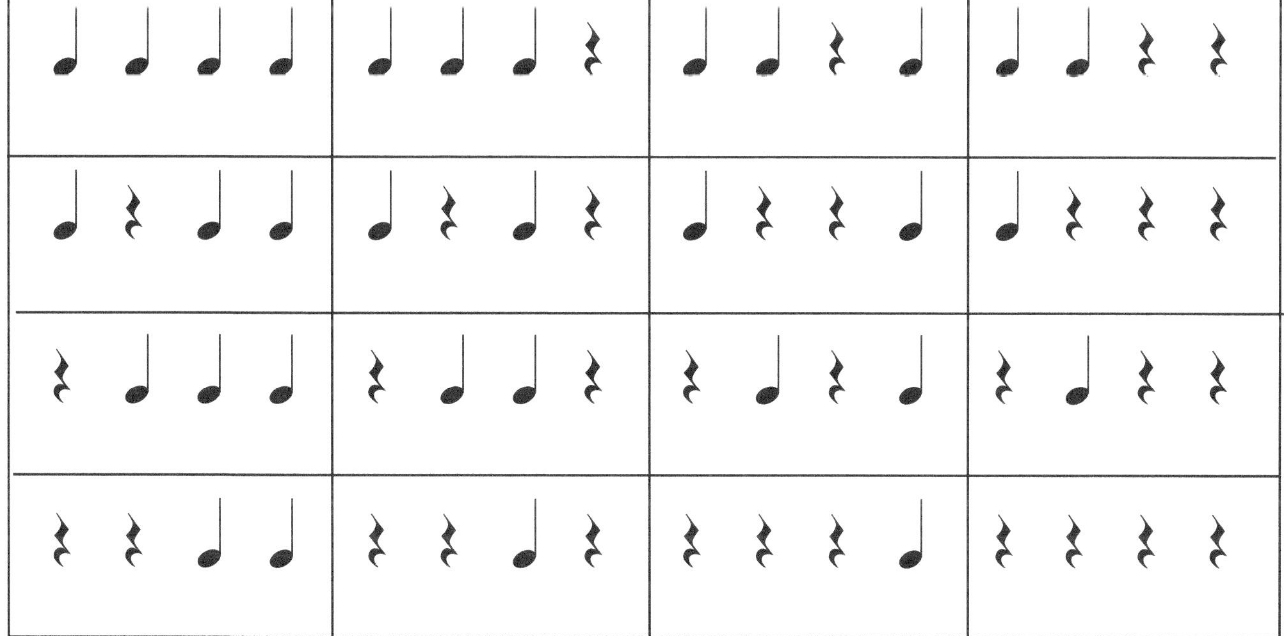

## Combining Rests

The previous table has a note or rest on each beat so you can see that every possible permutation is included. To use fewer marks on the page, we can combine two neighboring quarter rests within a measure to make a half rest, which is the equivalent amount of silence. For the last measure, with four beats of silence, we can write a whole rest instead.

When the half rest would cross beat 3, we may want to divide the overall measure into two equal parts, so there is always some kind of symbol on beat 3. This means keeping two quarter rests (cell 7 in the table below), or, when there are three beats of silence (cells 8 and 15), ordering the rests so that one starts on beat 3. This preference for showing beat 3 will also apply to rhythms we'll see later, so don't ignore it.

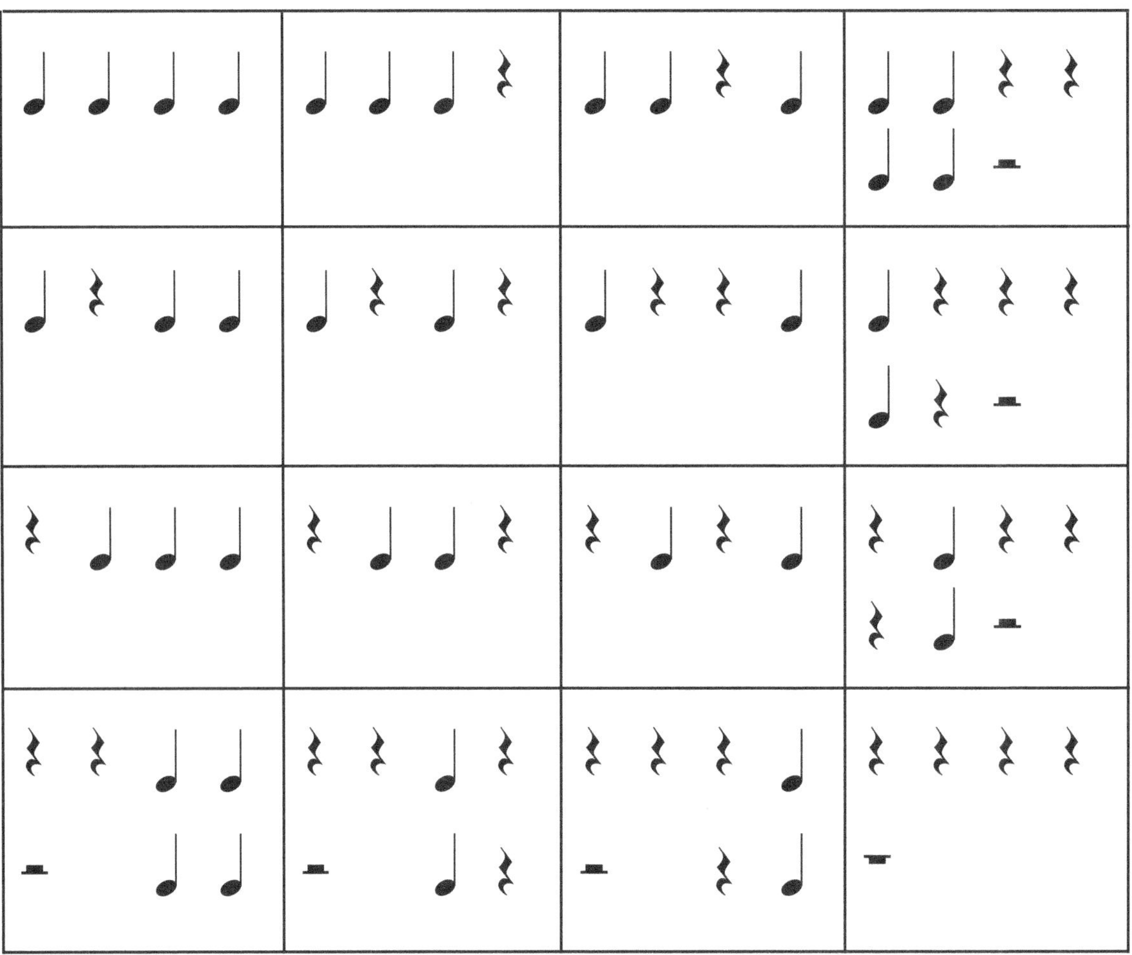

## Equivalent Attacks

Handclaps have practically no duration. When you clap rhythms, you're just playing the attacks and waiting through the duration, so clapping a half note sounds the same as clapping a quarter note followed by a quarter rest.

When considered this way—attacks only—the sixteen rhythmic permutations also include the sounds of all the half- and whole-note rhythms available in a four-beat measure. These equivalent attacks are shown in the following table, again with adjacent small rests combined into larger ones.

14

## Quarter-Note Vocabulary List

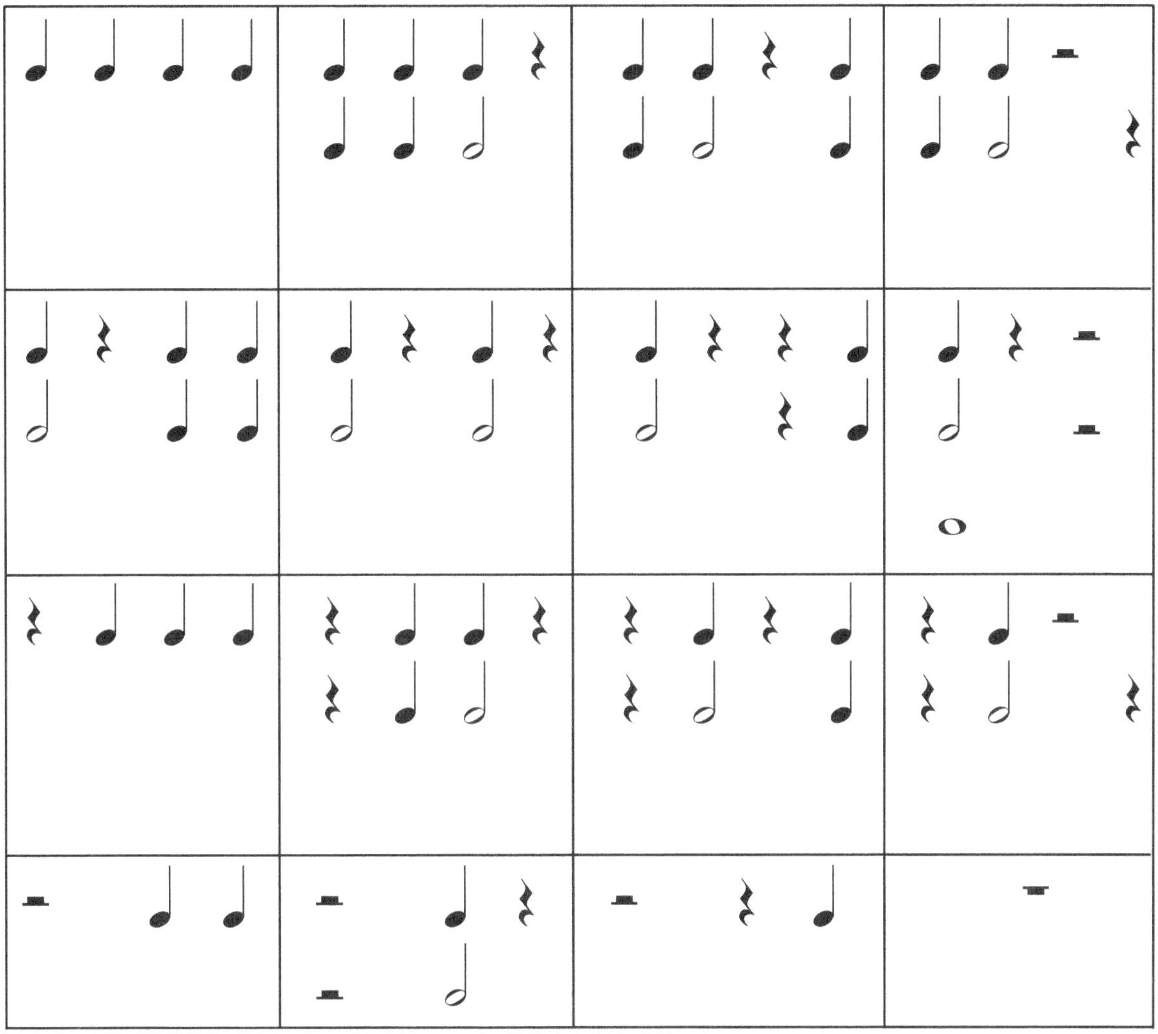

Now the table includes almost every rhythm you can write in a four-beat measure using quarter-or-larger notes and rests (see if you can write two more equivalent measures in cell 6). Clap the above measures while tapping your foot and counting aloud.

## Repeat Signs

A *repeat sign* is a double bar line with two dots that face in toward the section that is to be played twice. The outside lines are thick, to make this important sign easy to spot. When drawing repeat signs with a pencil, make them stand out by adding wings facing in toward the part that is to be repeated.

Play through the first repeat sign and just remember where it is. When you hit the second (left-facing) repeat sign, go back without stopping and play everything between the two signs again. Then continue on to play the measures that follow.

The measures in repeated sections may be numbered in either of two different ways. In the first, the repeated bars do not get extra measure numbers. In the example on the previous page, the numerals only go from 1-8, even though you actually play twelve bars of music when you read it.

In the second method, extra numerals get stacked up for the repeated sections as shown below. This may be done when other instruments are playing parts that change while your part repeats. A bandleader can call out any measure number and everyone knows where to start.

We'll also number some examples this way for study purposes in this book.

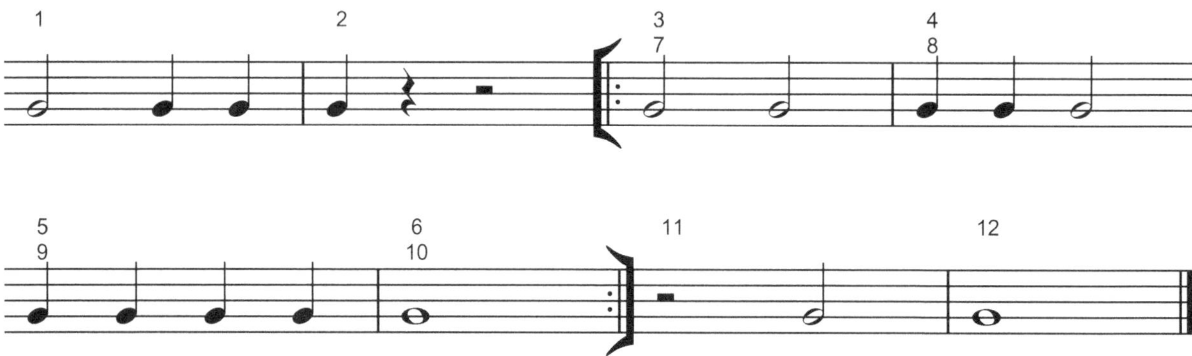

The repeat sign in the next example does not have wings, which is how they usually look in printed music. Now, when there is no right-facing repeat sign, it always means you start over from the absolute beginning of the piece. This is the only possibility, no matter how long the song—unless there's a mistake.

Exercise 12.

Write numerals below each measure in this example. Stack the numerals up in the repeated section to show the exact order to play each bar.

16

If you are writing a piece and you want a section to be played more than twice, use repeat signs along with a clear written direction; for example, "Play 3 times." Don't write "Repeat 3 times" because the reader won't know for sure if the part is played three times or four (literally speaking, the first time is not a repetition).

Measure 14, containing only a diagonal slash surrounded by dots, is a *one-measure repeat*. Play the contents of the previous measure again (from memory, while looking at upcoming measures, if possible).

Play 3 times

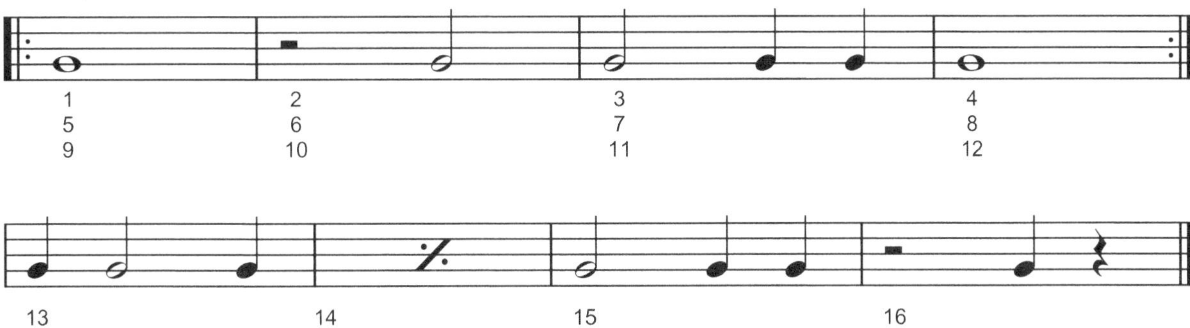

Two empty measures with a dotted pair of slashes in between signify a *two-measure repeat*. Play the preceding two measures again, for a total of four bars of music.

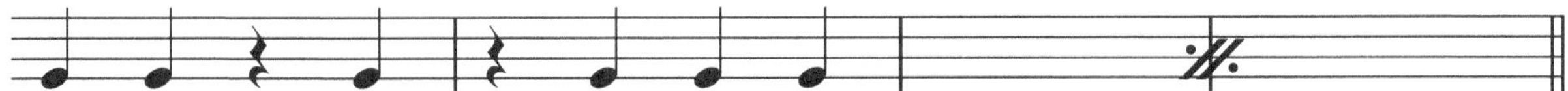

## Practice

1. Count in time with the metronome set at 50 beats per minute for two minutes. Tap your foot evenly so that it reaches its highest point off the floor exactly between the clicks.

2. Practice the quarter-note vocabulary list, reading the measures from left to right. Then read them in reverse order: read the final measure, then the second-to-last, and so on. Then try skipping around; for example, read down the first column and up the second. Be sure to practice all the equivalent-attack versions (whole notes and half notes).

Take in a whole measure at a glance. Once you know one, like a written word, you want to see it, identify it accurately, and play it without really thinking about each mark on the page. As soon as you know what you'll be playing, look ahead at the next measure, or, if you're already so far ahead you risk overloading your memory, look anywhere except at your instrument, as practice for when you'll be watching a conductor or video monitor.

3. Get some staff paper and draw four empty measures, with a double bar line at the end. Using whole, half, and quarter notes and rests, draw one random four-measure rhythm example per day, writing exactly four beat's worth of notation in each measure and no more. When you use a whole rest or whole note, nothing else will fit in the bar.

Make it easy to read, keeping the notes on the second line of the staff for now. Play your examples on the open G string, counting aloud and tapping your foot with the metronome.

# Chapter 3: Pitch

## Treble Clef

The first symbol on the staff at the beginning of a song, the *clef* defines the range of pitches that the staff will use. Music for guitar and many other instruments uses (we say it is "written in") the *treble* or "G" clef. The bottom of the treble clef encircles the second line of the staff, reminding us this note is a G. Draw some practice treble clefs on the staff below using these three steps.

1. Start with a vertical down-stroked line.
2. From the top of that line, draw a curving backward "S" shape that is smaller on the top, bigger on the bottom.
3. Finish by encircling the second line of the staff.

Once the second line is set as G, all the other letters of the alphabet fall into place. The line notes are E–G–B–D–F (**E**very **G**ood **B**oy **D**oes **F**ine), and the space notes spell F–A–C–E.

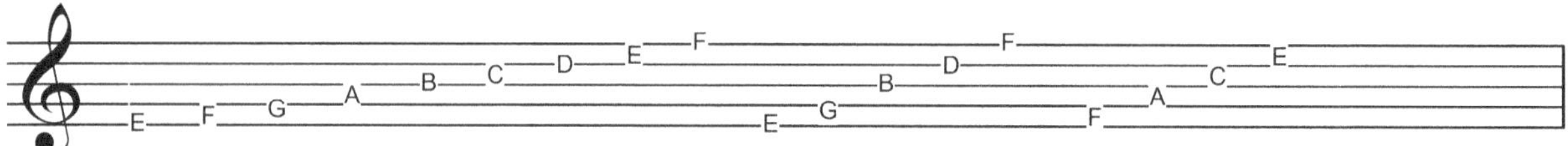


## The Musical Alphabet

When reading notes that move by steps up the staff, the name of the next note is always the next letter in the alphabet. We can mentally recite letters in alphabetical order as we play the corresponding pitches, without stopping to name every note by analyzing its staff location.

Notes go down just as often as they go up, so we need to learn the musical alphabet backward as well as forward. Memorize and recite the backward alphabet.

G F E D C B A

The alphabet is an endless repeating sequence; it can start anywhere, crossing from G to A.

F G A B C D E

It can, of course, also cross from A to G when descending.

C B A G F E D

Identify alphabet fragments, alone or among other notes.

## Exercise 13.

Circle the alphabet fragments in these series.

| | | | | |
|---|---|---|---|---|
| C A G F | D F G A | F E D C | G A F E D | C B A G D B A |
| F G A B | B C A D | F G B C | B A G F E | A C E F G |

## Fifth Position Natural Notes

For each fretboard location we must learn both a letter name and a note on the staff. Both are abstractions, so this takes some patience. If you've already learned to play some things by ear, by using tablature, or by looking at someone's fingers, you may have to fight a tendency to go back to those methods while reading.

First we'll learn only *natural* notes: the ones that are named using the only the letters A–B–C–D–E–F–G. A guitar has about 120 note locations, but we'll just start with a good range for reading melodies, near the fifth fret. The suggested reading position is often marked with a Roman numeral in guitar music.

## 3rd String

Here are the natural notes on the 3rd string at the 4th, 5th, and 7th frets: B–C–D.

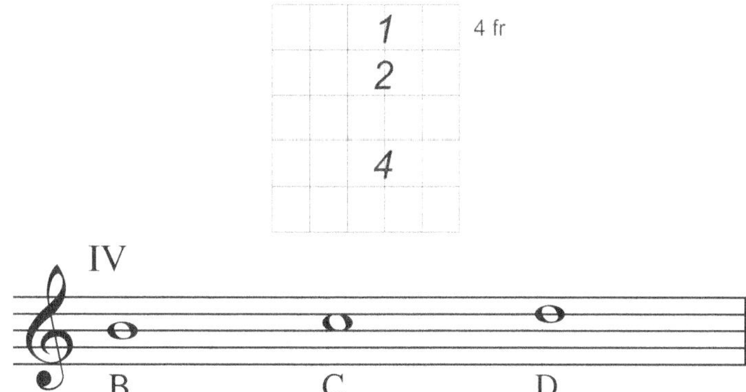


Place your 1st finger on the note B. From here on, do not look at your fingers, and do not take your hand off the fretboard. When reading, you need to look at the page and not at your hand. You will use your currently-fingered note, B, as a reference point for finding the next note you will play by feel.

### Verbalize

To memorize this note's name, repeat the following description aloud as you play.

"B, 3rd string, 4th fret, 1st finger."

The B note is on the 3rd line of the staff. Describe the staff location aloud.

"B, 3rd line."

**Visualize**

This time close your eyes; do not play, but mentally visualize 1) your finger playing the note, and 2) the note as it appears on the staff, as you repeat both verbal descriptions.

"B, 3rd string, 4th fret, 1st finger. 3rd line on the staff."

Now play the C with the 2nd finger, then the D with the 4th finger. Whenever possible we will follow a one-finger-per-fret rule. You may be using the 4th finger a bit more than you are accustomed to, but that's a good thing. On this string, for example, we do not use the 3rd finger because we're not playing the note that is directly beneath it.

Perform out-loud verbalization and eyes-closed visualization for the two new notes.

"C, 3rd string, 5th fret, 2nd finger. D, 7th fret, 4th finger."

The C note is on the 3rd space of the staff. The D note is on the 4th line. Say it aloud.

"C, 3rd space. D, 4th line."

## Half Steps and Whole Steps

The distance from one note to another is called an *interval*.

From B to C, one fret apart, is a *half step* interval.

From C to D, two frets apart, is a *whole step* interval.

On the staff, there is no obvious difference between a half step and a whole step. There is also nothing on the guitar to show us this, either, unlike on some other instruments. We just have to remember it: from B to C is a half step.

### Aural Recognition

Play the note C and then match it with your voice. The C is well within the singing range of all men, women, children, and small animals. Now play and then sing from the note C down to B. You are singing a half step. Now go the other way; sing from C up to D. That distance is a whole step. With time and practice you will hear the difference between a half-step interval and a whole-step interval.

## 2nd String

For the next three natural notes, E–F–G on the 2nd string, shift your 1st finger up to the fifth fret. Again, play these tones using one finger per fret only, without looking.

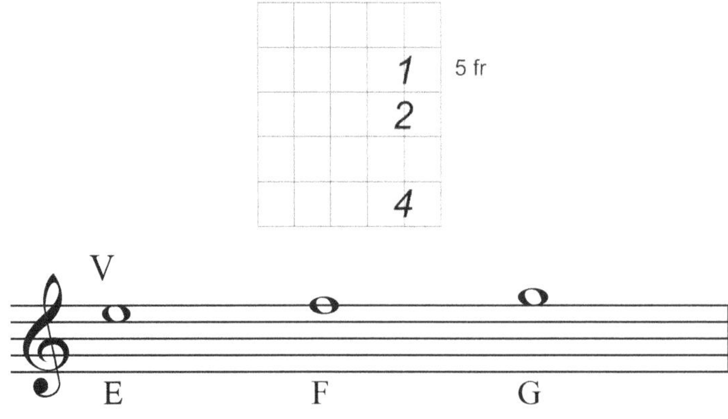

Perform out-loud verbalization for the new notes as you play them:
"E, 2nd string, 5th fret, 1st finger. F, 6th fret, 2nd finger. G, 8th fret, 4th finger."

Then repeat aloud while visualizing the notes on your fretboard instead of playing.

Now recite aloud the staff locations for the three notes.
"E, top space. F, top line. G, above the staff."

Notice that from E to F is another naturally-occurring half step. B–C and E–F are the only natural half steps. All other consecutive natural notes are a whole step apart. This includes the transition from D on the 3rd string to E on the 2nd string: that's a whole step, too.

Exercise 14.
Complete the Tab
Write a fret number on the correct string of the tab staff for the note given. Write the letter name between the notation staff and the tab. Then cover the tab with some paper and play the notation.

Exercise 15.
For each letter draw a quarter note on the correct line or space. Then play with the metronome.

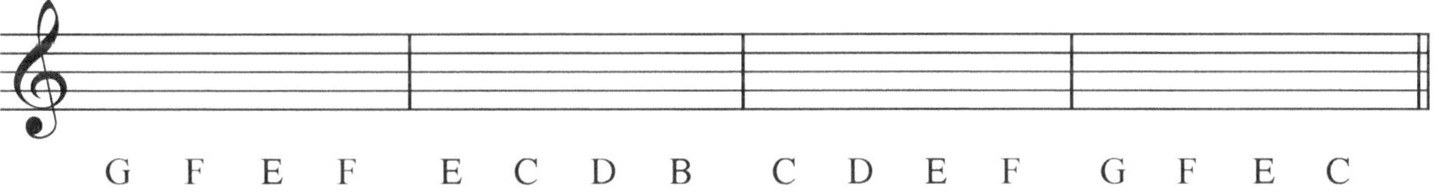


Exercise 16.
Finish translating this tablature into standard notation using quarter notes only. Write the note names in between the staves. When you're done writing, cover the tab and the note names, and play with the metronome.

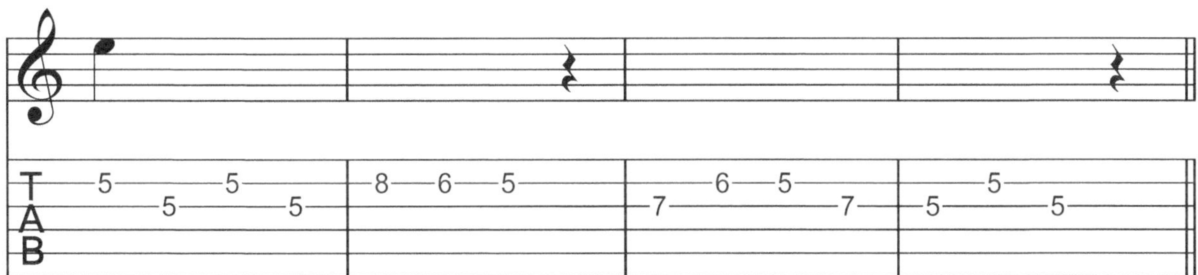

Exercise 17.

Finish translating this tablature into standard notation using notes only: whole notes, half notes, and quarter notes are needed. I've provided all the rests and some beat numbers that dictate the note durations you should use. When you've written it out, cover up the tablature and play with the metronome.

## Preparing to Read

With any luck, you'll have some time to look at any new music that comes your way before you have to play it. Making the right use of this time helps your execution, even if you just get a few seconds. Some of the tips I'll give you in this regard may seem obvious at first, but it's best to build good habits from the beginning. The list of things to do before you start to play will get longer as more topics are covered.

First, scan through the piece and find any repeat signs. In a live situation, no amount of note-reading ability will help if you miss the repeat signs and end up playing a different section from the band. Mentally trace the path these signs tell you to take. For example, "I play this section twice, then this section once. The final section is played four times and has these one-bar repeats in it."

Check the clef. We are only reading in treble clef now, but guitarists sometimes have to read parts originally meant for another instrument, and so may be written in another clef, especially bass clef.

Now find the highest and lowest notes. These determine your left-hand position. For most examples in this beginner-level book, we're staying at or near 5th position. Minimize position shifts when reading, especially at first. Later we will begin to change positions for things that work better in certain areas of the fretboard, like chords with notes in a specific order.

Next, quickly scan the piece and mentally (don't play them yet!) rehearse any parts that look harder than the rest. At our level, that means string changes, or any place where notes skip up or down on the staff. In spite of habit or instincts that tell you otherwise, these parts should be played without looking at your hands.

22

Finally, if you have the time, identify any repeated or familiar structures in the piece. Often there are some measures that are exactly the same as other ones in the piece, or the same as something you've already played many times elsewhere. Briefly check that they really are what you think they are, so that you can look ahead while playing those measures, especially the second or third time they come up.

**Practice**

1. Recite the names of the notes on the lines and spaces of the staff in treble clef.

2. For the notes B–G (the ones you have learned on the guitar in fifth position), name the string and fret.

3. Play all the notes you've learned so far, from B up to G, in steady quarter notes with the metronome set at 50 bpm. Perform the shift from fret 4 up to fret 5, along with the change from string 3 up to string 2, while looking away from your hands. Do not lift your 1st finger completely off the strings. Instead, slide the 1st finger up a fret and move it over to the next string; reverse the process when descending. As you play the notes, recite their letter names and positions on the staff.

4. Draw bar lines and then randomly-pitched quarter notes, four per measure, within the range you have learned: from B to G. Play your line of notes with the metronome. If you make a mistake, don't stop! Only review the weak notes **after** you're finished. The next day, repeat the process with a new example. Start on a different note each day.

# Chapter 4: Rhythm

## Time Signatures

The number of beats in each measure of music is called its *meter*. The *time signature* at the beginning of a piece dictates its meter, which controls how you tap your foot and count the music. Checking the time signature is another item on the list of things to do before starting to read.

The top numeral shows the number of beats per measure. The bottom numeral shows which kind of note (quarter, half, etc.) is counted as one beat. When writing a time signature, stack the two numbers directly on top of each other inside the staff as shown in the examples below.

Until now we've only used *four-four* meter, also called *4/4 time*. In this time signature, there are four beats per measure, and a quarter note counts as one beat. 4/4 may also be written as a big "C" that in medieval times was a broken circle representing imperfection. Nowadays people think of the "C" as standing for "common time."

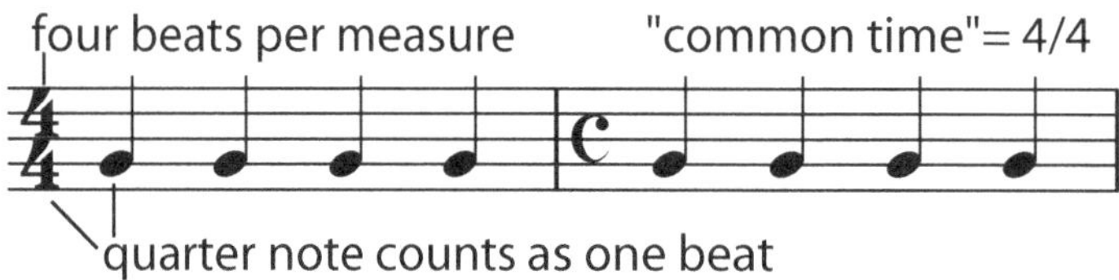


The number three corresponded to the Holy Trinity, so the *3/4 time* signature was considered "perfect" and written as an unbroken circle. Count off two bars of three ("one, two, three, one, two, three,") then continue counting as you clap this 3/4-time example. In this example, I've also included a *tempo marking* that shows how I'd like you to set the metronome.

Exercise 18.
At the end of each incorrect measure, write one note that is long enough to make the total note durations fit the given time signature.

Exercise 19.
This example is missing its bar lines. Draw them in so that the music fits the time signature.

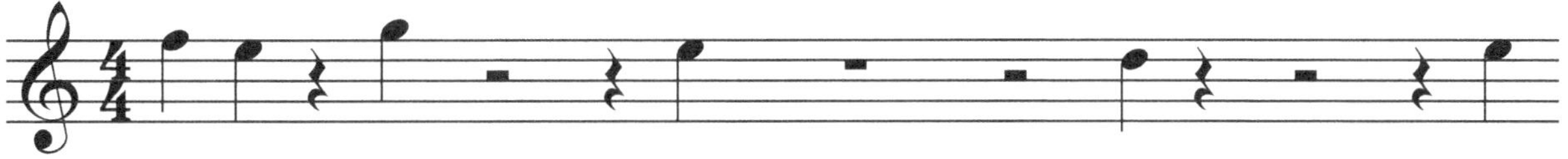

## Eighth Notes

By dividing a quarter note in half, we get an eighth note. In 4/4 time, we can fit eight eighth notes in a measure. There are two eighth notes per beat.

We draw eighth notes by adding a flag to the end of the stem. When the stem is up, the flag should hang down from the stem, then curve away and back in again. When the stem is down, the flag should defy gravity and fly upward. The flag is always on the right side of the stem. The rules for stem directions that we learned for half and quarter notes also apply to flagged eighth notes.

Draw random eighth notes on both sides of the center line, with proper stem and flag directions.

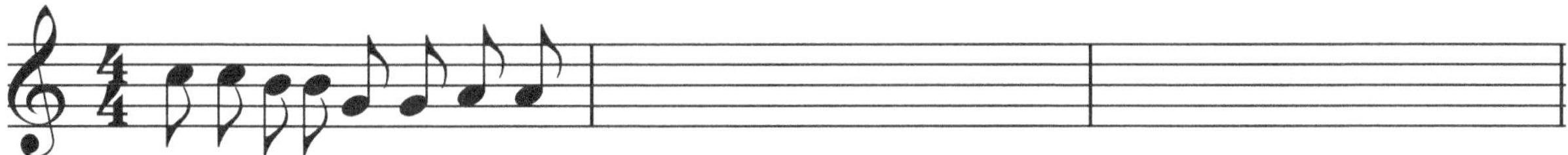

The eighth rest usually covers the two middle spaces of the staff. Draw it with a curved stroke from left to right, then a slash.

Exercise 20.
Write one rest on the right that is equivalent to all the rests on the left added together.

25

We can expand the pyramid of note values to include the eighth note and rest. Eight eighth notes equal four beats; equivalent in length to a whole note.

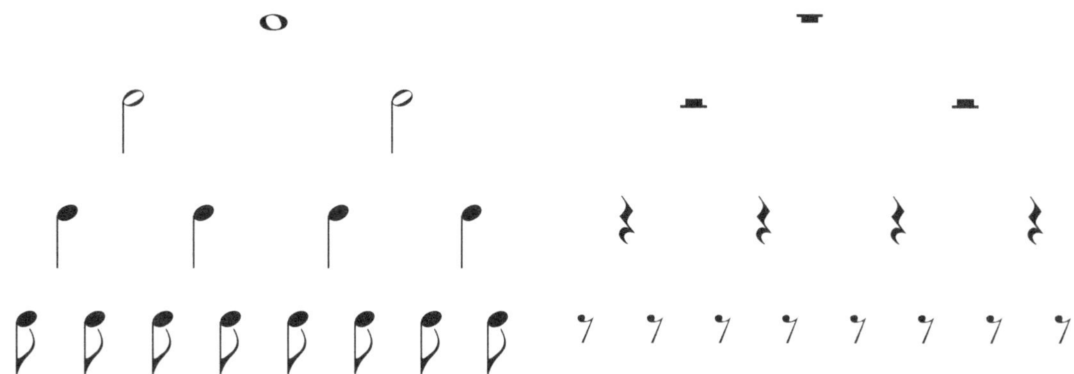

Exercise 21.
Write a note on the right that is equivalent to all the notes on the left added together.

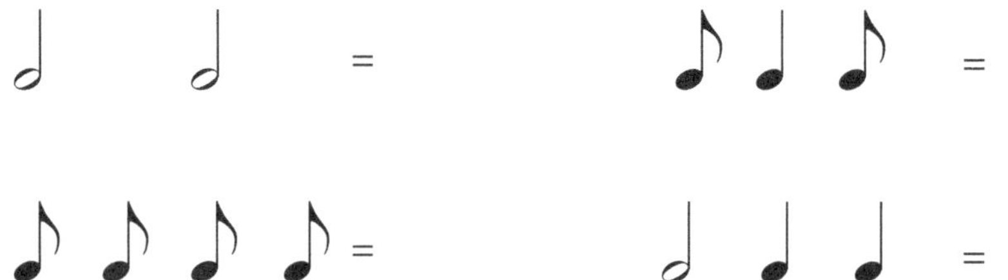

## Beams

For ease of reading, multiple eighth notes are connected by a *beam* that replaces the flags. Beams may not cross the third beat of the measure. Add your own measure of beamed eighth notes to this example.

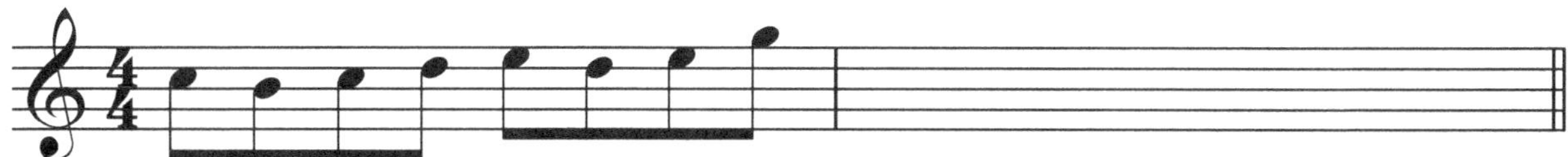

Beamed notes within a group must generally all be stemmed in the same direction—up or down. The note farthest from the center line determines which way the stems will go. The beam can help the reader by following the general direction of the melody, though it can't be curved, and the shortest stem in the group should still be two and a half spaces tall. This example is just for demonstration, because it contains low notes we haven't learned yet.

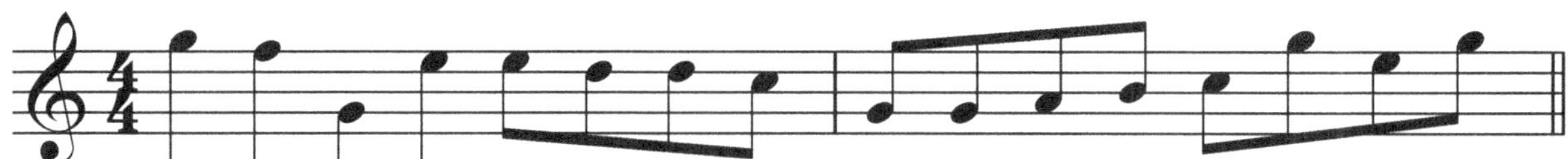

26

## Picking Direction

We count the eighth notes by including the word "and" in our counting, shown with an ampersand symbol (&) or a plus sign (+).

**1 + 2 + 3 + 4 +**

When playing eighth notes, continue tapping your foot in steady quarter notes. Don't let your foot speed up and tap every eighth note! Instead, imagine that your picking hand is connected to your foot by a rod. As the foot taps the floor on each number, your pick makes a downstroke. When the foot comes up on the "and," your pick makes an upstroke. You're using *alternate picking*, with downstrokes on the four beats in the measure. Now that we're looking at eighth notes, we'll call all four numbers *downbeats*, not just beat one. The upstroke "ands" are on *upbeats*.

If you're not used to it, coordinating these three actions should be practiced with the metronome, separate from reading: tapping your foot in quarter notes, counting aloud, and alternate-picking eighth notes.

To maintain rhythmic accuracy, your alternate-picking motion should continue whenever there are *any* eighth-note rhythms ahead of you in a measure. Look at the picking direction marks in this example containing notes and rests. I've shown the picking first with up and down arrows, then the way it is traditionally done, with the somewhat counterintuitive marks for down- and up-strokes placed only over the notes that are actually attacked. The pick continues its motion like the pendulum in a clock, so that when an attack is needed, it'll be right on time. Just move the pick slightly away from the strings until a note is to be played.

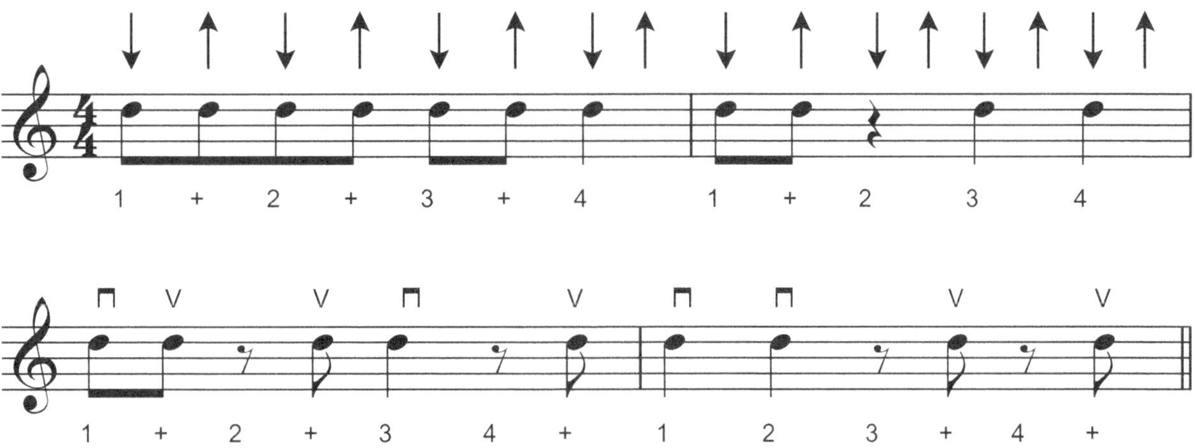


Exercise 22.

Write the correct picking directions for each note using traditional picking marks. Don't mark the rests.

Picking directions are written over the numerals where attacks are to occur. Write the correct notation for the rhythm. Add no rests; use notes that are long enough to keep attacks in the designated places and to create full measures according to the time signature.

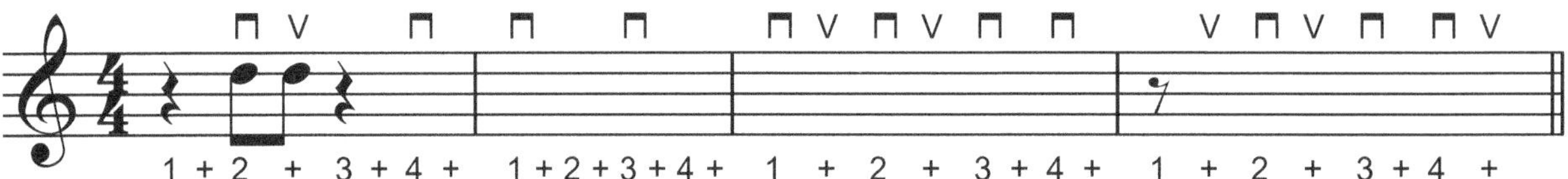

## Cut Time

Another popular meter is 2/2 or *cut time*, sometimes written as a slashed "C."

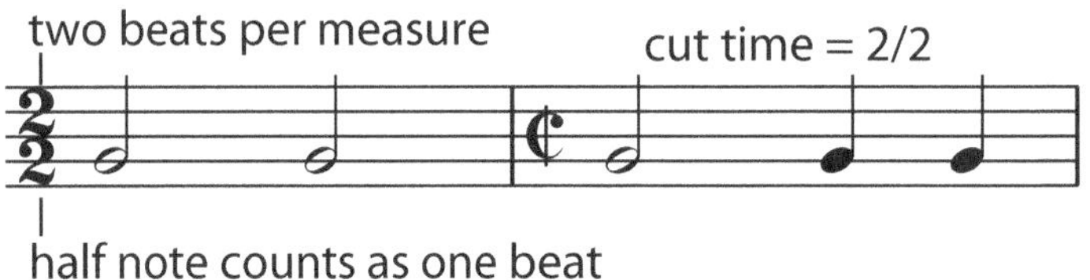


Cut time is used in folk or regional music styles all over the world. There are two beats per measure; a half note equals one beat. You can count it off like this: "one, two, one, two." Count off and clap this example. Only tap your foot once for each half note.

Since a half note is equal to two quarter notes, a measure of 2/2 is the same length as a measure of 4/4. You just tap your foot at half speed, which makes 2/2 good for uptempo music.

Try counting off the example above in 4/4 time and clapping it that way (ignore the beat numbers, counting to four instead of two). Start with the metronome set at 80, then repeat the example, gradually increasing the tempo each time until you reach about 160 beats per minute. Then switch it back to 80 bpm and count off the example in 2/2 time. The music tempo stays the same; the only thing that changes is the way you feel it and how your foot taps.

## Dots

A *dot* added to any note increases its duration by half. For example, if a whole note (four beats long) is followed by a dot, it is now six beats long. We can also say that a dotted whole note is the same as a whole note plus a half note.

The *dotted whole note* requires a time signature big enough to allow at least six beats in a measure.

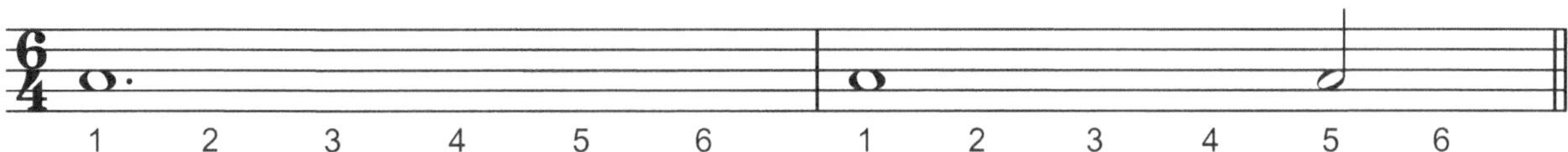

A *dotted half note* is also one and a half times its original value: three beats. This is commonly used to occupy a full measure of 3/4 time. It is equal in duration to a half note plus a quarter note.

A *dotted quarter note* is equal to a quarter note plus an eighth note: one and a half beats. If a dotted quarter appears on beat 1, the next thing after it starts on the "and" of 2. Slowly count and clap this example until your understanding is clear and you can read the dotted quarter note rhythm reliably with the metronome.

Exercise 24.
Write a note on the right that is equivalent to all the notes on the left added together. Sometimes a dotted note is what you need.

29

Exercise 25.

Add one note of the proper size (where needed) at the end of each measure to make the music fit the time signature.

Exercise 26.

Write the correct notation for the rhythm dictated by the **picking directions**. The numerals are only there to help keep your place. Add no rests; make the notes the correct length to fill the measure and keep attacks in the designated places. Some dotted notes will be needed.

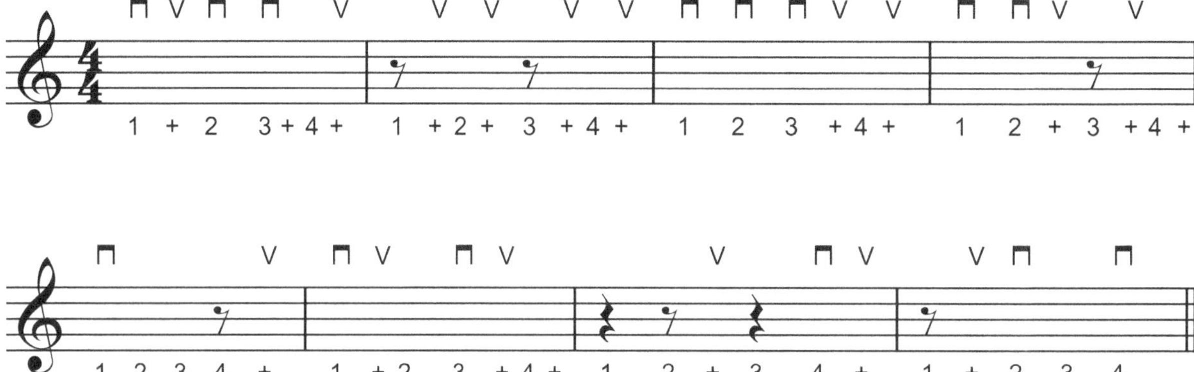

The table on the next page contains every possible way to fill **two beats** (half a measure of 4/4 or one measure of 2/4 time) with eighth notes and rests. It is similar to the quarter-note vocabulary list. The proportions are the same but the notes and rests are half the duration.

Exercise 27.

1. Find all the places where you can combine two eighth rests into one quarter rest and get the same silence. Write the equivalent rhythm below the original in the same cell.

2. Find the places where an eighth note is followed by an eighth rest. Write these equivalent-attack measures out again using a quarter note in those places.

3. Now find the places where an eighth note is followed by two eighth rests; write the measures out again using a dotted quarter note instead.

4. There's one more possibility for cells 8 and 16. They are equal, attack-wise, to a half note and a half rest, respectively. Write those in.

# Eighth-Note Vocabulary List

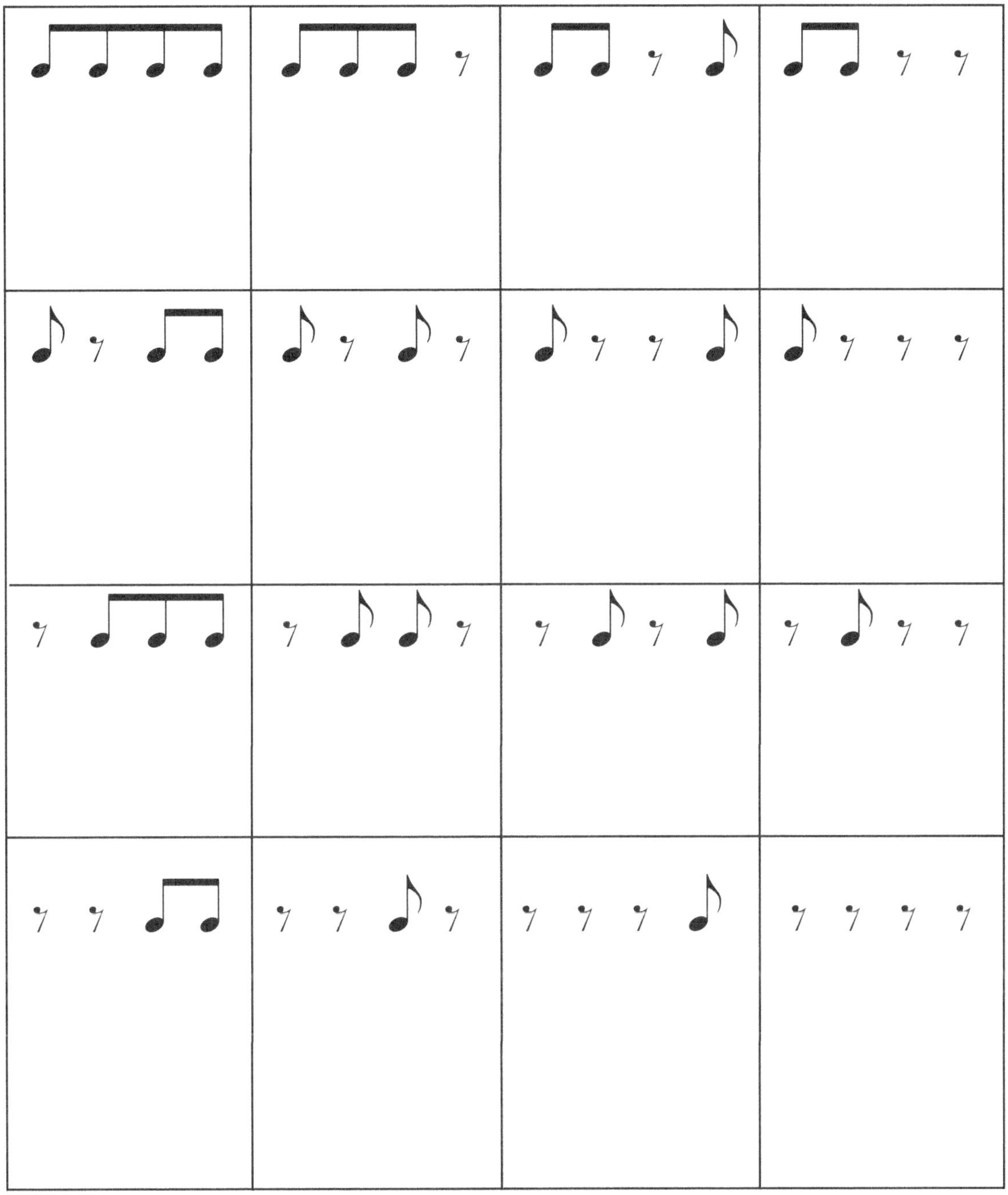

## Practice

1. Now that you know how dots work, go back to the quarter-note vocabulary list in Chapter Two and find the two measures where you can use a dotted half note to get the same attacks as those created by quarter notes and rests. Write those rhythms.

2. Practice alternate-picking in eighth notes while counting aloud, with your foot tapping along with the metronome, until it feels automatic. First count each number and all the "ands." Then keep the picking and tapping the same but drop the "ands" from your counting.

3. Practice reading the eighth-note vocabulary list forward, backward, and skipping around, eventually adding the new rhythms to your memory.

# Chapter 5: Intervals

## 4th String

The G note on the second line of the staff and the A note on the second space are found on the 4th string, at frets 5 and 7.

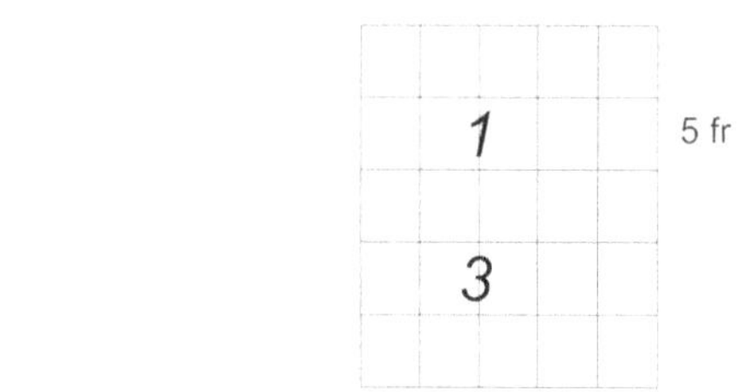

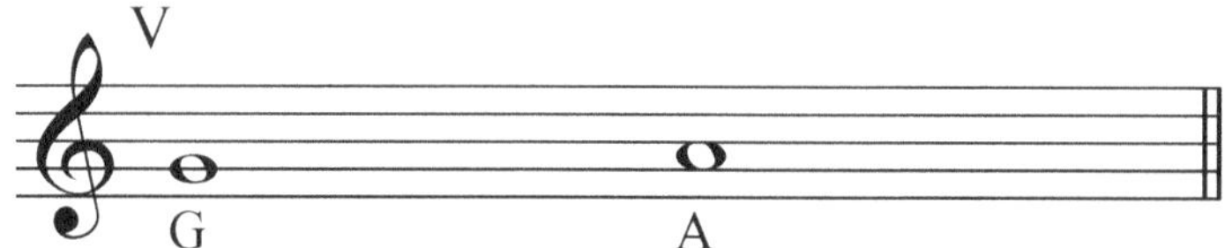



When playing these notes after the ones you already know on the 3rd string (B–C–D), shift your hand back to fifth position so that the G is played by the index finger. If these notes are followed by a 5th-string note in this position (which we'll cover soon) you'll want to use the fingering shown in the diagram. If you are going back to a B on the 3rd string the A may be played with the 4th finger.

As before, in order to make a strong mental impression of the new notes, verbally proclaim all aspects of each: the staff location, fretboard location, and the finger you use: "G, second line, 4th string, 5th fret, 1st finger. A, second space, 4th string, 7th fret, 3rd finger." Then look away  and visualize the locations of the notes on the staff and the fingerboard.

Now we have two G notes that we can read or write. The 2nd-string G is on the first space above the staff. The 4th-string G is on the second line. The interval of eight letters (GABCDEFG) or eight lines and spaces on the staff is called an *octave*.

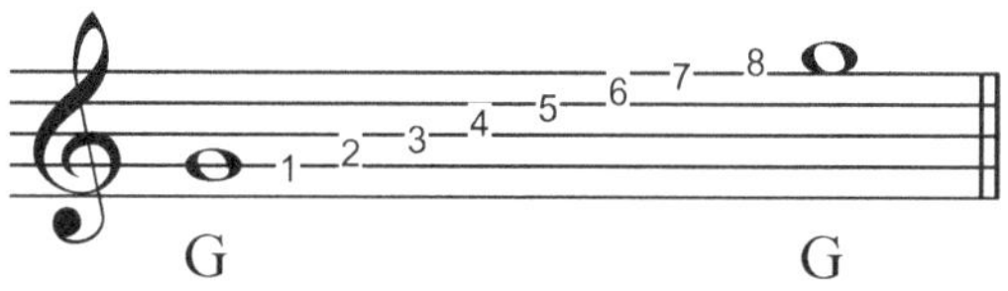



Exercise 28.

For each tabbed pitch, draw a quarter note on the correct line or space. Then cover the tab and play with the metronome.

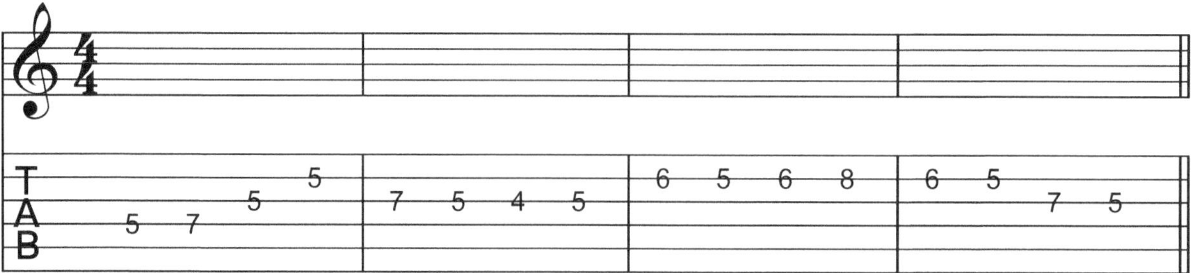

Exercise 29.

First read the notation along with the metronome. After you've read it, write the letter names and mark the note in each frame.

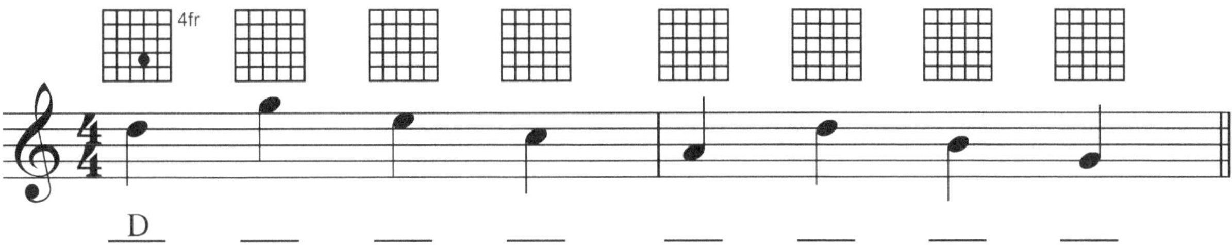

### A Reminder

Don't look at your fingers or at the guitar while you play. Keep your hand in position so you don't have to look.

If the music requires a lot of position-shifting (most of the music in this book does not), try sitting so that your fretting hand is near the line of sight between your eyes and the paper. Think of the marching lyres on the trumpets in a marching band; they put the music right in front of the players' fingers.

## Counting Intervals

There is no "zero" interval in music theory. We refer to the line or space (or letter) that we start from as "one," and count from there. Notes of the same pitch, in the same octave, are said to be in *unison*, from the Latin *unus*, for *one*.

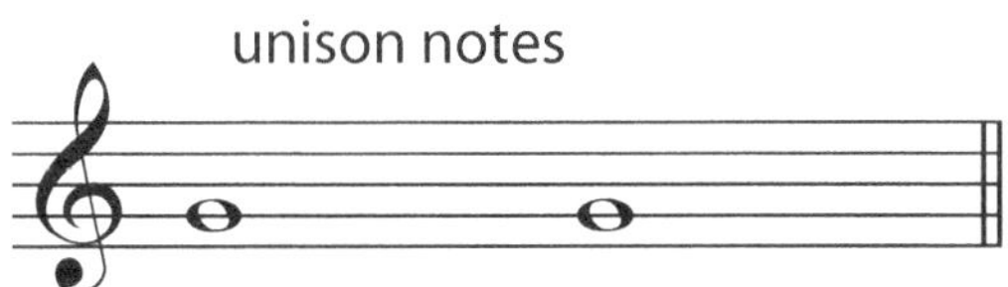


The whole-step and half-step intervals we learned are also called *2nd* intervals: A–B, B–C, etc. Notes that are a 2nd apart are always neighbors on the staff: one on a line and one on the next space, or vice versa. A whole step is also called a **major** 2nd. The half step is a **minor** 2nd. The staff naturally contains minor 2nds from B–C and from E–F only.

Exercise 30.

Next to the given pitches, draw noteheads that are a 2nd interval **higher**. Don't worry about the names or the fretboard locations for now.

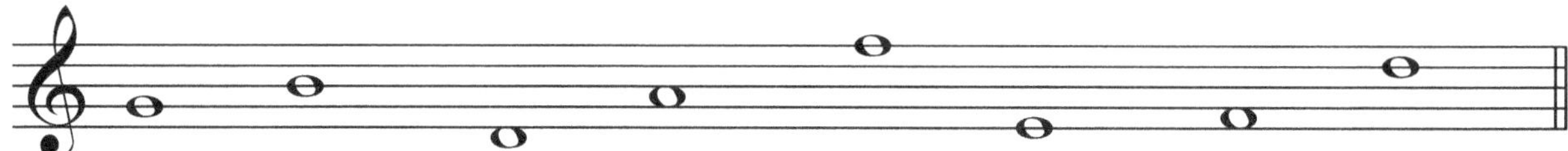

Exercise 31.

Draw noteheads that are a 2nd **lower** than the given pitches.

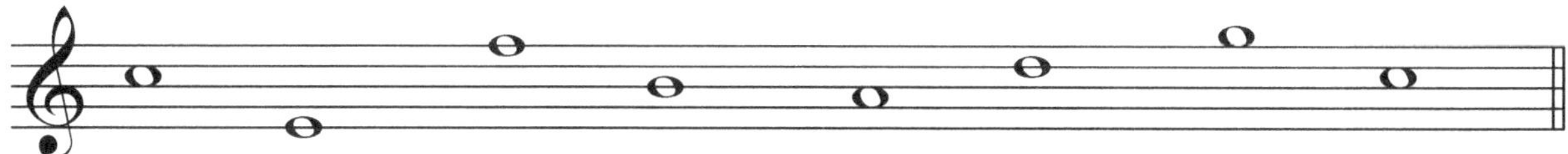

Like 2nds, notes that are an octave apart are always different: one on a line and one a space. They are divided by three spaces or lines (whichever you prefer to count).

Exercise 32.

Draw noteheads an octave **higher** than the pitches in the first measure. Draw noteheads an octave **lower** than the pitches in the next measure.

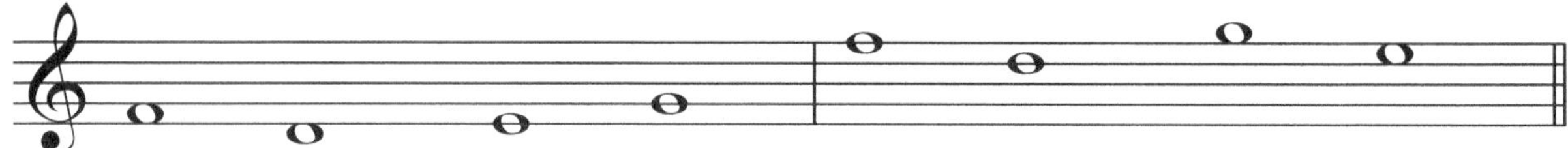

## 1st String

Notes on the 1st string in 5th position require the use of *ledger* (or *leger*) *lines*. These are short, disconnected line segments that extend the range of the staff. The first ledger line above the staff is the note A, which we play on string 1 at the 5th fret. Above the first ledger line is B, at the 7th fret. Remember that from B to C is always a half step? Good. That means that the second ledger-line note, C, is just one fret higher on the guitar. Play this note with the 4th finger.

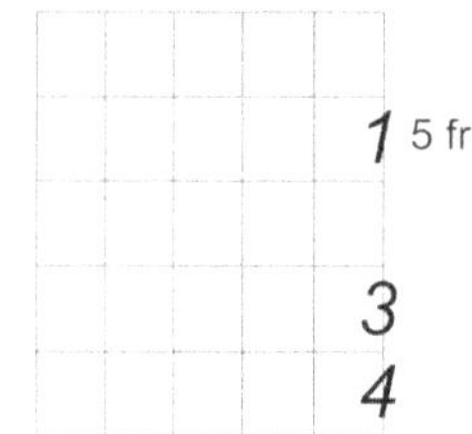


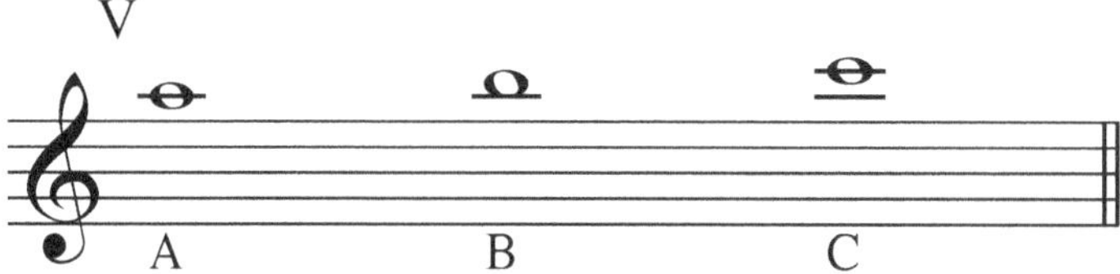

Since you've read a few verbal descriptions already, I think you can create and recite a description of the notes on the first string aloud without me giving it to you. What are those notes? Where on the staff? Where are they on the fretboard again? Which are the preferred fingers? OK, thanks.

Exercise 33.
Without playing or looking at your guitar, place dots at the correct spots in the 4th-position frames and write letter names in the blanks. Then play while looking at the notation only.

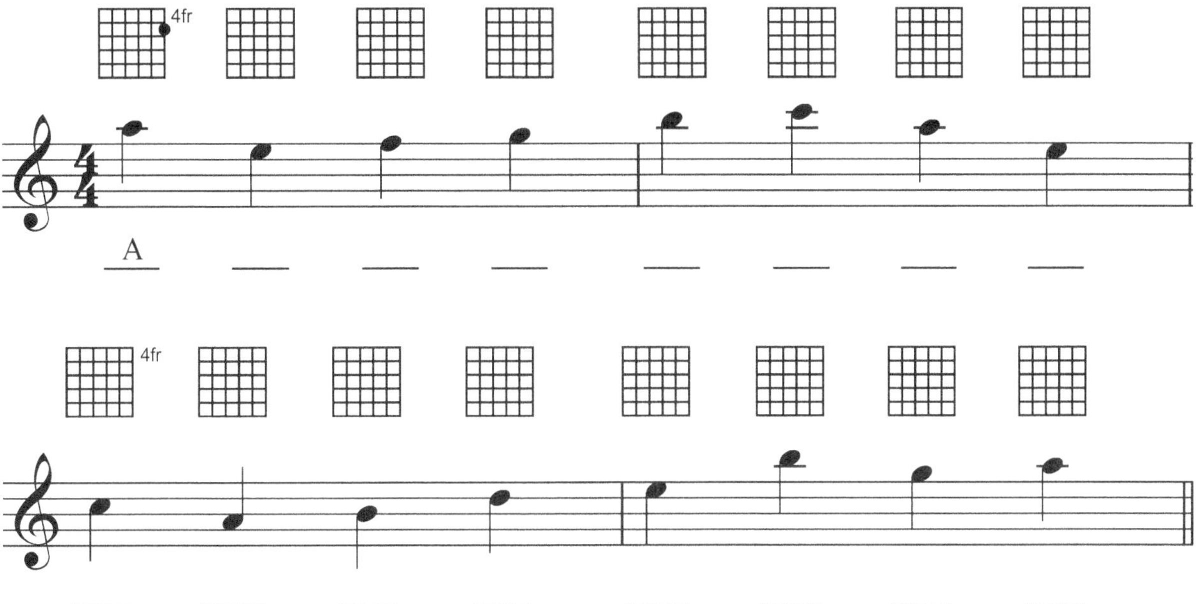

Exercise 34.
Draw the quarter notes on the staff; then write their letter names. Go for accuracy, then speed. Then play while looking at the notation only.

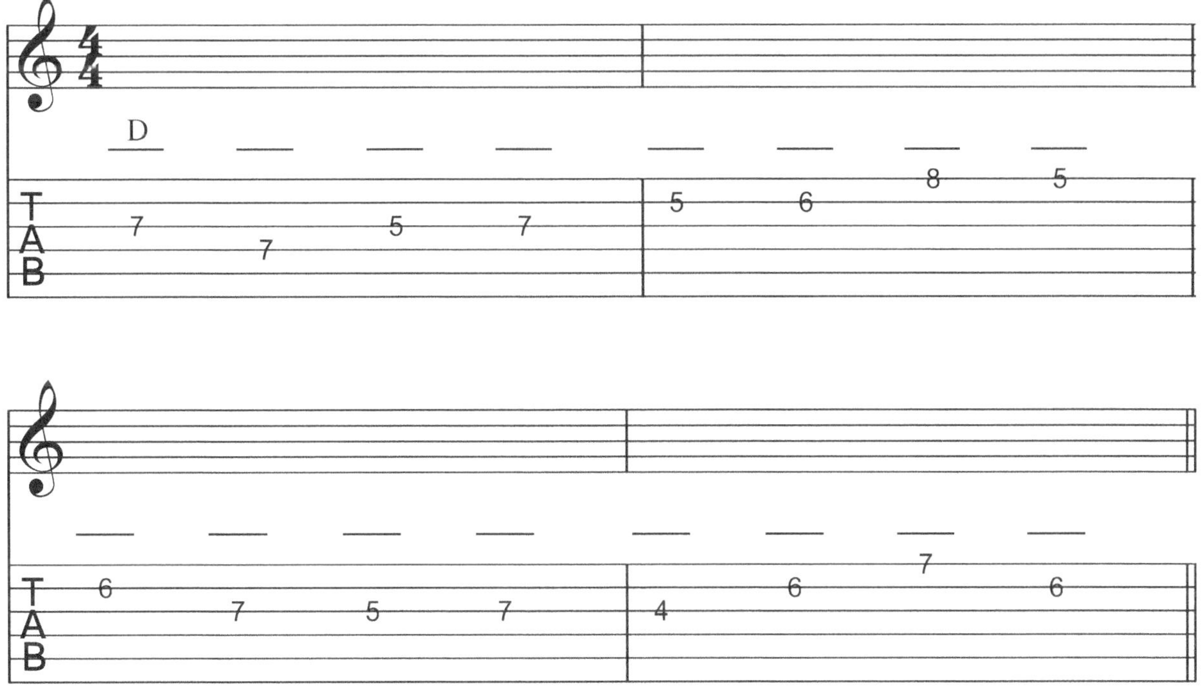

## Practice: Pitch + Rhythm = Music

Reading pitch and rhythm at the same time is tough unless all the different subskills are rock solid. Spend two minutes on each item in the following list every day for the next few weeks. When you get stuck while reading, think about whether one area is weaker than others so you can put in more work on it separately.

• Note Names on the Fretboard

Practice naming the notes we've learned in 5th position until you can do it without thinking. Randomly grab one of the notes we've covered on the neck and name it aloud. Draw fingerboard diagrams of notes with their names. Close your eyes, pick random letters from A to G and find them on the fretboard. Go for accuracy first, then speed.

• Notes on the Staff

Practice naming the notes on the staff until this too becomes automatic. Pick a staff location and name it as quickly as you can without making a mistake—no guessing! When that becomes easy, go the other way. Pick a letter and write the notehead on the staff. Finally, get some notated music and label each pitch with its letter name.

• Counting

We started the book with this because it's the backbone of reading and has to be strong. Practice tapping your foot and counting beats aloud in 4/4 or 3/4 time along with a metronome while reading a book or magazine to yourself. It will help internalize the beat-keeping reflex. Try counting to yourself and reading rhythms while carrying on a conversation with a reading partner.

• Rhythm Figures

Review and practice the rhythmic vocabulary lists from previous chapters. Write the rhythms out again, but now use a different pitch for each figure so that you start combining pitch and rhythm when you play them. Here are two eighth-note rhythms from the list as an example; write out the others on blank staff paper.

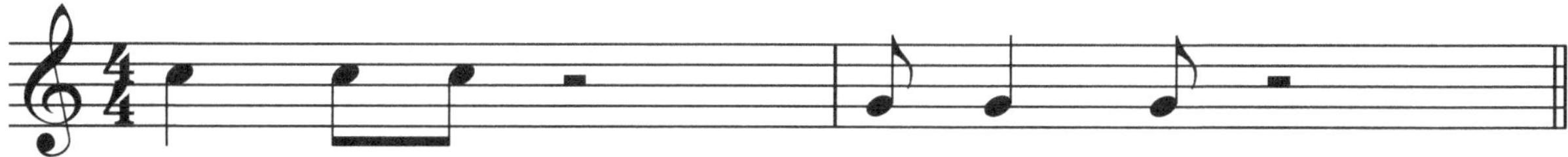

A common mistake is to lock into a repetitive rhythm because you're focused on the pitches. For example, if you are reading a melody with steady quarter notes, and the rhythm changes to eighth notes, you may forget to make the switch. These zone-outs especially seem to happen during passages with stepwise movement.

Practice this scalar example along with the metronome, maintaining awareness of rhythm and picking direction. Keep all upstrokes on the "ands" for now. If the tempo is too quick to read the eighth notes, read the entire example at a lower tempo. Don't rush long notes or drag short ones, even when rehearsing alone. Bad habits should not be reinforced in practice.

• Fingering

This is easy to overlook. If you're using bad left-hand technique—jumping up and down the fretboard using one finger—you'll force yourself to look down too much. Use all four fingers, play with one finger per fret whenever possible, and minimize the shifting. Go back to the fretboard diagrams and notation you've made and write the best fingering choice for each note.

One of the goals of reading is to increase your repertoire of songs and techniques. When you meet up with something that is new to you (e.g., a major-key melody in 3/4 time), don't expect to be able to read it as well as you can material that is more familiar. New material still must be learned and practiced.

These two examples combine pitches and rhythms we've covered thus far. Take as much time as you need until you are sure you're playing them as written.

## Sharps, Flats, and Naturals

These three signs are used to change the pitch of a note.

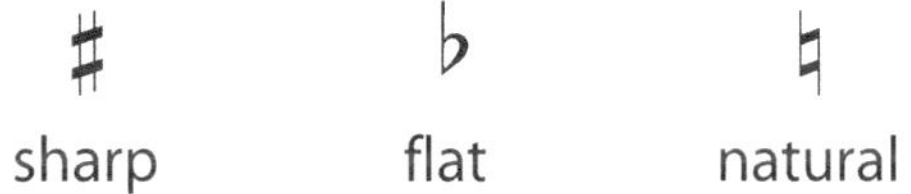


To ensure the right pitch is played, when one of these signs is used it is always drawn **before** (to the left of) the notehead. In verbal or written identification it comes **after** the letter.

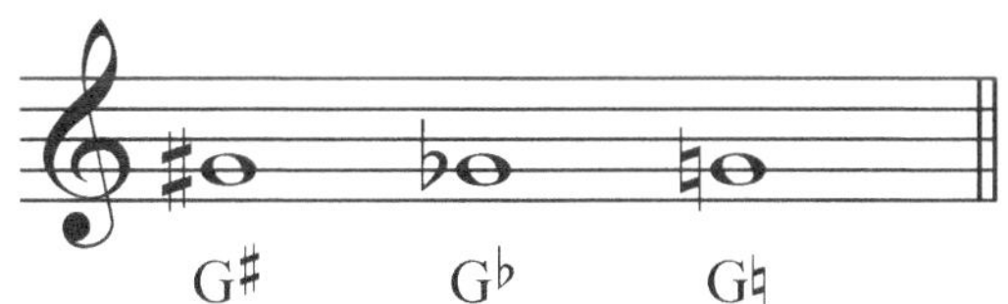

The body of each sign is about the same size as the notehead and is placed directly next to it. Each sign has a vertical part that makes it a little more than two spaces tall, drawn with vertical line segments that don't lean over. The horizontal lines on sharps and naturals should slant up a bit so they stand out from the staff lines. Finally, make sure you keep a point at the bottom of your flat signs so they are not confused with the letter *b*.

When sharps, flats, or naturals appear next to noteheads, they are called *accidentals*.

Draw four of each type, just to the left of the noteheads on this staff.

The sharp **raises** a pitch by a half step (one fret on the guitar). In the following example there is a new note for us, C♯, played on string 3, fret 6.

The flat **lowers** a pitch by a half step. In the example, the flat sign tells you to play the note one fret lower than E: an E♭ on the 2nd string, fret 4.

The natural **cancels** a previous sharp or flat, restoring a note to its natural pitch.

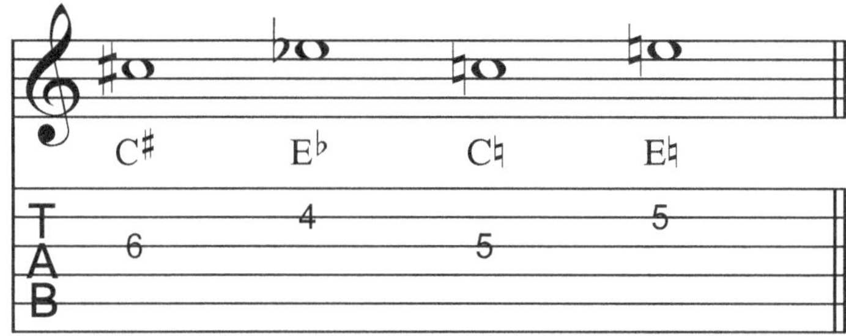


All the pitches we learned in earlier chapters may be called *natural notes*. Though they are usually named with letters alone, to change them back from a sharp or flat we have to call them A♮ (A-natural), B♮, C♮, and so on.

Exercise 35.
Draw noteheads with the prescribed signs in front of them on the staff at the given pitches. Don't worry about playing them yet.

Exercise 36.

Write the names of these notes. Remember that the sign comes afterward when writing the letter name.

—  —  —  —  —  —  —  —  —  —  —  —

## Accidental Rules

1. An accidental is canceled by the bar line.

2. An accidental on any note also applies to all later notes **on the same line or space** within the measure, until it is overruled by a later accidental.

3. Notes with the same name in a **different octave** are not affected by previous accidentals.

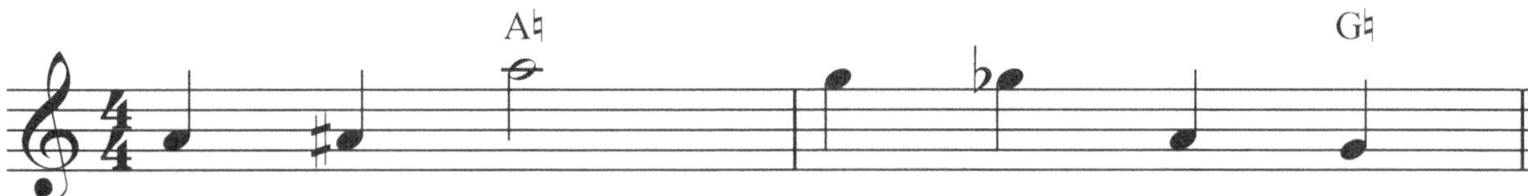


Exercise 37.

Keeping the accidental rules in mind, correctly name each note. Check your answers in the back of the book.

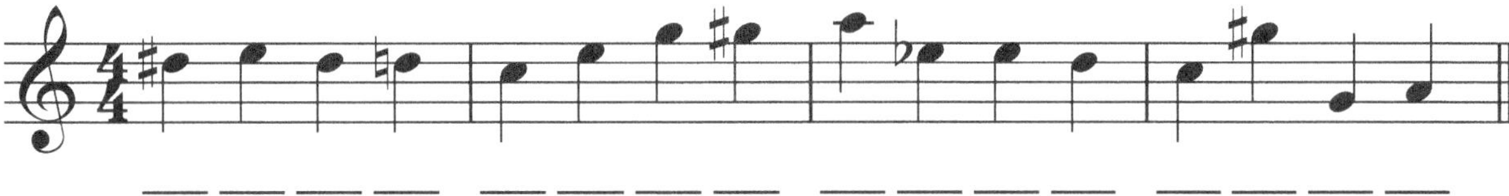

—  —  —  —  —  —  —  —  —  —  —  —

When changing the pitch of a note, you're faced with a choice. For example, to get the pitch in between D and E, do I use D♯ or E♭? There's no law, but it's best to look at the later notes and choose the accidental that necessitates the fewest accidentals be used overall, especially when they are in close succession. It's also easier to read if the noteheads on the staff follow the melodic direction. If all else is equal, use flat notes on melodic lines that go down, and sharp notes on lines that go up.

The selection of accidentals is sometimes best made by considering the chords behind the melody, whether actual or implied, but you don't have to worry about this if you are a beginner.

Exercise 38.

First write names for the notes in the blanks over the tab. Use a pencil so you can change your mind. Use the minimum number of accidentals to make the example easy to read. Then draw the eighth-note pitches on the staff, writing the noteheads first, then the accidentals, then the beams, then the stems. Though your choice of accidentals does not have to be exactly the same as those in the Solutions section, check to make sure you don't use more accidentals than are necessary.

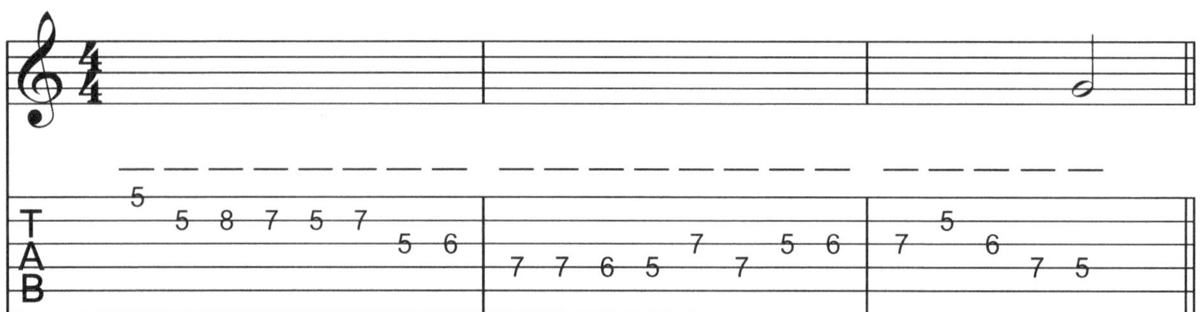

**Practice**

1. The list on page 36 contains many small items to practice in preparation for general melodic reading.

2. Go back to the examples with accidentals and work out how you'd most efficiently play them. Try to minimize position-shifting, and make written fingering notes if necessary. Take your time.

# Chapter 6: Ties

This section may present a challenge, but the rewards are worth the work. Make sure you can complete the written exercises, count and play all the examples, and understand the principles involved.

Besides the dot, the *tie* is another method for increasing the length of a note. The tie is a curved line between two noteheads of the same pitch. When two notes are tied together, only the first one is attacked, and the tone continues for the duration of both. In the example below, the ties cause the C notes to start on the "and" of 3.

Ties usually go on the opposite side of the note from the stem. For unstemmed notes, imagine where a stem would go if there were one and put the tie on the opposite side.

### Ties

A tie is not the same as a *slur*, which connects notes of different pitch via hammer-on or pull-off. For the last three notes in the example, only the first A is picked. The other two notes are played with a pull-off followed by a hammer-on. You may notice that when the stems change direction (as on beat 3), slurs go to the end of the stem, a detail you don't need to worry about for now.

### Slurs

## Duration Rules

Understanding the rules for correctly writing dotted and tied notes will also make it easier for you to read them, because either type of notation is only allowed to represent certain sounds. The general idea is to use the minimum amount of marks on the page while making sure the player knows where beats 1 and 3 are at all times.

1. Always have a note or rest on beat 3 when using quarter notes or smaller.

2. Do not exceed the available space in a measure.

3. Use the largest single note you can to get the desired duration unless it breaks rule 1 or 2.

4. For uneven lengths, use a dotted note instead of a tie unless it breaks rule 1 or 2.

Here are some examples of the duration rules in action.

1. Show beat 3 when using quarter notes or smaller. Like beams, ties are used to help us keep track of beat 3 in 4/4 time. A quarter note (or a dotted quarter note, measure 3) may not cross beat 3 of the measure, so the equivalent duration must be created with a tied note.

It's ok for a "hollow note" (whole, half, or dotted half) to cross beat 3. It's also ok for a quarter note or a dotted quarter note to cross beat 2 or 4.

2. If you want a note that is longer than the remaining space in the bar, use ties to make the note cross the bar line(s). The notation in each measure must add up to the time signature, and the downbeat of each measure must have something on it, showing beat 1.

Suppose we want a note that is six beats long, but the time signature only allows four beats per measure. We use a tie to join a whole note (four beats) to a half note in the next measure. Only the first note is attacked; the other provides the additional two beats of duration. The tone is now six beats long.

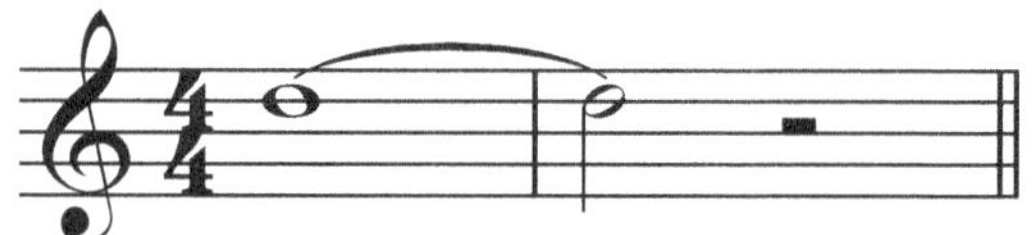

Here we want a note that is four beats long, but starting on beat 3. There are only two beats left in the measure, so we can't fit a whole note in. Instead we tie a half note (two beats) to another half note (two more beats) in the next bar. The total duration of the tone is four beats.

3. Use the largest note possible (while still showing beat 3 when quarter notes or smaller are used). There is no reason to tie together two half notes in the same measure when a whole note will do the job without breaking any other rule.

4. Use a dotted note instead of a tie when possible.

It may look strange, but it's common to tie a dotted note. Here, a dotted half note (three beats long) takes up beats 2, 3, and 4 of the first measure. If we want it to sustain until beat 2 of the second measure, we tie the dotted half note to a quarter note on beat 1. Now the tone is four beats long.

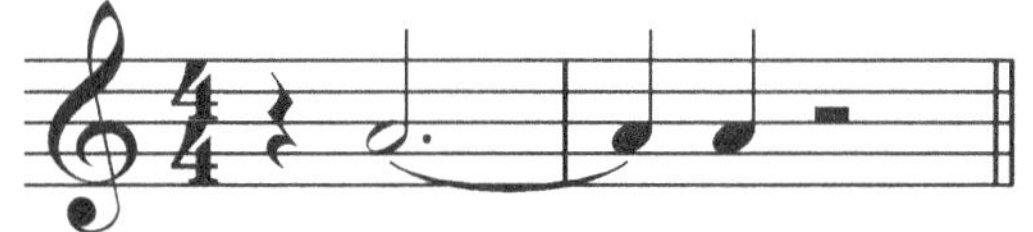

A dotted note may be tied to make sure beat 3 of a measure is visible.

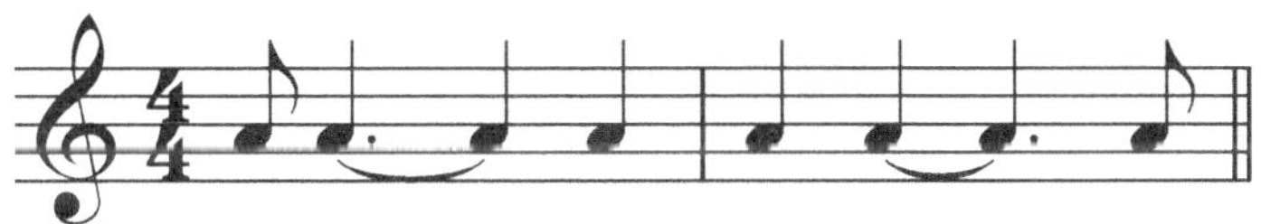

Exercise 39.

Add just **one note** where needed at the end of each measure to make the notation fit the meter. Use dotted notes where necessary.

## Writing Rhythms

Part of *ear training*—a complete subject of its own—is *rhythmic dictation*: writing the rhythms you hear using correct notation. The best way to start doing this is to break the job into small steps. For now, we'll assume we have a rhythm we already know how to play, and want to notate it.

First, count aloud while playing the rhythm, and listen for a strong recurring downbeat where it feels natural to say "one." This gives you the time signature. I am imagining a rhythm in 4/4 time for the demonstration.

Next, count the number of bars in the entire figure. We'll work with a rhythm figure that is two measures long. You can always break an example into one-measure or even smaller time frames. We can only use notation that we've learned, so we can't write anything smaller than an eighth note for now. With dots and ties, however, this includes well over 65,536 possibilities in two bars.

Play the rhythm with strict alternate picking that follows the tapping of your foot as we studied in Chapter Four. (After we're finished, you can go back to a different picking pattern if you prefer.) If any upstrokes are used, then the rhythm contains at least some eighth notes. Write out two measures of steady counting that includes the smallest rhythmic unit played. If there are no upstrokes, then no "and" marks (+) are needed.

```
1 + 2 + 3 + 4 + | 1 + 2 + 3 + 4 + |
```

Now, with pencil in hand, hum the part while tapping your foot. Don't worry about rhythmic notation yet. Just mark a dot at every place where there is an attack. Watching your foot can help.

```
.       .       .       | . .     .     . .   |
1 + 2 + 3 + 4 +   1 + 2 + 3 + 4 +
```

Next, does any tone cut off before the next one starts, creating a rest? Let's mark the start times of these silences with circles.

```
.       . o     .       | . .     .     . .   |
1 + 2 + 3 + 4 +   1 + 2 + 3 + 4 +
```

When you are satisfied that your marks are over the right beats, then count up the durations required to put the attacks where they need to be. For instance, my second attack falls on the "and" of 2, so the first note must be three eighth notes long: a dotted quarter. The third item is a rest on beat 3, so the second note is only an eighth. Continue translating the marks into notation, following the rules for dots and ties. A tie is used to show beat 3 in the second measure here.

Read the notation you've written with a metronome, making sure it resembles the original rhythmic example and fits the time signature you've chosen.

Exercise 40.
Using dots or ties where necessary, draw notes so that the meter is obeyed and that notes and rests only happen on the marked beat numerals below the staff.

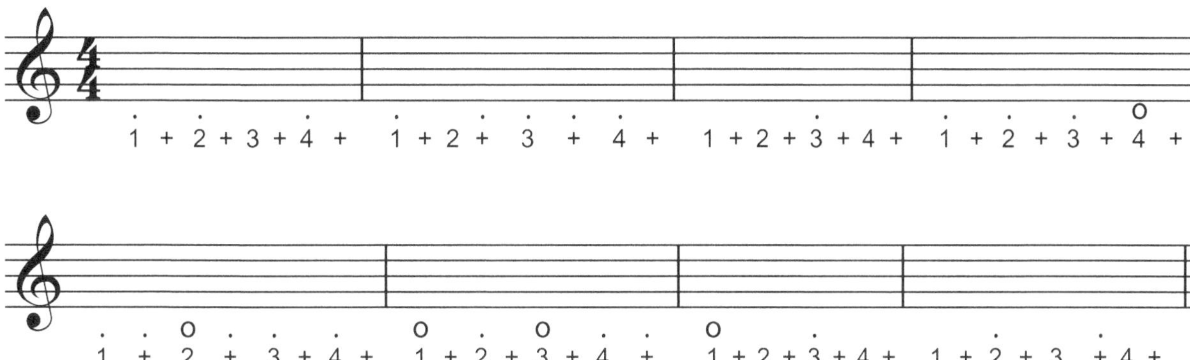


## Tied Accidentals

When a note sporting an accidental is tied across the bar line, the accidental persists for the duration of that note only, then it is canceled. Play this example, letting the C♯ sustain for its full written value.

## Adding Up Rests

Ties are **never used** on rests. Ties are used to remove note attacks, which rests do not have, so tying them is not needed. Dots are also **not used** in 4/4 time on the rests that we've learned thus far. Exceptions to the "no dotted rests" rule will occur in certain situations that we will see later. For now, we'll complete the desired duration of silence using the biggest rest allowed by duration rules 1 and 2 (they're on the first page of this chapter), adding successively smaller rests as needed. No dots, no ties.

In this example we want six beats of silence, starting on beat 3. There are only two beats left in the first measure, so we put a half rest on beat 3 and follow with a whole rest in the next bar.

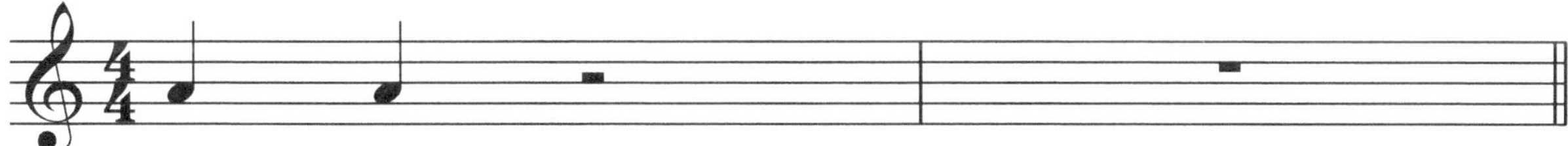

Use smaller rests to make sure there is something on beat 3 in 4/4 time when quarter notes (and especially eighth notes) or smaller are present.

Exercise 41.

Fill up the missing parts of each bar with correctly written rests so that the notes fall on the beats indicated.

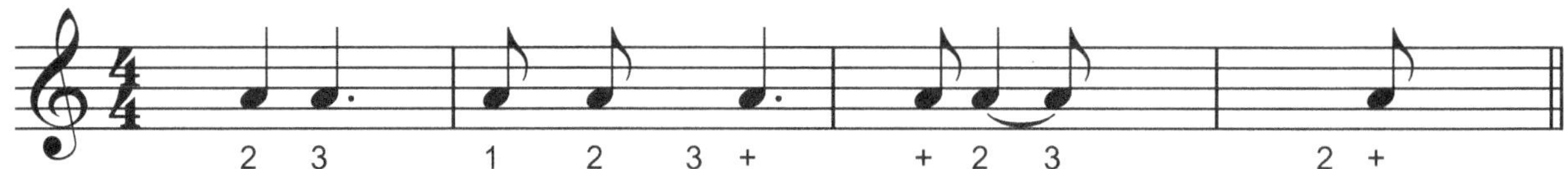


In a special exception made for convenience, a whole rest is used to signify a full measure of silence in **any** meter with fewer than four beats per bar. These are just called *bar rests*, and have the whole rest in the center of the measure.

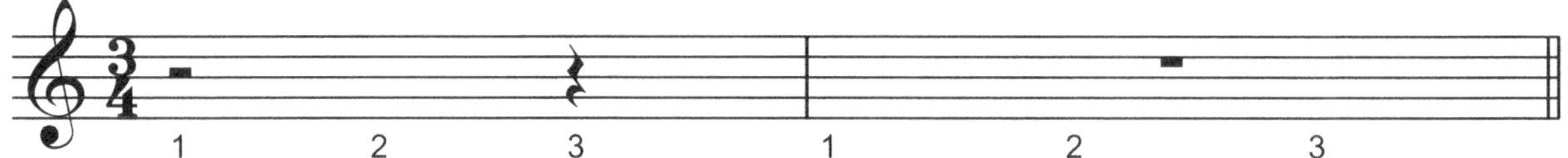


Multiple measures of rest may be indicated by a solid block with a number written over it. In this example, you count four measures while someone else plays another part. Then come in at measure 5.

There are more conventions for writing beamed notes, rests, dots, and ties, some of which we'll see in later chapters.

## Pickups

A song may start on a beat other than the downbeat. Rather than fill up the beginning of the first measure with rests, a special measure is allowed that does not have the full number of beats described by the time signature. This is called a *pickup measure*, which contains *pickup notes*. The pickup bar does not get a measure number.

When a pickup measure is used, it's best to use a two-bar countoff to make sure you start playing at the right time. While tapping the foot in in steady quarter notes, count two half notes aloud, then start counting in 4/4 during the pickup measure: "One! Two! One, two, three!" Then the pickup phrase (in this example) starts on the "and" of beat 3.

46

**Practice**

Play this chapter's examples with the metronome, being careful to continue counting through tied and dotted rhythms. If you lose your focus for a second, you may feel like you have fallen very far behind. This can lead you to jump too far ahead, thinking that is what is needed to catch up. (This is different from when you know where you are and are just **looking** ahead.) In fact you have probably only been lost for one or two beats.

Keep the foot tapping, and find the last note you were on when you felt yourself getting lost. In a group, the others would probably only be one or two beats ahead of that spot, and if you keep your eyes right there until you hear where everybody is, you can jump back in more easily.

The topics in this chapter require lots of practice. Write out and play some of your own more-complex rhythms. One way to do this is to just combine any two examples from the quarter and eighth-note vocabulary lists, tying the last note in the first to the first one of the next. If the duration rules allow, combine the two tied notes into one larger (or a dotted) note.

If you have someone to practice with, write a one- or two-bar rhythm example, then play it with the metronome repeatedly so they can transcribe it. Then switch places and transcribe the other guy's rhythm.

# Chapter 7: Scalar Reading

**5th String**

Here are the natural notes on the 5th string at the 5th, 7th, and 8th frets: D–E–F.

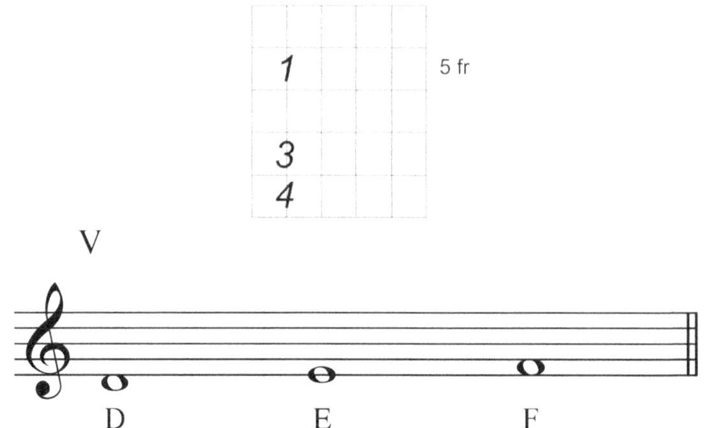


Place your 1st finger on the note D. Once your other fingers are poised, one per fret over frets 6-8 on the 5th string, try not to look at them, and do not take your hand off the fretboard.

**Verbalize**

To memorize this note's name, repeat the following description aloud as you play.
"D, 5th string, 5th fret, 1st finger."

The D note you're playing is on the space below the staff. Describe aloud the staff location for D.
"D, below the staff."

**Visualize**

Repeat both verbal descriptions, but this time close your eyes; do not play, but mentally visualize 1) your finger playing the note, and 2) the note as it appears on the staff.
"D, 5th string, 5th fret, 1st finger. Below the staff."

Now, keeping to the one-finger-per-fret rule, play the E with the 3rd finger, then the F a half step higher, with the 4th finger.

Perform out-loud verbalization and eyes-closed visualization for the two new notes.
"E, 5th string, 7th fret, 3rd finger. F, 8th fret, 4th finger."

The E note is on the 1st line of the staff. The F is on the 1st space. Say it aloud.
"E, 1st line. F, 1st space."

Mentally connect the positions of these pitches on the staff with their correct fretboard locations in the proper octave. For instance, we know D notes in two different octaves: one on the 5th string, and one an octave higher, on the 3rd string. We now have almost two octaves of natural notes to keep track of.

Notes with the same name in different octaves are not freely interchangeable when you are reading. Playing the wrong one can disturb the shape of a melody.

Exercise 42.

For each tabbed pitch, draw an eighth note on the correct line or space, and write the name of the pitch. Then cover the tab and the letters, and play with the metronome set at 50 bpm.

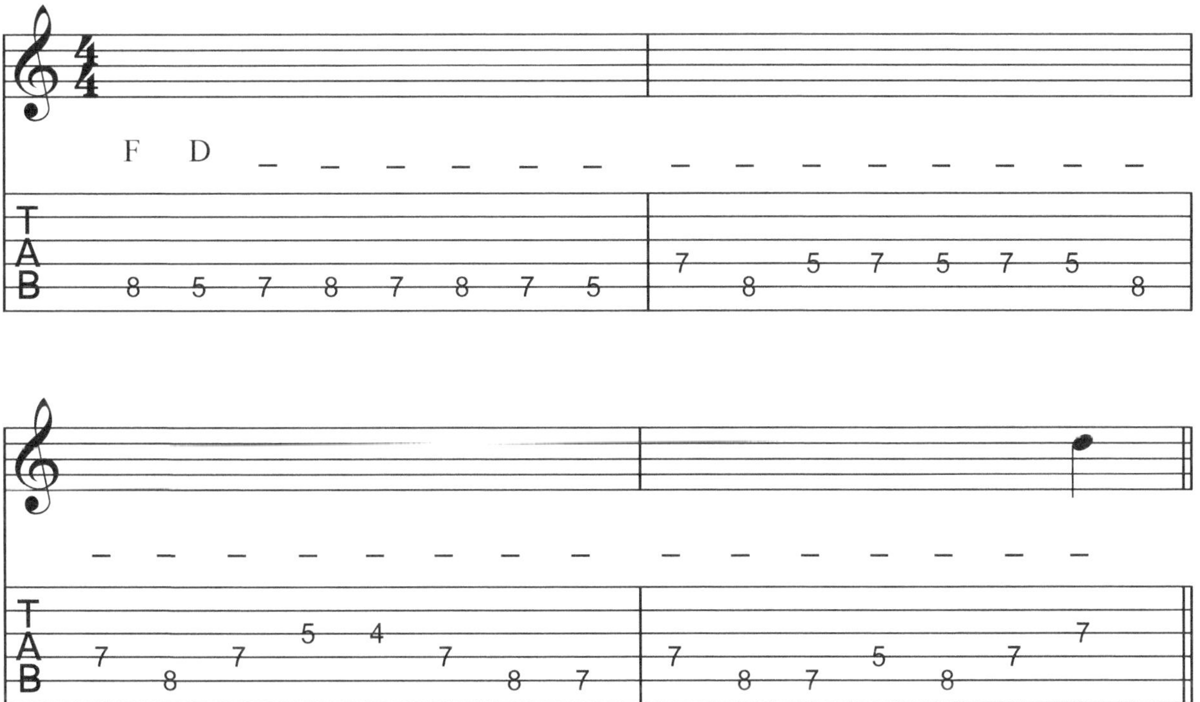


Exercise 43.

Read the notation on the next page along with the metronome, naming the notes aloud as you play. After you've read it, write the letter name for each note below the staff.

## The Blue Danube

name notes:

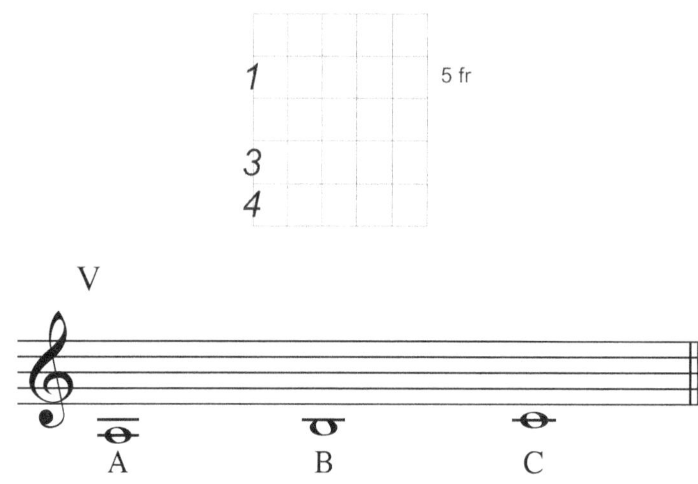

## 6th String

These complete our range of natural notes available in the 5th position. The A is on the second ledger line below the staff and is played with the 1st finger. The B is below the first ledger line, played with the 3rd finger. The C is played with the 4th finger, and is the first ledger line below the staff.



Close your eyes as you recite the staff and fretboard locations of these three notes. Then plant your hand on the 6th string in 5th position and play the notes while reciting the information aloud. As before, the new notes have duplicate letter names to those we've already learned. Our reading range now includes the notes A, B, and C in three octaves. Play and name all the natural notes we have learned in this area of the fretboard. Notice that the letter names of pitches on the 6th and 1st strings are the same.

Exercise 44.

Without playing or looking at your guitar, write the letter names of the notes. Then play with the metronome. Finally, write the numbers at the correct spots on the tab staff.

Exercise 45.

Translate the tab into notes on the staff, following the beat numbers to create the correct rhythmic notation. Any necessary rests have already been provided; you will only write notes. Then cover up the tab, and play.

## Major Scales

On the staff, a scale is a series of notes going up or down in 2nds—line, space, line, space. 2nd intervals are also called *steps*, so scales are said to have **stepwise motion**.

The *major scale formula* has half steps from 3-4 and from 7-8, with whole steps between all other notes. This is an important fact to memorize. Most music theory depends on the major scale formula in some way. Because there are already half steps from E–F and from B–C, the C major scale follows the formula without needing any sharps or flats.

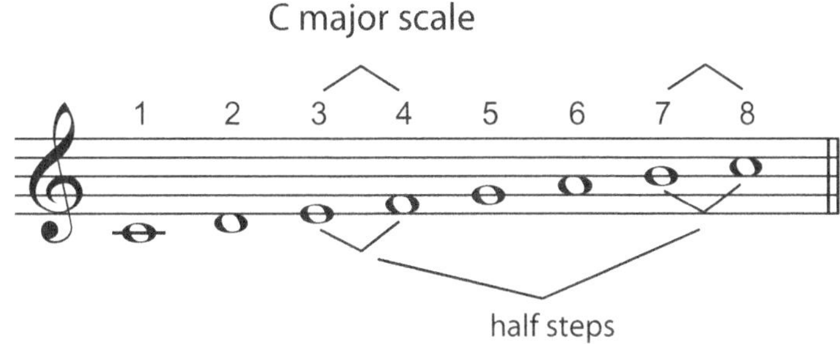


Practice the scale until you can play it from memory, naming the *scale degrees* (another word for steps 1-8) aloud. Practice playing it from any starting note, and then proceeding up or down. For example, here is the C major scale descending from its 7th degree (B), starting on beat 2.

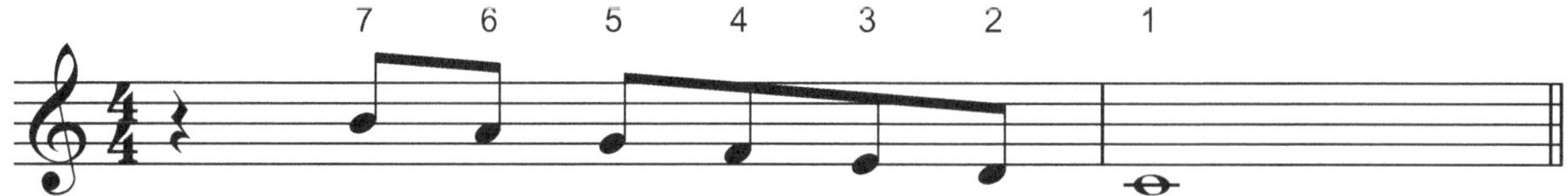


You can play a written scale or a part of a scale without stopping to name every single note, just as you read words correctly without naming every letter. (We will learn to identify exactly which scale we're seeing in later chapters.) You still have to read every note—you just don't have to **name** each one, and you don't have to read them **one at a time**.

I'm not saying in any way that you may make assumptions or just play something "sort of like" what is actually on the page. A single note or accidental symbol can make what looks like one melodic idea into a completely different one, just as one letter can change the pronunciation and meaning of a word—and therefore that of a sentence.

The point is that we recognize larger patterns and give ourselves more time to focus on the parts that are unusual. For example, here is stepwise movement (starting and ending on the 4th degree) of the C major scale, starting on the "and" of beat 1, but with one **skip** on the "and" of beat 3. Recognize the two scalar chunks and the note that you will skip over, then play the example from F to F, starting on the correct beat after a countoff.

Think about the risk that comes with scalar reading. If you don't skip the B note and instead just run the rest of the scale, then every note you play from that point until the end is *wrong,* even though you think you're reading it perfectly! If you make this mistake (and it's a common one), everything is late by an eighth note.

Even in the first scalar reading examples, I made sure to include a rhythmic element, because keeping track of the downbeats has to be your priority—no matter what. All the "right" pitches in the world are wrong if they are played at the wrong time.

If, instead of recognizing the scale, you named every single pitch as you went along, missing one pitch would not affect the others, as long as you counted the beats correctly. There might be more mistakes, but they'd be smaller.

The larger the pattern you recognize as you read, the bigger any mistakes can be, and the greater the potential for a rhythmic meltdown. So be sure the pattern really is what you think it is, and keep that count going! The idea behind pattern recognition is not to be lazy. It's to make the process as efficient as possible so you can eventually sightread things in real time that you couldn't before. You still have to see and read every note. If your counting and recognition of individual pitches on the staff are not developed enough, keep reviewing those fundamentals as you start working on this new skill.

Now, with that warning in place, even when there are only two notes a scale step apart, you'll save mental energy by only identifying one of them. The other note can be reached by moving along a scale pattern, with your fingers following a programmed reflex. The free time gained allows you to look ahead, thereby increasing your overall accuracy.

Exercise 46.

Circle all the scalar fragments in this example.

Learning and practicing your scales, separate from reading, will help your reading comprehension.

To get a G major scale, we follow the major scale formula, with half steps from 3-4 and 7-8, starting at G. Every F note must be changed to an F♯ as a result. We play all the same notes as those in the C major scale, with the exception of the F♯.

Here is the G major scale, starting from its root on the 4th string and ending on its 2nd-string root an octave higher. Play the G major scale beginning with your 2nd finger. Make sure you know where those roots are.

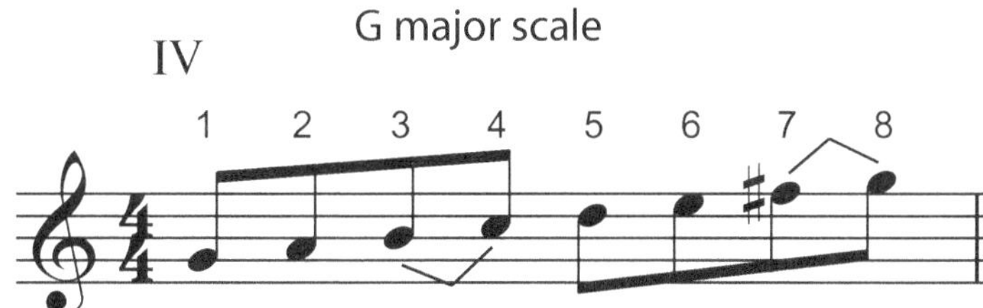


Now practice the G major scale including all the notes you can reach in this position. Play the lower F♯s on string 4, fret 4. Start on the 4th-string G root, then play all the way up to C on the 8th fret of string 1. Then descend all the way to the 6th-string A. Then ascend and finally stop on the 4th-string G root.

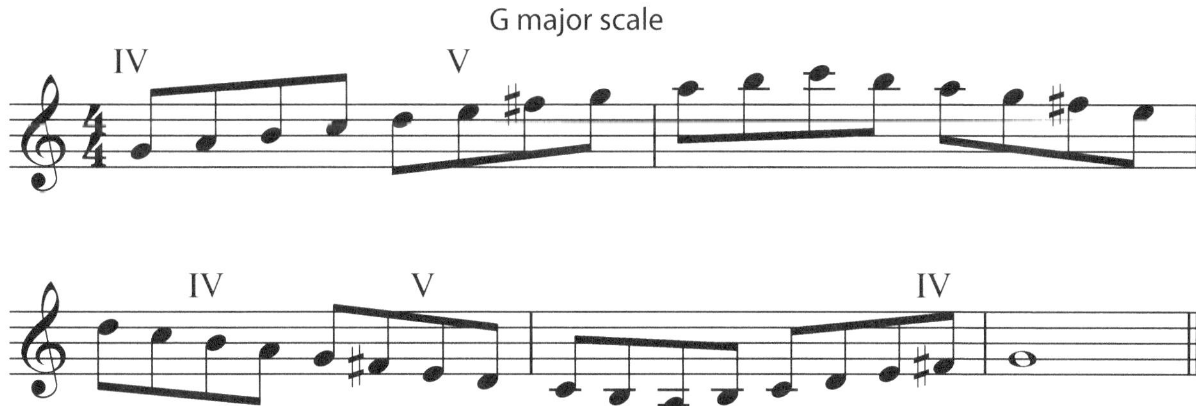


Name the scale, G major, and then its pitches aloud as you play, making special note of the locations of the G roots and the F♯s. Play it again while reciting the scale degrees 1-7 aloud. When you reach the 8th degree, call it 1 and start the numbers again. Practice playing it from any degree and then proceeding up or down.

Exercise 47.

Using the major scale formula to make sure each note is correct, write the major scales indicated. Don't put two noteheads on the same line or space; each note in a scale gets its own spot on the staff. Use accidentals to place half steps from 3-4 and 7-8. Check your answers in the back of the book.

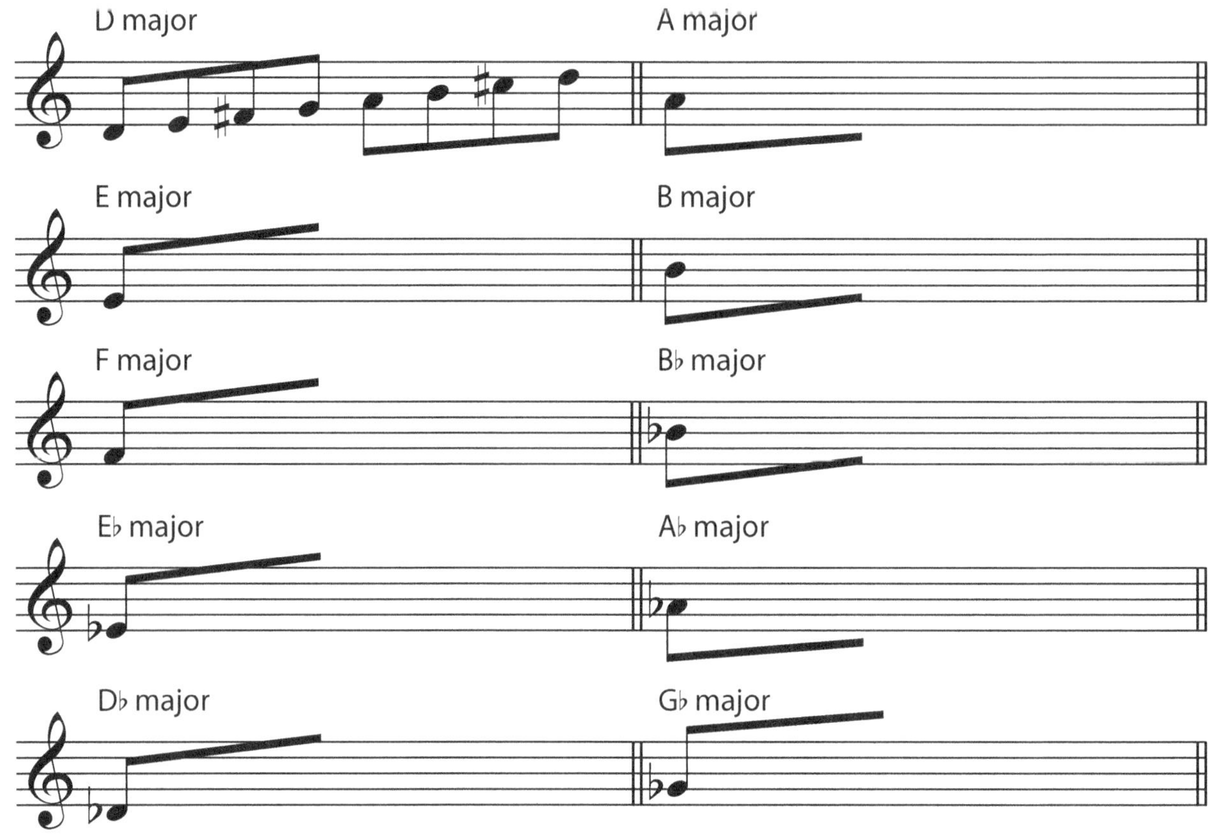


Exercise 48.

The scales shown below are major scales, but they don't always start from the root. Name the scale by using the major scale formula: 1 2 3^4 5 6 7^8. (Hint: find and mark the half steps first.)

54

## The Fretboard

By limiting our reading to the 5th-position area of the fretboard, we've been easing some of the challenges presented by the guitar. One such challenge is that the same pitch on the staff can be played in more than one fretboard location. I don't expect you to read in these other locations until later, but looking at them now will help you understand the scale patterns.

For example, besides the 6th string at fret 8, where we've been playing it, the C on the first ledger line below the staff may also be played on the 5th string at fret 3. The next C, on the third space, may be played at four (or five, if you can reach the 20th fret) different locations. Only three of those are shown here.

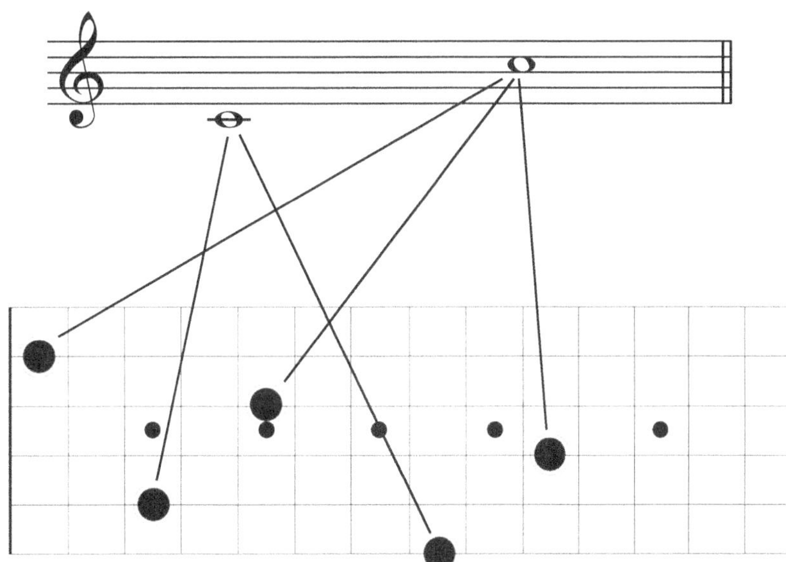

By placing the 1st finger successively on each C, at frets 1, 3, 5, 8, and 10, while at the same time reaching to the next C higher up the fretboard with the 3rd or 4th finger, we get five distinct overlapping **root shapes** for C. Each corresponds to a fret-hand position where we could read the same notes of the C major scale, with variations in available range and fingering possibilities for each position. The five shapes for C start over at the 13th fret, which you can see here as the second instance of pattern 1.

**C Root Shapes**

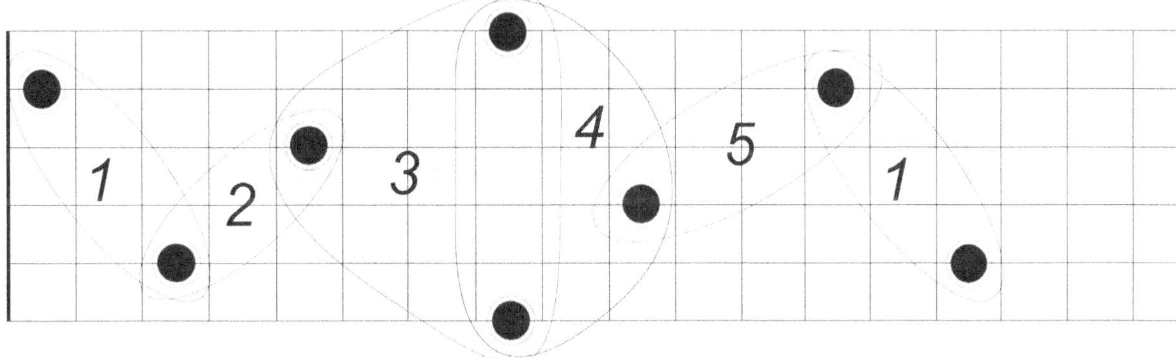


Root-shape patterns 3 and 4 (marked with irregular outlines) are the only adjacent patterns that share two roots, on the 6th and 1st strings. The shaded area is pattern 3, which we've been reading in throughout the book.

Play and memorize the five root shapes with their numbers. Describe them aloud as follows, but do not include specific fret numbers or staff locations in your descriptions. Once learned they will help you find the notes on your instrument.

"Pattern 1, roots on strings 2 and 5."
"Pattern 2, roots on strings 5 and 3."
"Pattern 3, roots on strings 3, 6, and 1 ."
"Pattern 4, roots on strings 6, 1, and 4."
"Pattern 5, roots on strings 4 and 2."

The five patterns of root shapes stay the same for all twelve unique pitches. For example, by moving each dot closer to the body by one fret, we get all instances of the pitch C$\sharp$ (or D$\flat$), which is always a half step higher than C$\natural$.

### C$\sharp$ or D$\flat$ Root Shapes

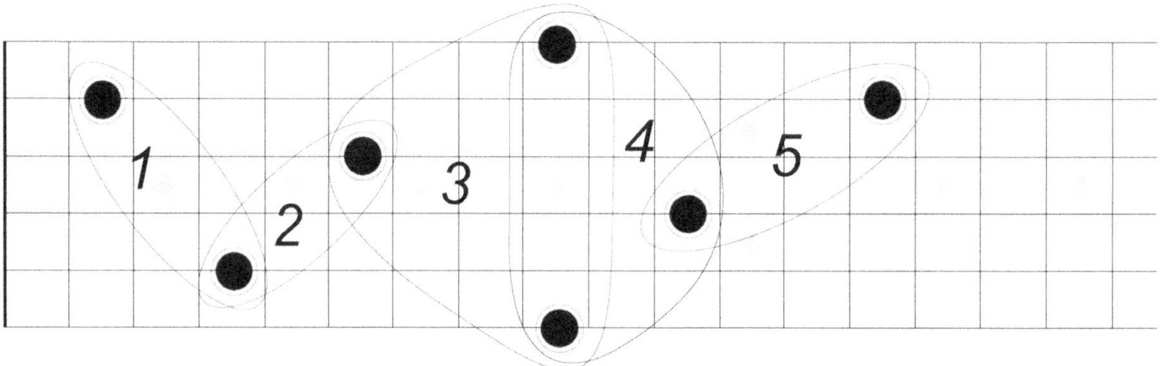

Moving them all up by another fret gives us the five root shapes for the note D natural, with pattern 5 heaving into view on the open 4th string.

### D Root Shapes

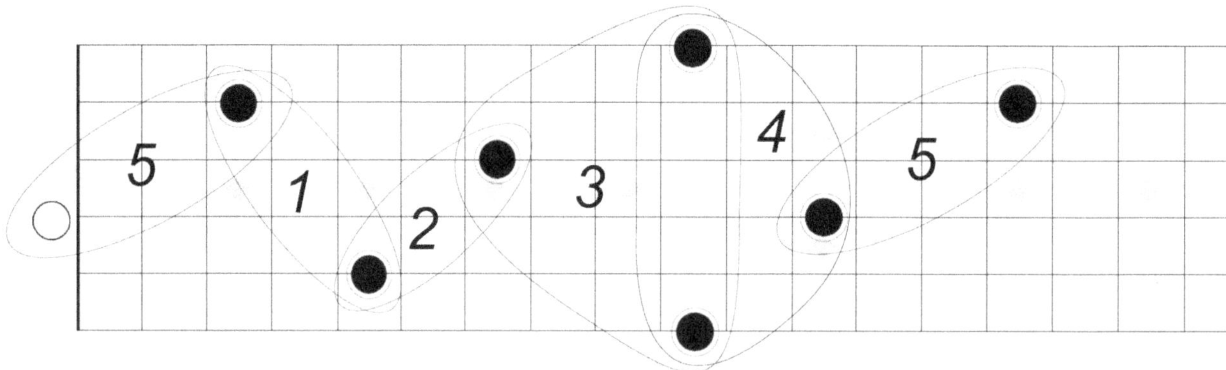

Exercise 49.

Move up the notes in the previous diagram by two frets to mark every E on this diagram, then circle and label the five root shapes. Include the open low and high E strings in pattern 4.

Exercise 50.

Mark every G note on this neck diagram, then circle and label the five patterns of root shapes. Include the open G string.

For each root shape, there is a distinct fingering pattern for the major scale. From our methodical study of all the natural notes in 5th position, we've already learned pattern 3 of the C major scale. Staying near the 5th fret helps us learn the names of the notes on the neck in that area, but it means that new scales we learn won't look the same. For example, the G major scale we looked at in 5th position has its roots on strings 4 and 2. The location of the roots show us it is a pattern-5 scale.

### G Major Scale, Pattern 5

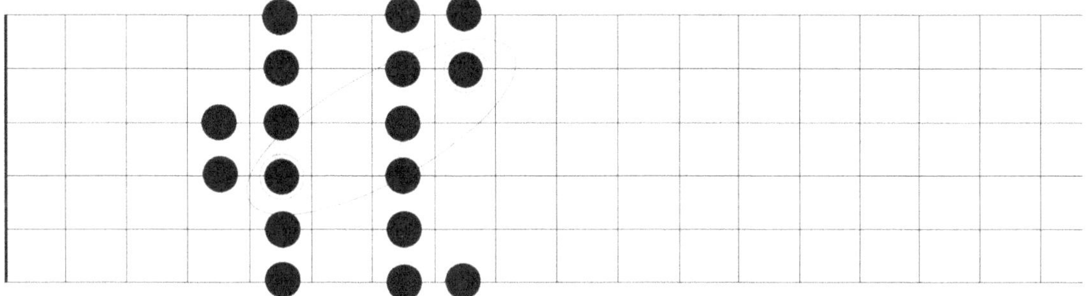

The five patterns are the result of the guitar's two-dimensional fret-and-string grid and its oddly-tuned 2nd string. The same melody usually looks different when played at another position, which is why we're staying with 5th position for now. Even so, all five major scale patterns will be needed in order to read music in different keys while staying in this area of the fretboard.

## Major Scale Patterns

In these frames, the scale degrees are written instead of fingering dots. Count the degrees aloud as you study them one at a time, spending as many weeks as you need to memorize each pattern. Each degree has a different musical character and functions.

Pattern 1

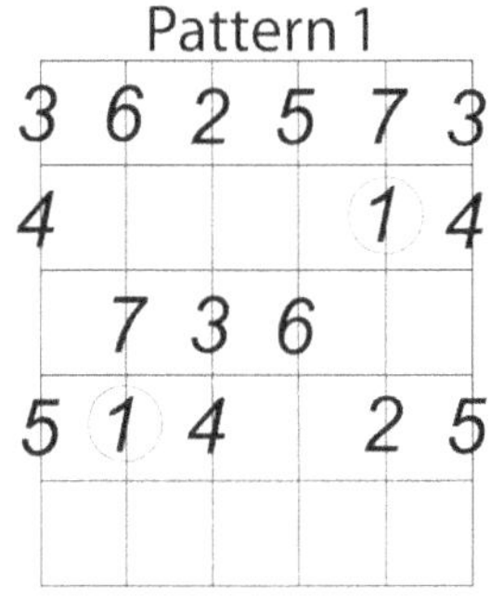

Pattern 2

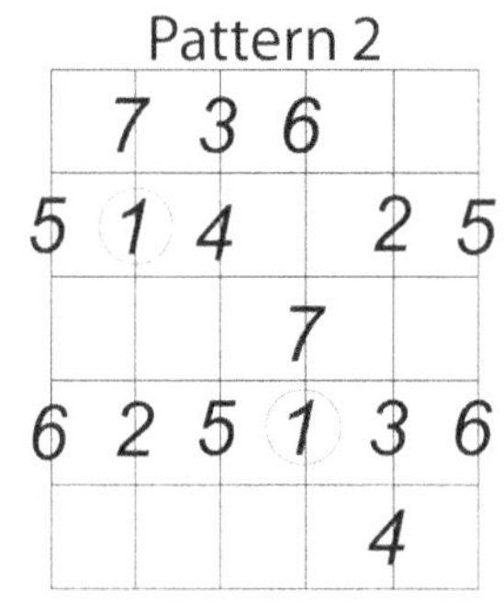

Pattern 3

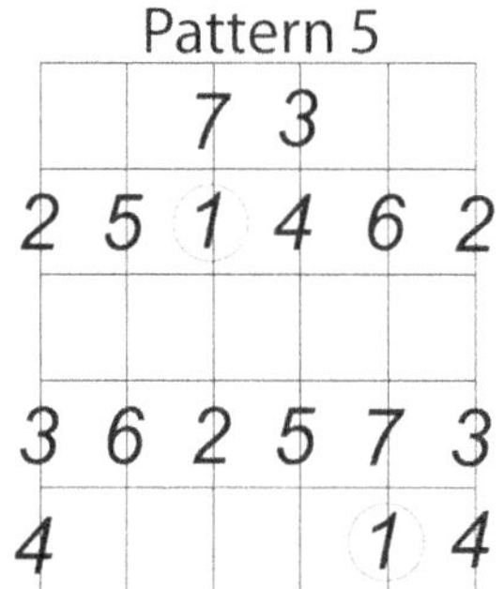

Pattern 4

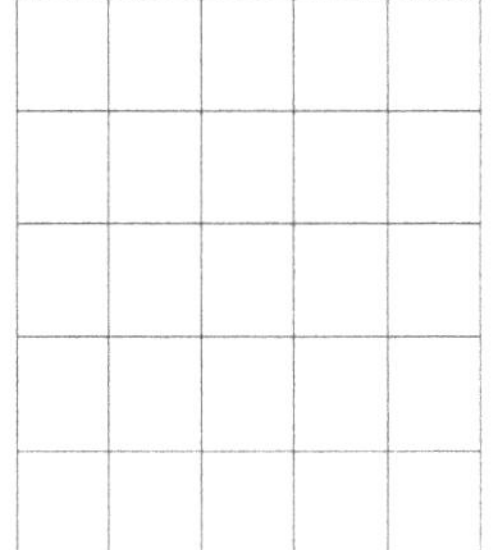

Pattern 5

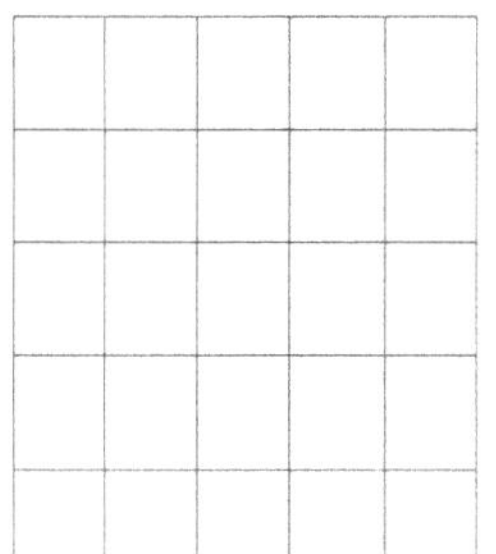

Exercise 51.

Draw the 5 patterns of the major scale for yourself. To make sure you don't run out of room, don't place a root on the first fret of the frame. Then cover the above examples and follow the major scale formula, placing a half step from 3-4 and from 7-8 every time. Check your patterns against those shown above.

Understanding the fretboard layout requires time and patience. Take encouragement from knowing that the guitar gives you only five distinct major-scale fingering patterns to learn, which is not bad compared to some other instruments.

**Practice**

1. Begin the process of committing the five major scale patterns to memory, one at a time. This can take several months of daily practice.

2. Practice starting the major scale patterns from any scale degree. For example, play pattern 4 of C major in 7th position, but start from E on the 7th fret of string 5.

3. Place your hand in 5th position, pick any note, and name it.  We'll make it a root. Play a note an octave higher or lower that is within reach of the hand. Name the root shape the two notes create. This determines which major scale pattern is closest to you. Play that pattern, naming the pitches. Write the scale on the staff using the correct accidentals. Repeat the process with a new root.

# Chapter 8: Triplets

## Eighth-Note Triplets

The "3" in the example below tells us to jam three notes into the time normally taken up by only two notes of the same value. Each beamed group in this example adds up to one beat in total duration. When writing a triplet, the "3" goes at the stem end of the notes. Write some eighth-note triplet groups below in the empty bar.

To be sure your triplets are not played unevenly (an easy mistake to make), set your metronome at 180 bpm, then tap your foot only once every three clicks. The metronome is now playing steady eighth-note triplets for you. Count them by adding the syllable "*a*" ( pronounce it "uh") for the third note of the triplet. Clap and count each click: "1 & a 2 & a 3 & a 4 & a." Tap the foot only on the numbers. Repeat until it's smooth and relaxed.

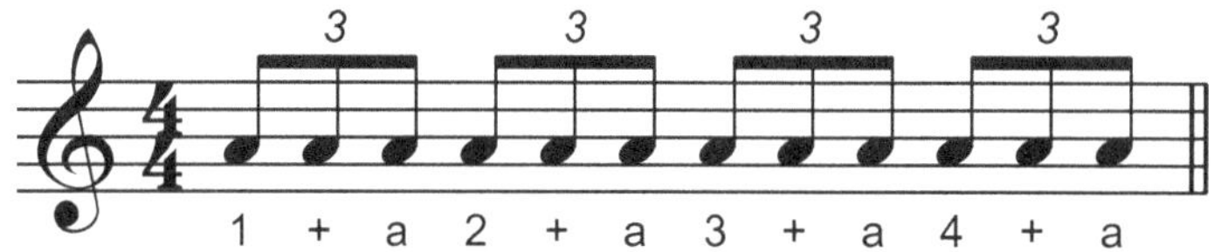


Then set the metronome back to 60 bpm and practice counting and clapping triplets, while tapping your foot in quarter notes as always. There should be three evenly-spaced claps per beat. It may take some practice because your foot still has to tap quarter notes. Don't let your foot copy the triplet rhythm.

Now count and clap the next example, using the metronome to ensure you don't change the overall tempo. The triplet makes you clap and sing faster because it has more notes, but the underlying beat stays the same. Repeat the example until you can smoothly switch between the three given note values. Don't let the *straight* eighth notes on beat two become unequal in duration.

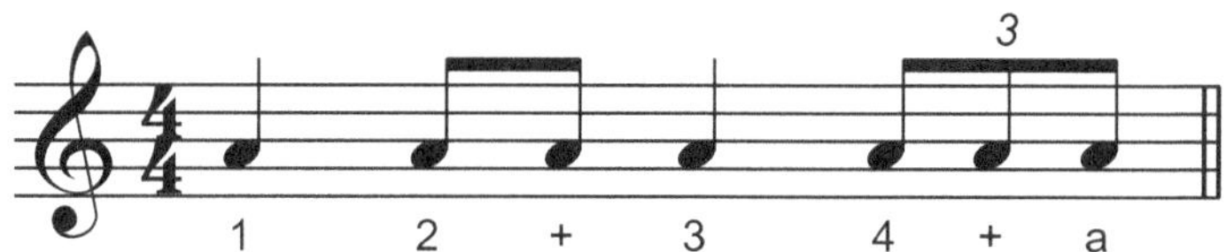


Once you can clap the previous two examples, trade the claps for guitar notes and play with the metronome. Notice that the odd number of notes in a triplet creates a change in picking direction. For now, I'd like you to pick a downstroke on every downbeat in the measure.

## The Shuffle

By omitting the middle attack in a triplet, we get notes only on the beat and the "a." A bracket around the "3" is used to show that the notes and rest fit into one beat. Count all the syllables, but clap only on the first and third in each beat.

A *shuffle* is the same as above but replaces the rest on the "and" with a sustain by using a quarter note. Play this using downstrokes only for now.

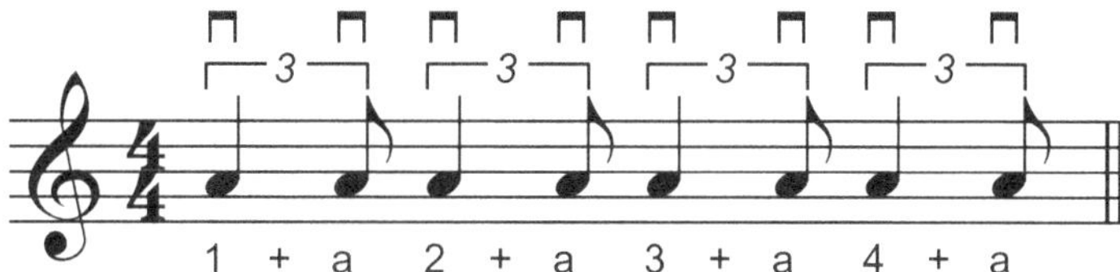



The *reverse shuffle* is a triplet rhythm with the third attack removed. Here it is in both versions: with a rest, and with a duration through the "a." Clap on the beat and on the "ands" only. Play with down-up picking.

Confirm that you are clapping these rhythms correctly by adjusting the metronome up to 180 bpm to play every triplet eighth note as before.

After you have had a little practice playing triplets with downstrokes on every foot-tap, go back and try all the examples in this chapter with alternate picking. This will mean that for continuous eighth-note triplets, your hand and foot will move in opposite directions on downbeats 2 and 4. For shuffles (and rests), keep your hand moving steadily in between attacks.

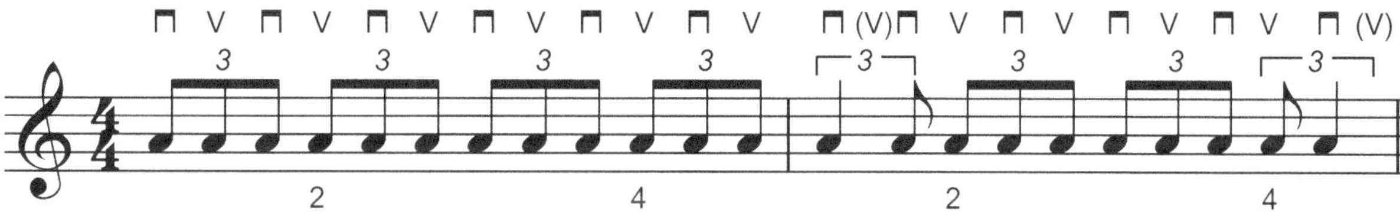



The two ways of picking (repeating down-up-down only vs. alternation) create slightly different-feeling triplets. The down-up-down way is good for creating accented parts with a strong groove. The alternate-picked triplets might sound too "stiff" in that situation (because the notes are all about the same volume) but are good for playing fast lines of evenly-picked notes. Practice both ways with strong strumming motions, keeping the unwanted strings from ringing by damping them with the unused parts of your fretting hand.

Exercise 52.

Write the count below and the two sets of possible picking directions above this example. Play slowly while counting aloud, then with the metronome set as low as necessary—perhaps 40 bpm. When you play it, focus on the notation; the count and picking are just there to help you learn.

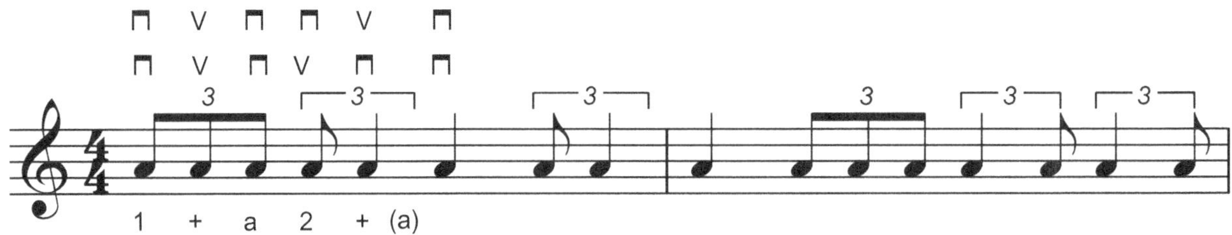

Exercise 53.

This example contains quarter notes and triplet eighth note rhythms, including shuffles and reverse shuffles. From the given count, write notation so that there is an attack on each written number, "+," or "a." Bracket the "3" for any triplet rhythm that does not have a beam.

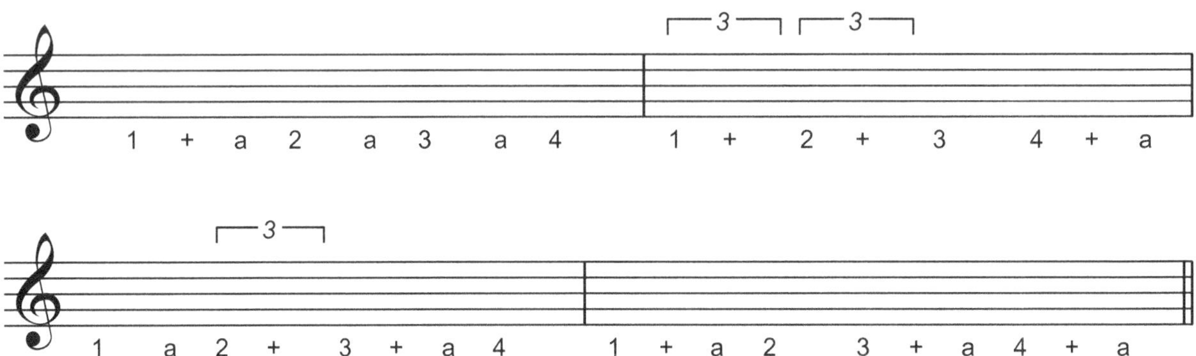

Finally, let's try alternating between measures of straight eighth notes, which should be exactly uniform in duration, and shuffling eighth notes, which create a bouncy feel because the first note is longer than the second one in each beat.

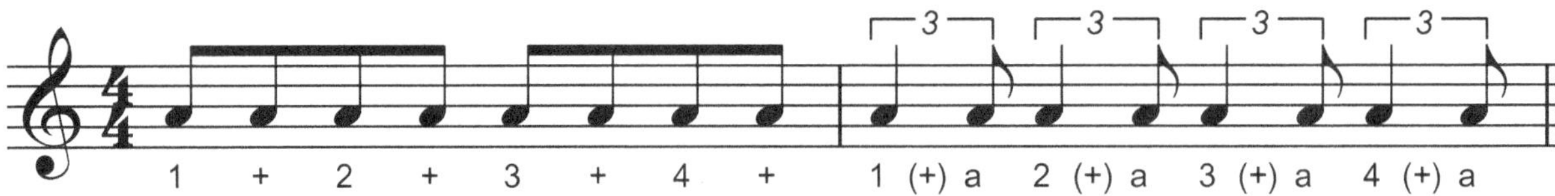

This table contains all the ways to fill one beat with eighth-note triplet attacks, along with most of their equivalent-attack versions. Beams should be used on neighboring eighth notes within beats.

## Eighth-Note Triplet Vocabulary List

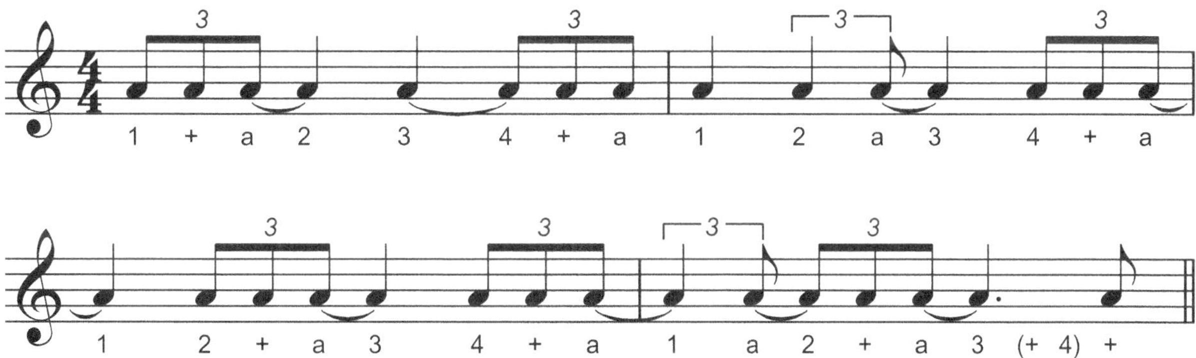

Start the metronome and practice playing the cells of the table, first reading across each line, then down each column, then in a diagonal pattern from the edges to the center (from cell 1 to cell 8, then 4 to 5, 3 to 6, and 2 to 7). Memorize them so you can look ahead or away while playing.

## Tied Triplets

Triplets may be tied across beats and bar lines. As with the basic tied rhythms we studied, only the first of two or more tied notes is attacked. Count through the others; they only contribute duration.

Count and clap this example, then play with the metronome. Accelerate your picking motion to triplet speed during any beat with a "3" over it, even when you are not picking all the attacks in the beat.

Exercise 54.

The long notes in this triplet lick are marked with fret-hand vibrato. Use forearm rotation for the smoothest type. Write the count below, then try playing it with different picking methods and write the one you prefer over the notation.

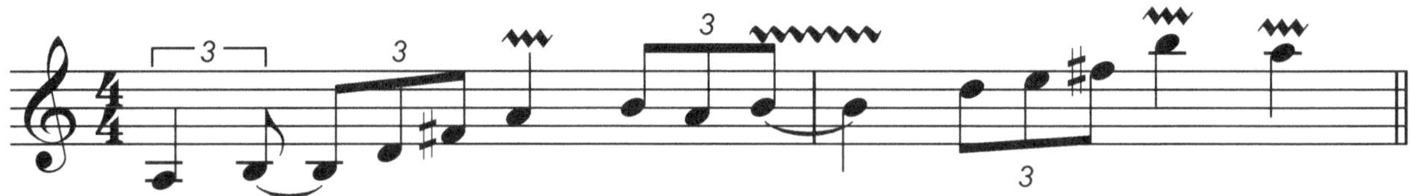

Exercise 55.

From the given count, write notation so that there is an attack on each number or syllable, translating the pitches from the tablature. There should be no rests in this example. Use tied notes to fill up any extra duration so that the time signature is respected. Bracket the "3" for any triplet rhythm that does not have a beam.

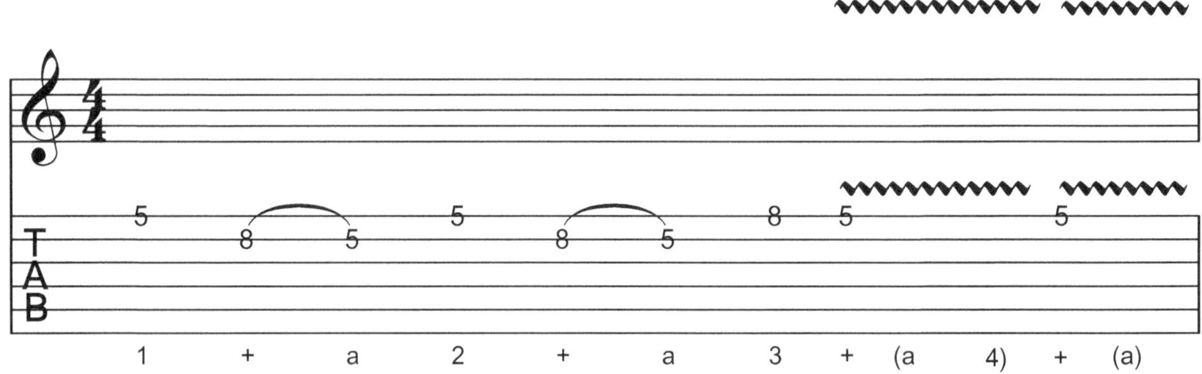

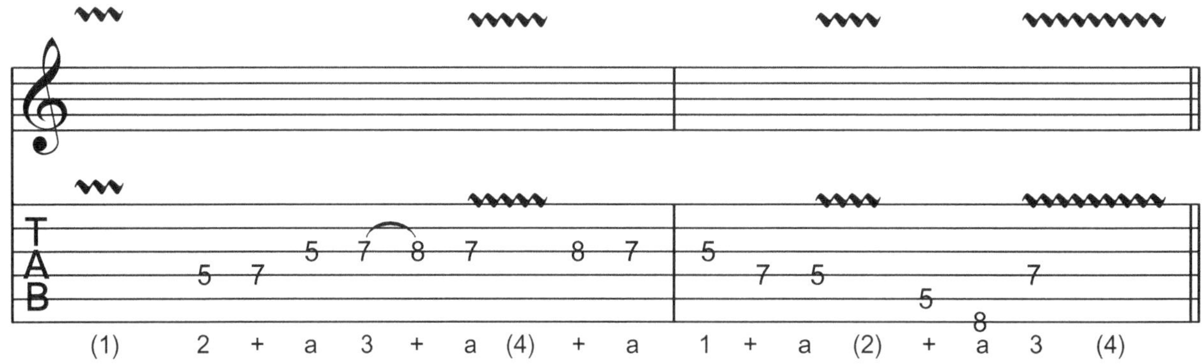

## Compound Meters

When a song uses triplet rhythms all or most of the time, the composer has a way to avoid writing all the 3s and brackets. This is a *compound meter*, where each beat divides into three notes. The beat is a **dotted note** (usually a dotted quarter note) in a compound meter. Compound meters also use a dotted rest (an exception to the earlier rule) to show one beat of silence. The opposite of a compound meter is a *simple* meter like 4/4, where each beat contains two eighth notes.

The most common compound meters are 6/8, 9/8, and 12/8. Divide the upper numeral in the time signature by three to find the number of times your foot taps in each measure. For example, you'll tap

64

your foot four times per bar in 12/8 time. Count the four beats aloud as if it were 4/4 time. There's no need to count up to twelve!

The two measures below should sound exactly the same. Notice that the metronome marking for a compound meter must also use a dotted note.

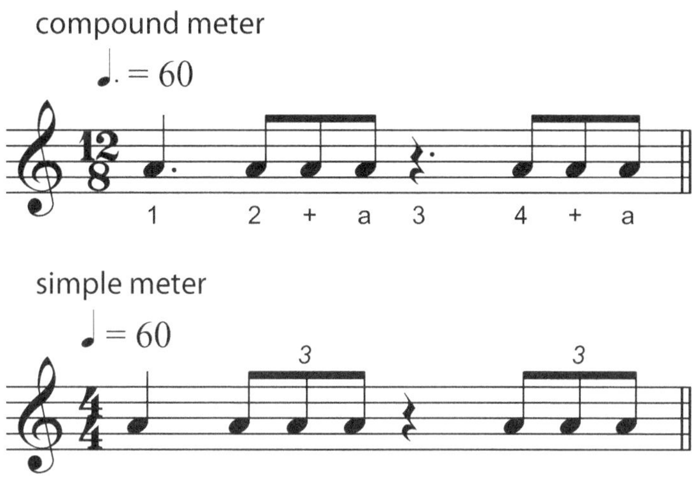


Exercise 56.
From the given count, write notation so that there is an attack on each written number or syllable, referring to the tablature to find the pitches. Use tied notes to fill up any extra duration so that the time signature is respected. The only rests in the example are already provided.

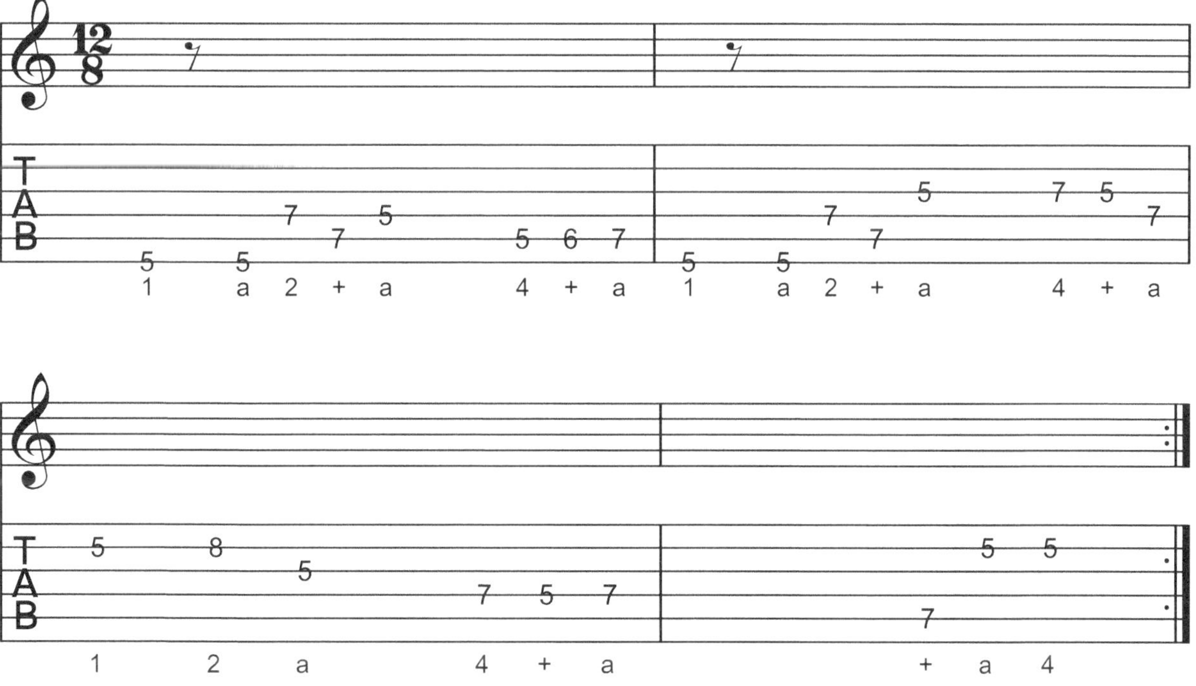

# Chapter 9: Intervallic Reading

You should be able to write major scales on the staff and play major scale fingering patterns for this lesson.

Groups of intervals form melodic patterns and variations that often occur repeatedly in the same song. A complete study of intervals is a topic for a book of its own, so we'll just learn enough to use them to help us recognize these patterns, thus speeding up our reading overall. A small dose of theory will make it easier to understand intervals on the staff, and from there, the chords and melodies that use them. The actual intervallic reading we'll start with after this explanation won't be as hard as the theory, so hang in there.

All intervals are classified as one of two basic kinds, or *qualities*.

- The **major** intervals are 2nds, 3rds, 6ths, and 7ths.
- The **perfect** intervals are unisons, 4ths, 5ths, and octaves.

The major and perfect intervals are the same sizes as the ones measured **from the root** of the major scale. In the C major scale, for example, there is a major 2nd (abbreviated **M2**) from C to D, a major 3rd (**M3**, two whole steps) from C to E, a perfect 4th (**P4**, two whole steps plus a half step) from C to F, and so on.

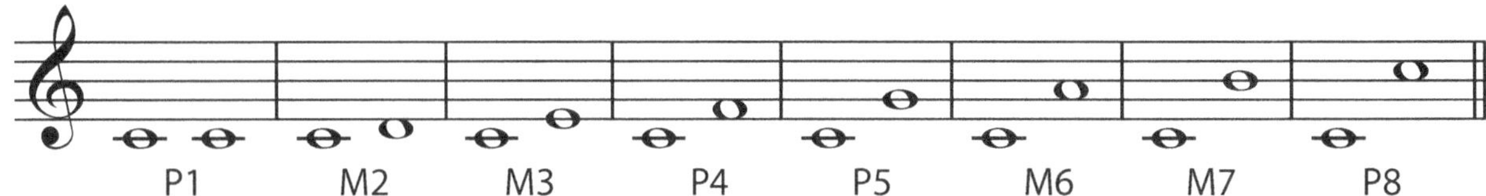


Exercise 57.

Count the lines and spaces and then write first the quality (**M** for 2, 3, 6, and 7, or **P** for 1, 4, 5, and 8) and then the *quantity* (1-8) of each interval. Then play them all.

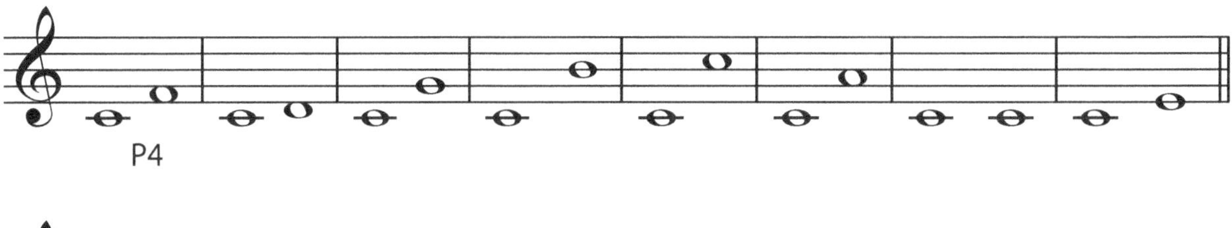

Exercise 58.

Here is the same exercise, this time with all intervals starting from the root of the G major scale. Write the quality (M or P) and quantity (1-8) of each interval. Then play them all.

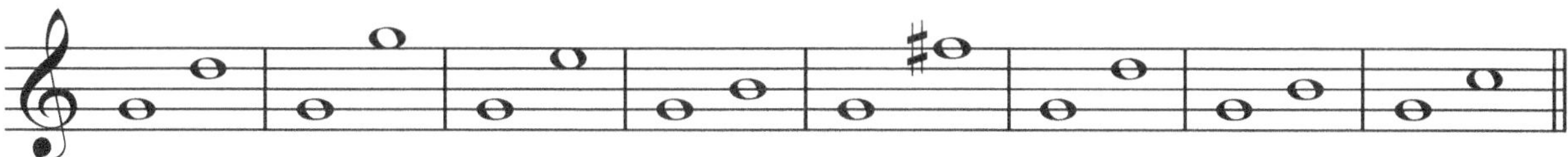

If we add an accidental to (or change an existing accidental on) one of the notes in an interval, its **quality** changes depending on which of the two kinds it is: major or perfect. Moving the notes farther apart in pitch—by raising the higher note or dropping the lower one—is called *augmentation*. The opposite, *diminution*, happens when the change moves the notes closer together, shrinking the interval.

This table summarizes how an interval's quality changes when you put an accidental on one of its notes.

## Interval Quality Table

| | | | | |
|---|---|---|---|---|
| | Augmented | | Augmented | |
| Augmentation ↑ (growth)<br><br>Diminution ↓ (shrinkage) | **Major 2, 3, 6 ,7** | | **Perfect 1, 4, 5, 8** | |
| | minor | | | |
| | diminished | | diminished | |

Following the table, we see that:

• augmentation of either major or perfect intervals by one half step makes them augmented in quality.

• diminution of major intervals by one half step makes them minor in quality.

• diminution of both minor and perfect intervals makes them diminished in quality.

• diminution of an augmented interval results in a major or perfect interval, depending on how many letters (or lines and spaces on the staff) separate the two notes: major (2, 3, 6, 7) or perfect (1, 4, 5, 8).

• augmentation of a diminished interval produces either a minor or perfect interval, and so on.

The only way to change the number (or *quantity*) of an interval is to move a note to a different spot on the staff.

These sample intervals have their qualities changed by the addition of accidentals. Name the notes and count to verify the correct interval names.

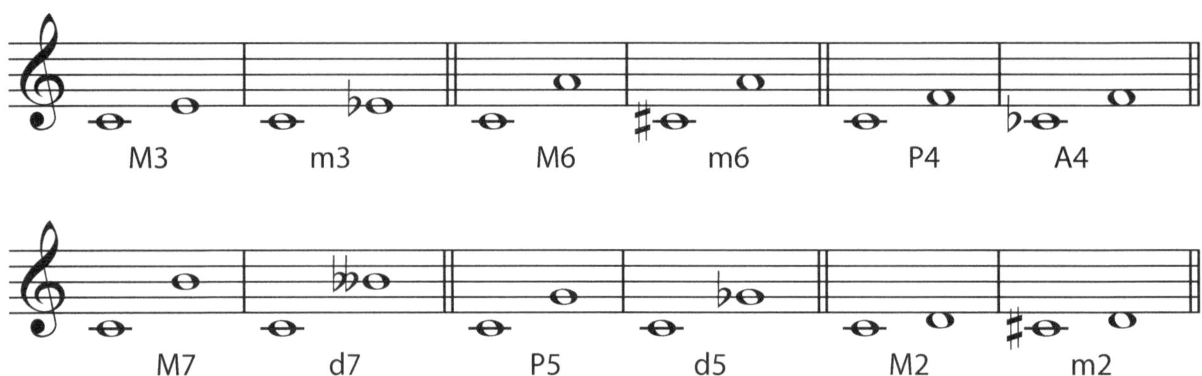


Cover up the solutions below and answer.

What do you get if you:
1. Diminish an augmented 6th?
2. Augment a diminished 3rd?
3. Augment a diminished 5th?
4. Doubly diminish a major 7th (diminish it by two half steps)?
5. Augment a perfect octave?

Solutions
1. Major 6th.
2. Minor 3rd.
3. Perfect 5th.
4. Diminished 7th.
5. Augmented octave.

Exercise 59.
Write the name of the interval, starting with the quality (big M for major, small m for minor, A, P, d) and then the quantity (1-8). Then play the intervals.

68

Exercise 60.

Write the name of the interval, including quality (M, m, A, P, d) and quantity (1-8). Use a correctly-spelled G major scale—the major 7th is F♯. Then play the intervals.

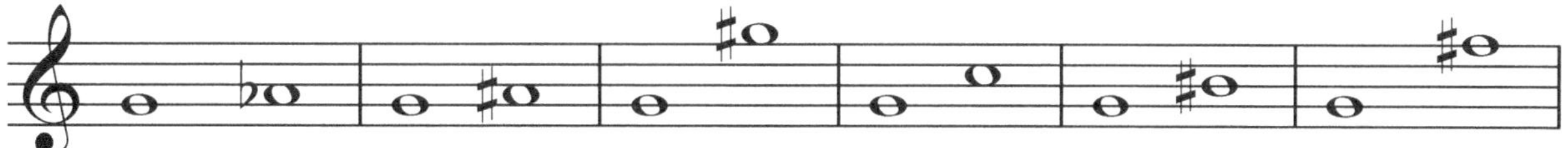

You may notice that an augmented 2nd is the same as a minor 3rd in absolute size: three half steps. There are many of these *enharmonic* intervals. They sound the same but are written differently on the staff.

You can determine the interval formed by any two notes by thinking of the lower note as the root of a major scale. If the higher note is a member of that scale, then the interval they form must be perfect or major. If the higher note is not a member of the scale then the interval is one of the other qualities. We're not going to practice that deductive process, however, since we have not practiced spelling major scales on the staff starting from every possible note. We know enough about intervals for our immediate purpose.

## Diatonic Intervals

We also find some minor, augmented, and diminished intervals if we measure between notes of the scale other than the root. For example, between steps 2 and 4 is a minor 3rd. Since they're still in the scale, these intervals are said to be *diatonic*. This important musical term has Greek roots.

*Dia-* means across, as in *diameter*: a measure across; *tonos* means *tone*; and *-ic* means *of*, making the word an adjective so it can modify other nouns. Something that is diatonic, then, is "of a span of tones," meaning that it comes strictly from a scale. We can say, for example, that the notes G and A are **diatonic to** the G major scale.

Since the phrase "the diatonic scale" is often used to compare the seven-tone major scale to a *pentatonic* (five-tone) scale, it might look like *dia-* means seven; but the prefix for seven is *hepta-*. A *heptatonic* scale is any scale of seven tones, while "the diatonic scale" means one that follows the major scale formula.

Any notes that do not belong to the scale are called *non-diatonic* notes. We can say, for example, that F and A♭ are **non-diatonic** to the G major scale.

We'll learn to read diatonic chords, arpeggios, and melodies, all of which are made of diatonic intervals, which consist only of diatonic notes!

## 2nds

A diatonic 2nd goes from any note in a scale to the one above or below. From 3-4 and from 7-8 are minor 2nds. Major 2nds (whole steps) separate the other notes, starting from 1, 2, 4, 5, and 6.

When you practice a major scale you are playing in diatonic 2nds. When reading a scalar melody, you will automatically get the correct major or minor 2nd as long as you stay diatonic (within the scale pattern). For this example, review the entire pattern-3 C major scale in 5th position, then stick to it as you read the piece.

## 3rds

When two notes are a 3rd apart, they are on adjacent lines or spaces.

Similar to the way the major scale formula produces all major 2nds, except for two minor 2nds (from 3-4 and from 7-8), you'll notice it produces diatonic 3rds of two different sizes.

Beginning on steps 1, 4, and 5 are major 3rds, consisting of two whole steps. Usually we play these across two strings. Diatonic minor 3rds are found on steps 2, 3, 6, and 7, and consist of a half step plus a whole step; a 3-fret distance when played on one string. Again, when playing diatonically, remember the scale pattern and you'll get the appropriate major or minor 3rd.

The 3rd is also sometimes called a *skip*. When you see a diatonic 3rd in the music—two notes on neighboring lines or neighboring spaces—it's not necessary to read both notes by name. Just follow the major scale pattern and skip one scale step.

On the next page is an ascending and descending sequence of diatonic 3rds in the C major scale. It is a two-note melodic pattern repeated on each step of the scale. The pattern is played four times in the first measure. Look at the music first and think about the sequence of notes you will be playing. Recite the scale degrees aloud:

1-3, 2-4, 3-5, 4-6, 5-7, 6-8, 7-9, 8.

Recite the descending version:
8-6, 7-5, 6-4, 5-3, 4-2, 3-1, 2-7, 1.

Then play it while looking away from the page. If you are very familiar with the scale shape it should be possible, if difficult. It may help to recite the number of the starting note of each two-note group aloud as you play.

70

<h1 style="text-align:center">Diatonic Thirds in C major</h1>

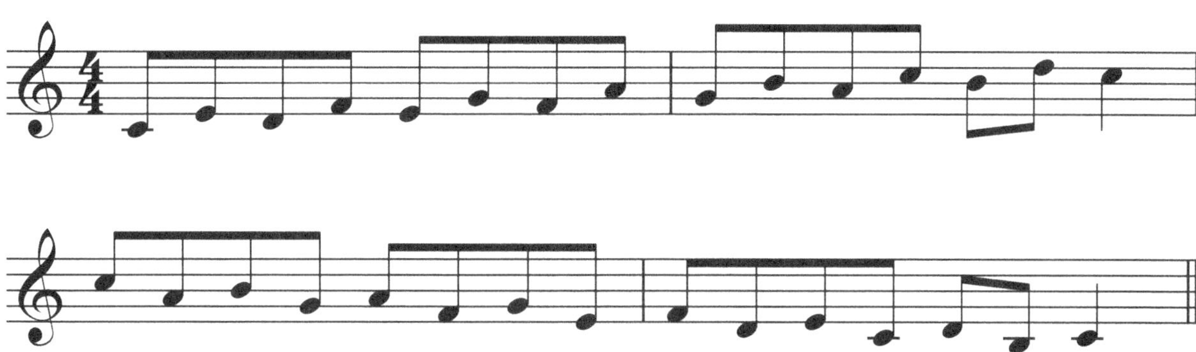

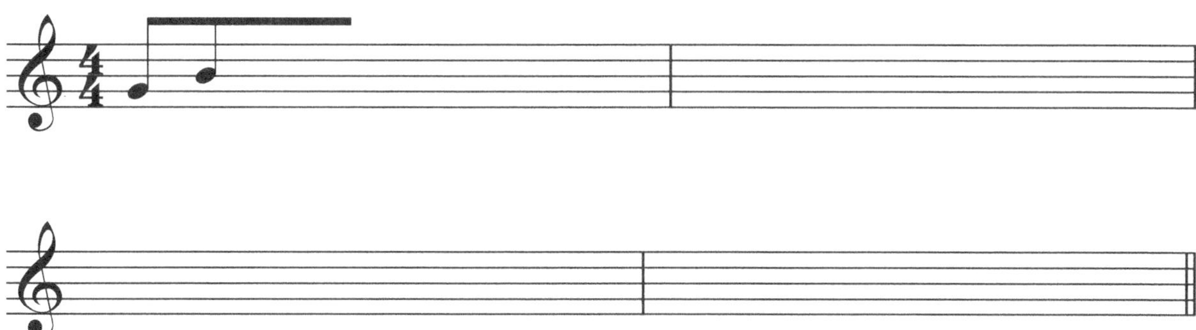

Exercise 61.

Write the diatonic 3rd sequence using the G major scale, starting from G on the 4th string, and ending with G on the 2nd string. Remember to put a sharp on F to make a correct G major scale. Circle around and stop on the roots in bars 2 and 4 as I did in the previous example, just to keep the rhythm even.

Exercise 62.

In the exercises above, label each diatonic 3rd as major or minor.

Memorize and practice playing diatonic-3rd sequences in each scale pattern you know, as a technique exercise. Sing the numbers aloud.

## The Skipping Alphabet

After steps, skips (diatonic 3rds) are the most important interval to recognize, as they form the basis for chord construction. When letters are in alphabetical order but every other letter is skipped over, you're spelling a chord or *arpeggio* (the notes of a chord played one at a time). On the staff, this is a series of noteheads on lines only or on spaces only. If you learn the chord as a unit, it won't be necessary to name every note. This is a long-term practice item that works both ways: you'll learn to write your music faster if you can easily rattle off the notes in a chord. To start the learning process, memorize and recite the skipping alphabet in both directions.

A C E G B D F

G E C A F D B

An actual chord or arpeggio will usually use fewer than seven letters.

C E G

D F A C

A F D

G E C A F

B D

Exercise 63.

Circle the 3rds (skips) in the music, mentally rehearse, then play.

**Practice**

Recite the skipping alphabet forward and backward, starting from each of the seven letters.

# 4ths

A 4th appears on the staff as the next bigger interval than a 3rd: two notes, one on a line and one on a space, with a line and a space in between. Learn to recognize this shape as a 4th on sight.

There are perfect 4ths starting from each degree of the major scale, with the exception of the 4th from step 4-7. It is three whole steps, an augmented 4th.

4ths are usually easy to play on the guitar. Instead of the stretchy string-skipping augmented 4th from F to B in this position we could move up and use the B at string 4, fret 9. Here is a diatonic-4ths exercise in the key of C in 5th position.

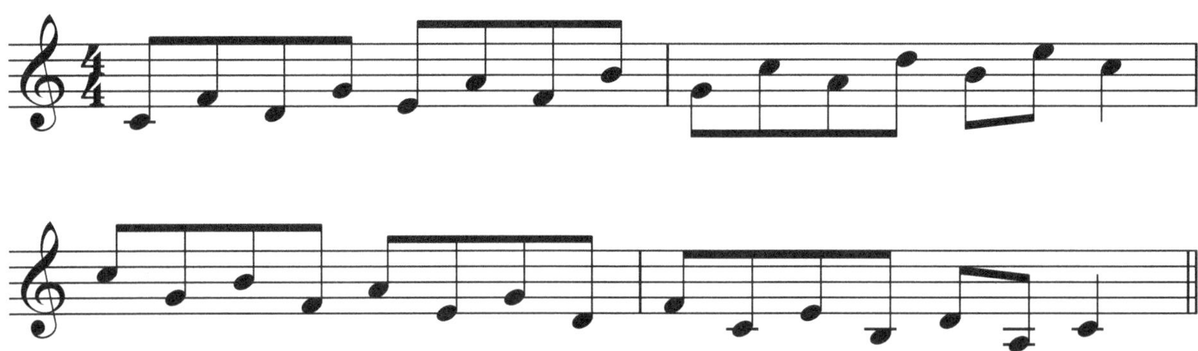

Exercise 64.

Write a series of diatonic 4ths ascending and descending the G major scale. Remember to put a sharp on F.

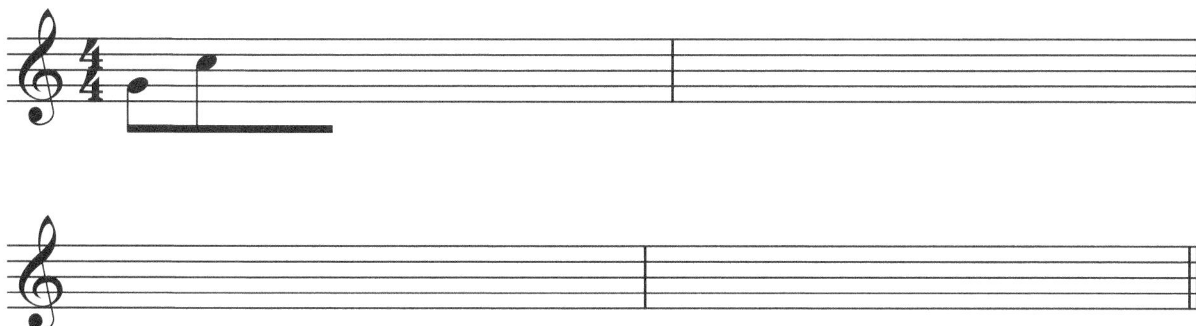

Find and label the augmented 4th from the 4th to the 7th degree in the above exercise.

## Practice

Recite the alphabet in ascending and descending 4ths.

A D G C F B E

A E B F C G D

## 5ths and Larger

5ths are notes both on a line or both on a space, but farther apart than the comparable 3rd. The major scale has perfect 5ths on every degree, with the exception of a diminished 5th from 7 up to 4 in the next octave. The second half of this example jumps up an octave to stay within our reading range.

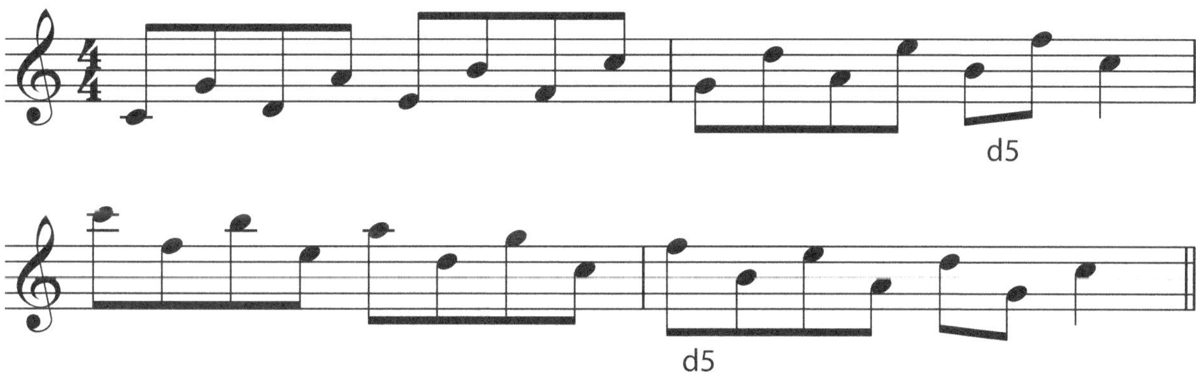


Exercise 65.

Write a series of diatonic 5ths ascending and descending the G major scale.

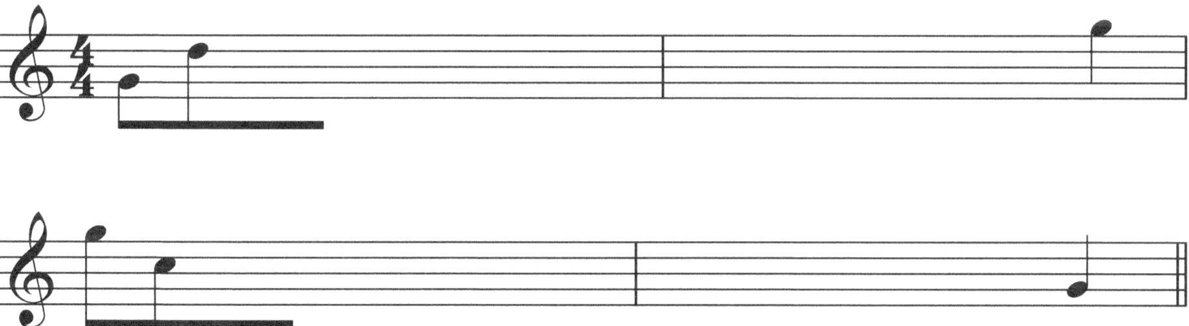

## Exercise 66.

Write a series of diatonic 6ths ascending and descending the C major scale.

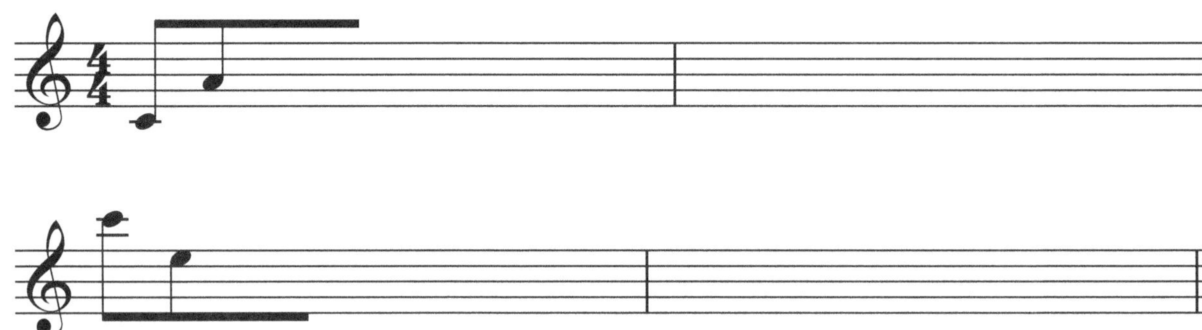

## Exercise 67.

After each given note, write a notehead that is higher by the diatonic interval indicated.

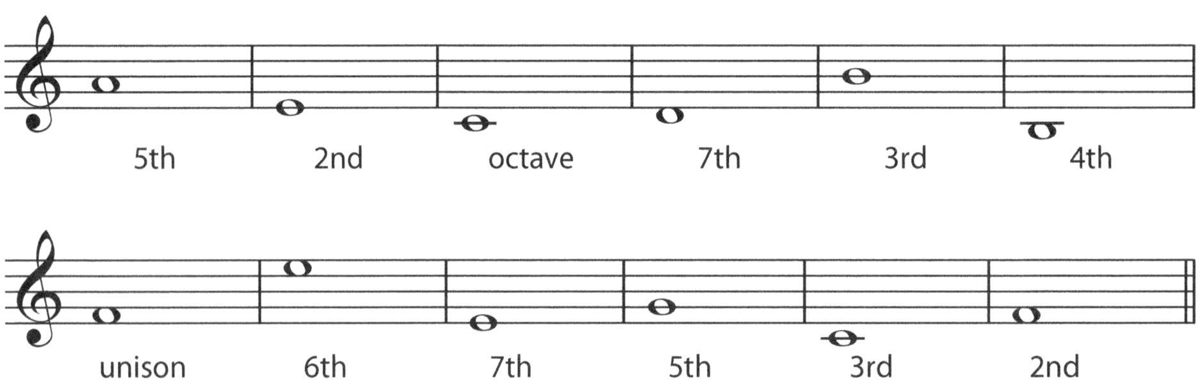


## Exercise 68.

After each given note, write a notehead that is lower by the diatonic interval indicated.

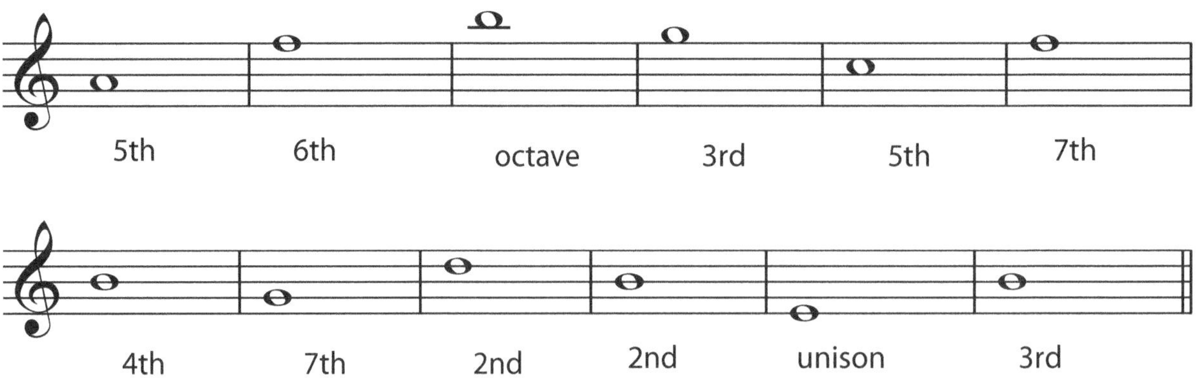

**Practice**

Practice diatonic 3rds, 4ths, 5ths, and 6ths sequences with a metronome. They are an excellent way to relieve the monotony of practicing scales, so apply them to other patterns that you know. Write the new sequences out on staff paper and gradually memorize the interval shapes on the fretboard. Learning these exercises will help you to play more melodically.

All the talk about recognizing scales and intervals and playing them without reading the individual pitches is **not** meant to suggest that you don't have to know how to read pitches! Accurate pitch recognition is a must. Beyond it, however, it is important to continue to develop pattern recognition. For example, the following series of notes is easier to play accurately when you recognize it as an ascending diatonic 3rd followed by a descending diatonic 3rd, over and over.

# Chapter 10: Key Signatures

A single scale dominates a piece of music at a given time. Rather than continually write the accidentals needed to create that scale, we can put them at the beginning of the song or section, in a *key signature*. The first—and often the only—key signature is right after the clef, and before the time signature. Many songs don't change keys at all.

Unlike the accidentals we've seen, which only apply to notes on the same line or space within the same measure, a key signature affects notes in every octave and throughout every measure of the song, unless it is overruled by accidentals or a new key signature.

For example, if a piece consistently uses the G major scale, which requires the note F♯, we put a sharp sign at the beginning on the top-line F. The reader will play every F as an F♯ in every octave throughout the piece. The G is the *tonic* note of the piece, which is said to be in the *key of* G major.

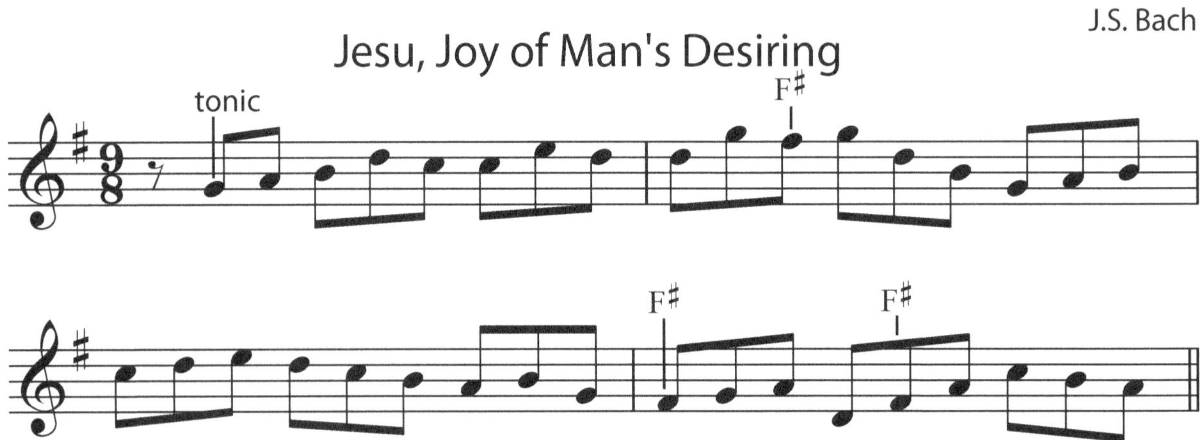


Now we know two key signatures: C major, which has no sharps or flats, and G major, which has one sharp. In reading, it's best to progress slowly, working with one key for awhile before learning to read in another one. On the other hand, we don't want to get stuck reading in one key only.

Thinking of written notes as being part of a scale fingering pattern whenever possible helps you remember which notes are correct, helps you hear where the tonic note is (G in this case), and helps you understand and therefore play the music better. If instead you just try to remember to apply a sharp to every F, you're doing it the hard way, which you'll realize as the number of sharps or flats in the key signature goes up.

## Sharp Keys

This is the **order of sharps** that are added to create successively harder sharp keys.

Each new sharp is a 5th higher or a 4th lower than the previous one, depending on which way you want to count. You might memorize the sharps with a mnemonic of your own making. **F**red **C**an't **G**et **D**readful **A**lice to **E**at **B**eans is one a student gave me.

The C major key signature (no sharps or flats) uses the natural half steps from E–F and from B–C as degrees 3-4 and 7-8, following the major scale formula. The first sharp key, G major, requires an F♯ so that the notes follow the major scale formula from G to G, with half steps from 3-4 (B-C) and from 7-8 (F♯-G). The second sharp key, D major, keeps that F♯ note so that there is a half step from 3-4, and also requires C♯ so that the major scale formula is followed at step 7-8.

Hide the solutions below and answer these questions.
1. What is the 7th degree in the key of A major?
2. What is the 7th degree of B major?
3. What is the 7th degree of D major?
4. What is the 7th degree of E major?
5. What is the 7th degree of G major?
6. Where are the half steps in any major scale?

Solutions
1. G♯
2. A♯
3. C♯
4. D♯
5. F♯
6. From 3-4 and 7-8.

Sharps are always applied on the staff in the same order, following the pattern of two, three, and two on each diagonal, which gives a predictable symmetry and keeps you from having to use ledger lines when writing key signatures. On your list of things to practice, add memorization of the **order of sharp keys**.

Each successive sharp key is a **5th higher.**

Exercise 69.
    Name the following major keys.

Exercise 70.
    Write the key signatures on the staff, using the correct order of sharps.

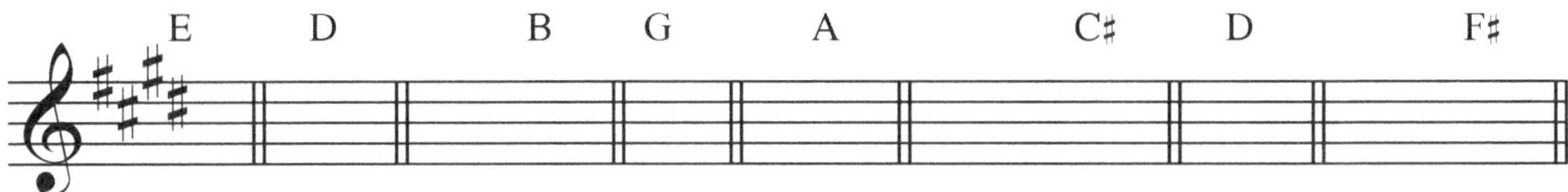


## Flat Keys

Flat keys are created by applying flats in the following order. Memorize the **order of flats**.

$$B^\flat \; E^\flat \; A^\flat \; D^\flat \; G^\flat \; C^\flat \; F^\flat$$

Flats are applied to the staff in a predictable order: two on each diagonal, with the final one, $F^\flat$, by itself on the 1st space.

Again, the C major scale, with no sharps or flats, naturally has half steps from 3-4 and 7-8. The first flat key is F major. We create it by placing a flat on the note B, which creates a half step from 3 to 4. The pre-existing natural half step from E to F completes the major scale formula in the key of F. The second flat key is $B^\flat$ major. It contains $B^\flat$ as its root, and it needs a flat on step 4, to make it follow the major scale formula.

Answer these questions. The solutions are on the next page.
1. What is the 4th degree in the key of F major?
2. What is the 4th degree of $E^\flat$ major?
3. What is the 4th degree of  $B^\flat$ major?
4. What is the 4th degree of $A^\flat$ major?
5. What is the 4th degree of $D^\flat$ major?
6. Name the thing that determines where the half steps are in a major scale.

Solutions

1. B$\flat$
2. A$\flat$
3. E$\flat$
4. D$\flat$
5. G$\flat$
6. The major scale formula: half steps from 3-4 and 7-8.

Each new flat key has all the previous flats plus one more, with the tonic being a 4th higher every time. Memorize the **order of flat keys** produced by this process.

The key signature with seven flats (C$\flat$ major) is rarely used because the same pitches can be more easily obtained by writing in B major (five sharps) instead. Similarly, the key signature with five flats (D$\flat$ major) is more likely to be used than the sharp key that produces the same pitches (C$\sharp$ major with seven sharps).

Exercise 71.

Name the following major keys.

Exercise 72.

Write the key signatures on the staff, using the correct order of flats.

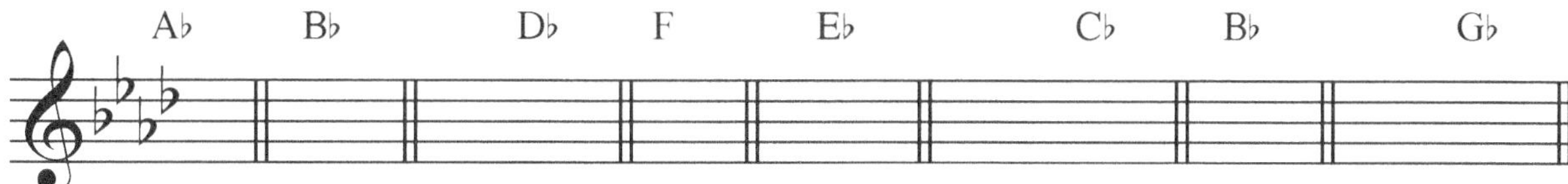


## Practice

Make flash cards with the key signatures on one side and the name of the key on the other. Memorize the order of sharps, the order of flats, and the keys they produce.

## Guitar Shortcuts for Key Signatures

When you see a key signature on a piece of music you need to identify it as quickly as possible, but with great accuracy. Since the guitar's strings are tuned in 4ths (with a single exception), we can use it to help us remember the sharp and flat key orders and find the key for a piece of music. If you are a hands-on player, you'll like this method.

The first sharp key, G major, is represented by the G note on the 3rd fret of the 1st (thinnest) string on your guitar. Its key signature is one sharp, F♯, which puts the 7th degree of the G major scale a half step from the tonic.

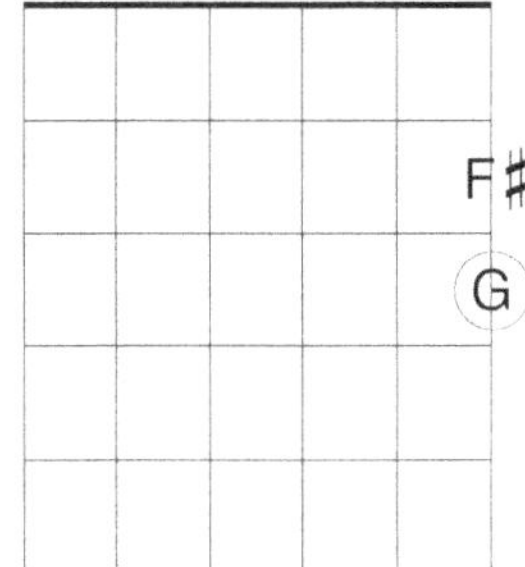


The second sharp key, D, is represented by the D note a 4th lower, on the 2nd string. The key signature keeps the F♯, and adds C#, putting the half step between 7 and 8 in the D major scale.

Because of the tuning difference between the 2nd and 3rd strings, the next descending 4th is one fret lower. This is A, and we can use it to remember that there are three sharps in the key of A major.

The next three sharp keys are E, B, and F♯, and by imagining a seven-string guitar (or being blessed by the demonic gods of metal to actually have one), you can tell that seven sharps give you the key of C♯ major. The sharp needed to form the major scale for each successive key is on its 7th step, which is a half step below the tonic every time. Each successive key uses all the sharps from before, plus this last one.

<— more sharps

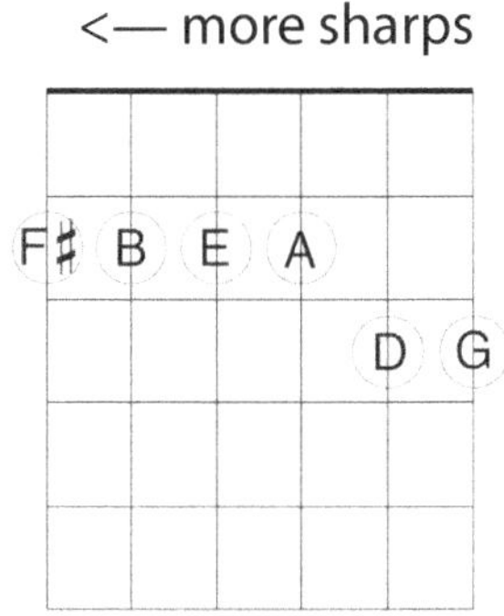


Barre the shape with your 1st and 2nd fingers as if it were a chord, but don't strum it. Use it to read and write sharp key signatures.

The approach is similar to help us remember the order of flats and flat keys, but starting from the 6th string. The first flat key is F, with the key signature containing the note a 4th higher: B♭.

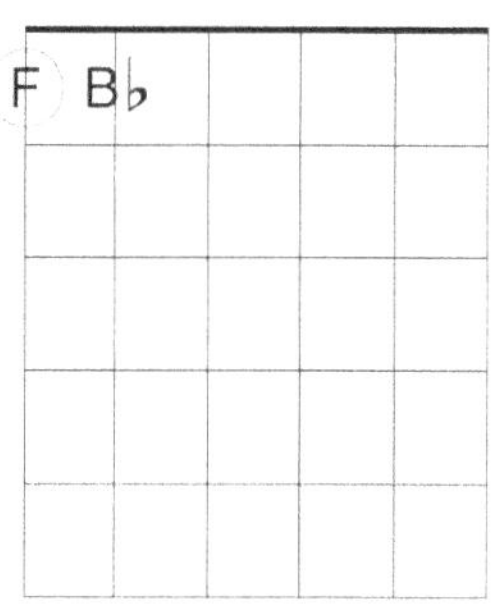


more flats —>

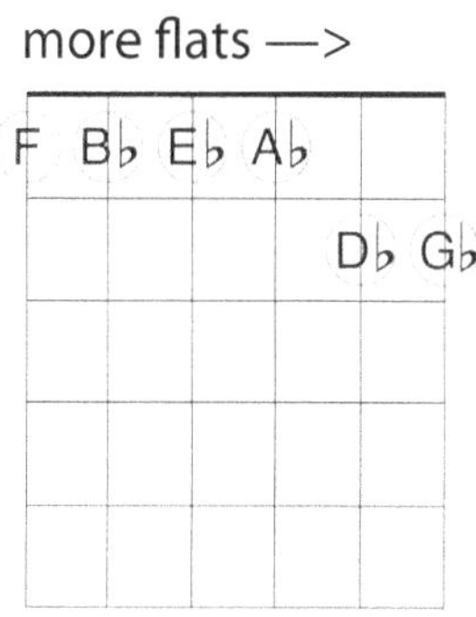


The scheme continues through the same shape, with the key of B♭ containing B♭ and E♭, the key of E♭ containing B♭, E♭, and A♭, and so on. An imaginary high A string added to the guitar would show that the key of G♭ requires the addition of C♭, and the key of C♭ requires the addition of F♭ to the staff.

## Preparing to Read

The key signature is a new item on the checklist for getting ready to play:

1. Repeat signs
2. Clef, key signature, and time signature
3. Range of notes
4. Harder parts
5. Repeated or familiar figures

Learn your scale fingerings, and remember to use them when reading. The range of notes **and** the key signature tell you exactly which scale patterns you can use. Then find any accidentals and mentally rehearse how you'll play them.

## Minor Keys and Scales

Each major key has a *relative minor* key that is represented by the same key signature. The relative minor key always starts on the 6th degree of the major scale. For example, the key signature for C is the same as the key signature for A minor. We find this by counting up six steps from C to A.

```
C  D  E  F  G  A  B
1  2  3  4  5  6  7
```

The relative minor of G is E minor. Both have one sharp in the key signature.

```
G  A  B  C  D  E  F♯
1  2  3  4  5  6  7
```

The principle also goes the other way. G is the *relative major* of E minor.

Exercise 73.
Name both keys that these signatures may mean.

Instead of counting up six steps, we can quickly find the relative minor scale by moving down two diatonic steps (three frets on the same string) from the root of the major scale. The fingering for a minor scale is the same as for its relative major; only now a different note in the pattern is used as the tonic. The natural notes we've been reading may be in the key of C, or they may be in the key of A minor. The difference is mainly determined by the chords that the composer uses or has in mind when writing a melody. It's not absolutely necessary for us to know immediately which was intended—major or minor—as long as we read the notes correctly, but learning to hear the composer's intent will help us read more easily in the long run.

We can identify minor scales just as we do major ones, even without the help of a key signature. The minor scale formula has half steps from **2-3** and from **5-6**. It is a displaced version of the major scale formula.

```
minor:                    1  2^3  4  5^6  7  8
                   C  D  E  F  G  A  B  C  D  E  F  G  A
Major:   1  2  3^4  5  6  7^8
```

A half step in music is one of the cues we use to figure out what scale is being played. For example, there is a half step from A to B♭ in this example. It could be 3-4 in F major, or 7-8 in B♭. It could also be 2-3 in G minor, or 5-6 in D minor. Because the phrase ends on G (and because it feels like G is the tonic), I think it is in G minor. Play the B♭ on the 4th string at fret 8.

Exercise 74.

Name both scales that these pitches may come from.

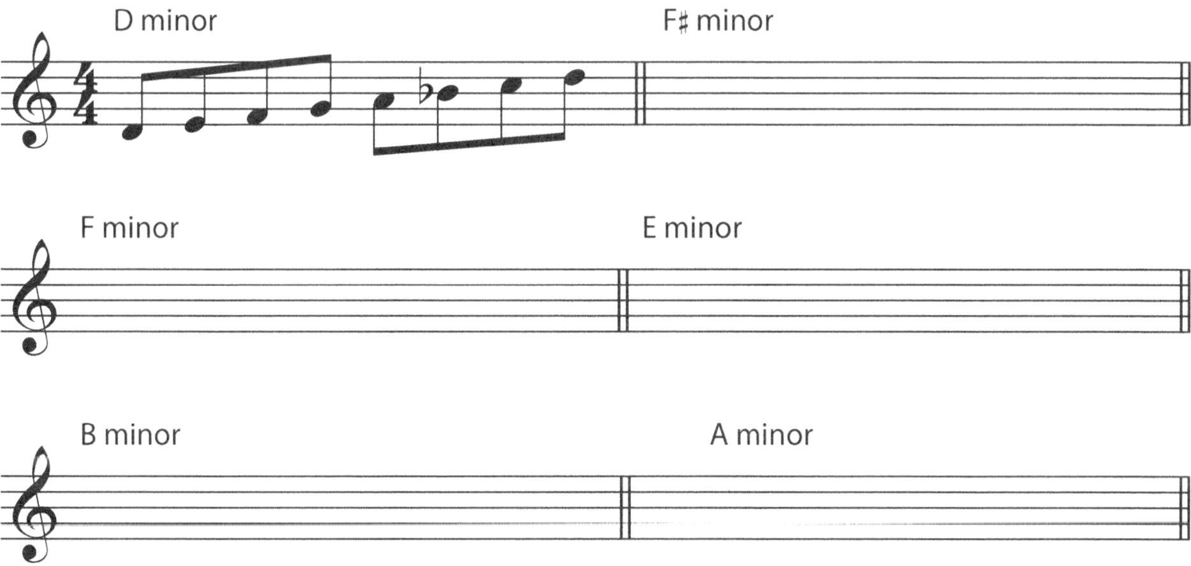

Exercise 75.

Write the indicated scales on the staff using the minor scale formula. Use accidentals instead of a key signature.



**Practice**

1. Write minor scale patterns on frame diagrams, using the major scale patterns on page 58 for reference. The patterns of notes stay the same; only the scale degree numbers will be different. Practice the patterns with the metronome, this time starting and stopping on the root of the minor scale instead of the relative major.

2. Add the names of relative minor keys to your flash cards so you can memorize them along with the major keys that share their signatures.

# Chapter 11: Roadmaps

The repeat signs we learned are one of several symbols (sometimes called *chart directions*) that define the path we will follow through a piece. Checking the roadmap is first on the list of things to do before starting to read.

## Numbered Endings

Often a section is repeated note-for-note except for its final measures. Numbered endings with repeat signs save us from writing the entire section out again just to change the last bar. In this example, play measures 1-3, then play the first ending, with the bracketed "1." Then obey the repeat sign, playing bars 1-3 again, but **skip over** the first ending and play the second ending. Then continue with the bars that follow.

Multiple numbered endings imply how many times to play the section. In this example, the section is played three times, each time with a different ending.

Here, the section is played four times, alternating between the two endings.

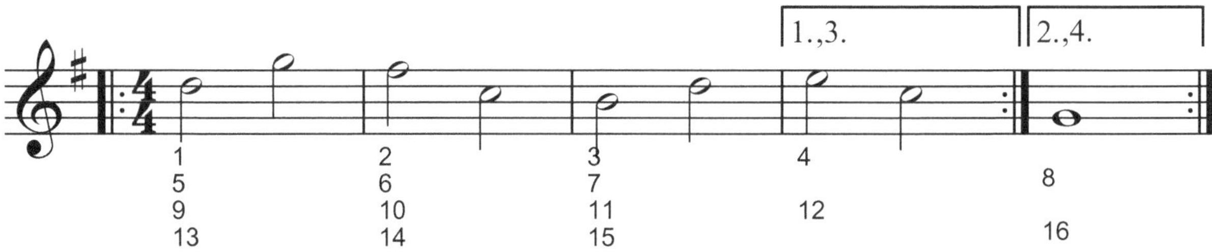

## D.C.

The letters *D.C.* stand for the Italian *da capo*, literally meaning "from head." When you see this instruction, which is usually written over or just after the final measure of a section, you are to immediately jump to the absolute beginning of the song (the "top" or "head") and play from there.

When "taking the D.C." you still obey one- and two-bar repeat slashmarks, but it is customary to **disregard** all section repeat signs that you have already followed, playing only the final ending in any sections that were previously repeated. This custom may be overruled by writing *D.C. (repeats good)*, or *D.C. (take repeat)*, etc. Follow the measure numbers in this example to see how a D.C. works when the *repeat good* direction is not included.

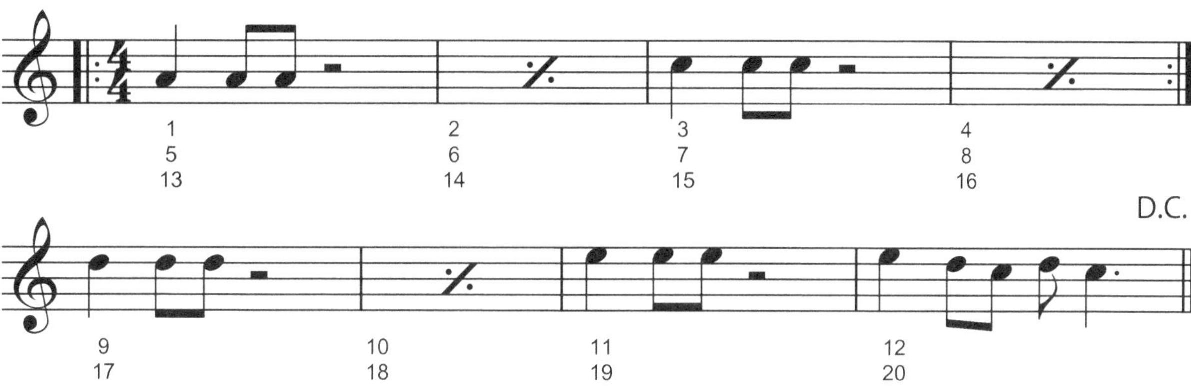

## D.S.

This is an abbreviation of *dal segno*, meaning "from the sign." The sign it refers to is the letter *S* with dots on either side, and a slash.

When you see the sign for the first time, play past it but make a note of where it is for later. When you reach the *D.S.* instruction, jump back to the sign and continue reading. The same customary rules for repeats as used for *D.C.* also apply when following *D.S.* instructions: don't take any repeats unless you're told otherwise.

## al Fine

*Fine* (pronounced *feenay*, "end") is used to mark the final measure to play **after** following a *D.C.* or *D.S.*

The first time you pass by the *fine*, ignore it and read on. After following the *D.C.* or *D.S.*, stop when you play the note or measure marked *fine*.

Use of the *fine* is only necessary if there is a *D.C.* or *D.S.*, which should then say *D.C. al fine* ("from head to the end") or *D.S. al fine* ("from the sign to the end").

## al Coda

Italian for "to the tail," *al coda* may appear instead of *al fine*. The *coda* itself is a final section written after all the others. The *coda mark* is a circle with a cross in it.

There are always two coda marks on the piece when this direction is used. The first is at the place you'll be jumping **from**. The second marks the place you'll be jumping **to**. Before you start playing, make a note of the locations of the two marks. Mentally rehearse the measures before and after the jump.

As you play the song, the first time you see the coda mark, **pass it by** and keep playing. Later you will see either *D.C. al coda* or *D.S. al coda*. Return to the top or to the sign as directed, then play until you reach the first coda mark. At that point, jump to the second coda mark.

A *coda* mark is only needed if a part of the song has to be skipped over.

Exercise 76.

On staff paper, create a song chart using blank measures, to which notes could be added later. Use chart directions so that all repeated music will only be written down one time. Here is the form of the song:

Intro (4 measures)
Verse 1 (8 measures)
Verse 2 (same as Verse 1, but its last bar is different from the last bar of Verse 1)
Chorus 1 (8 measures)
Verse 3 (8 measures that are the same as Verse 2)
Chorus 2 (4 measures that are the same as Chorus 1 first 4 measures)
Coda (4 measures, played twice for a total of 8 measures, plus one extra final measure)

## Sixteenth Notes

By dividing an eighth note in half, we get a *sixteenth note*. A sixteenth note written by itself gets two flags. Add a few of your own sixteenth notes at random pitches on both sides of the center line, with proper stem and flag directions. Flags always go to the right side of the stem.

There are four sixteenth notes per beat in a simple meter like 4/4. We count with two more syllables (*e* and *a*, pronounced "ee" and "uh") to time sixteenth-note attacks: 1 e + a 2 e + a 3 e + a 4 e + a. When playing sixteenth notes, do not change the way you tap your foot. Tap the foot only on the quarter-note downbeats as usual. The upstroke of the foot still corresponds to the "and" (+).

Sixteenth notes within the same beat may be beamed together with other sixteenth notes and eighth notes. A sixteenth note only needs to have a double beam on one side. The second beam cannot touch the stem of an eighth note. Copy these beamed figures in the space provided.

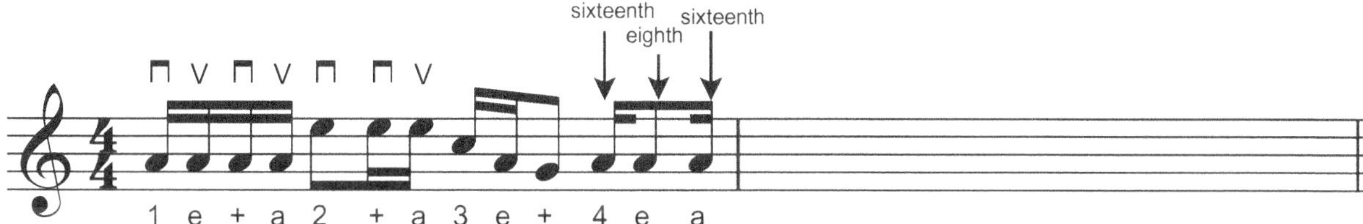


Along with sixteenth notes comes the dotted eighth note, which is equivalent to an eighth note plus a sixteenth. You may also think of it as three sixteenth notes tied together. There are two possible ways this rhythm can appear (if we don't count tied rhythms and compound meters). In the sixteenth-dotted-eighth combination (shown on beat 3 in the next example), the notes are spread out slightly from the crammed-together position their exact values would suggest. Pay very close attention to the picking directions in the examples that follow.

The *sixteenth rest* is like the eighth rest, with an extra flag added. Two adjacent sixteenth rests in the same beat are combined to form an eighth rest.

Sixteenth-note beat division produces an exception to the "no dotted rests" rule. When a lone sixteenth note starts or ends a beat, a dotted eighth rest (three sixteenths long) may fill the rest of the beat.

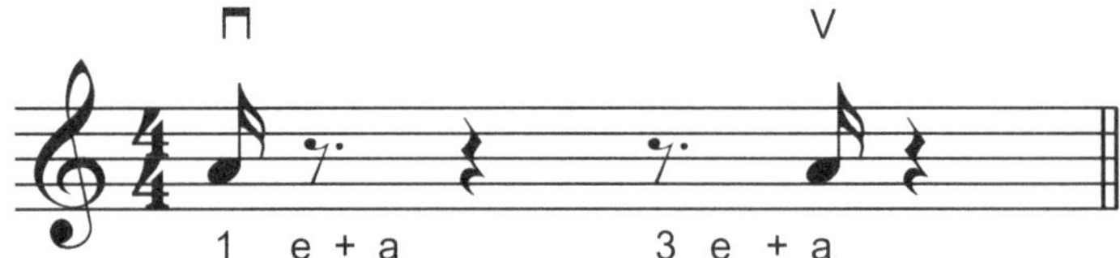

A note or rest must be written to show the downbeat of any beat where sixteenth notes are used (not just beats 1 and 3 as with eighth notes). Break a longer note into two smaller ones tied together if necessary to follow this rule. In the first line of this example, a dotted eighth note covers "1 e and," three sixteenth notes in total. There is only room for one more sixteenth note before beat 2. To extend the duration, a tie must be used, as shown in measure two.

We can expand the pyramids of note values to include the sixteenth note and rest. Sixteen sixteenth notes equal four beats; equivalent in length to a whole note.

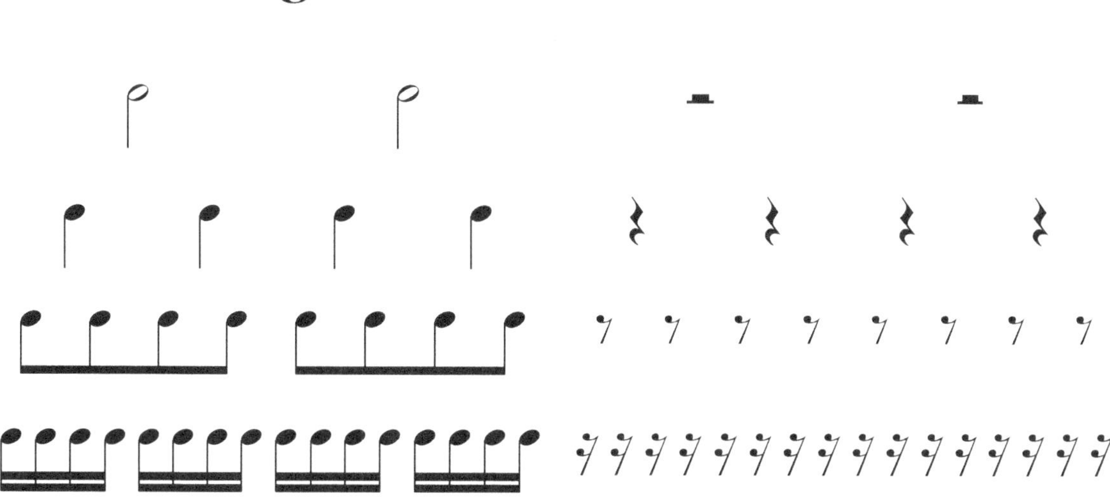

## Exercise 77.

Write the corresponding count below these note attacks.

## Exercise 78.

Write correction notation for the given attacks on one pitch of your choice.

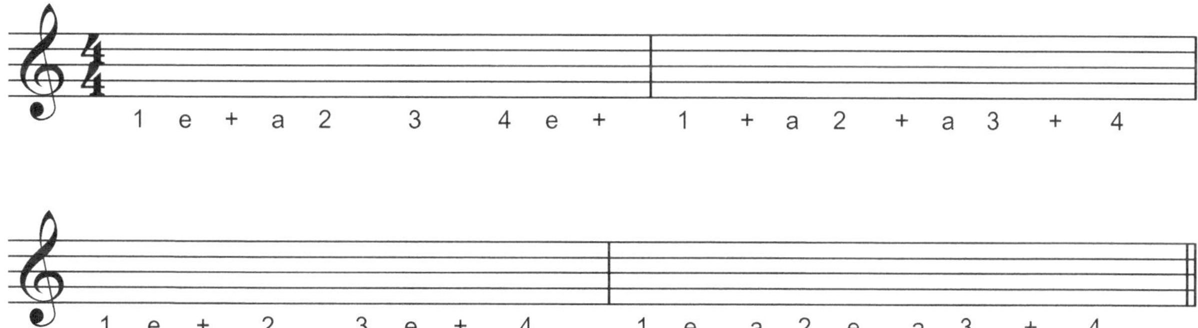

# Sixteenth-Note Vocabulary List

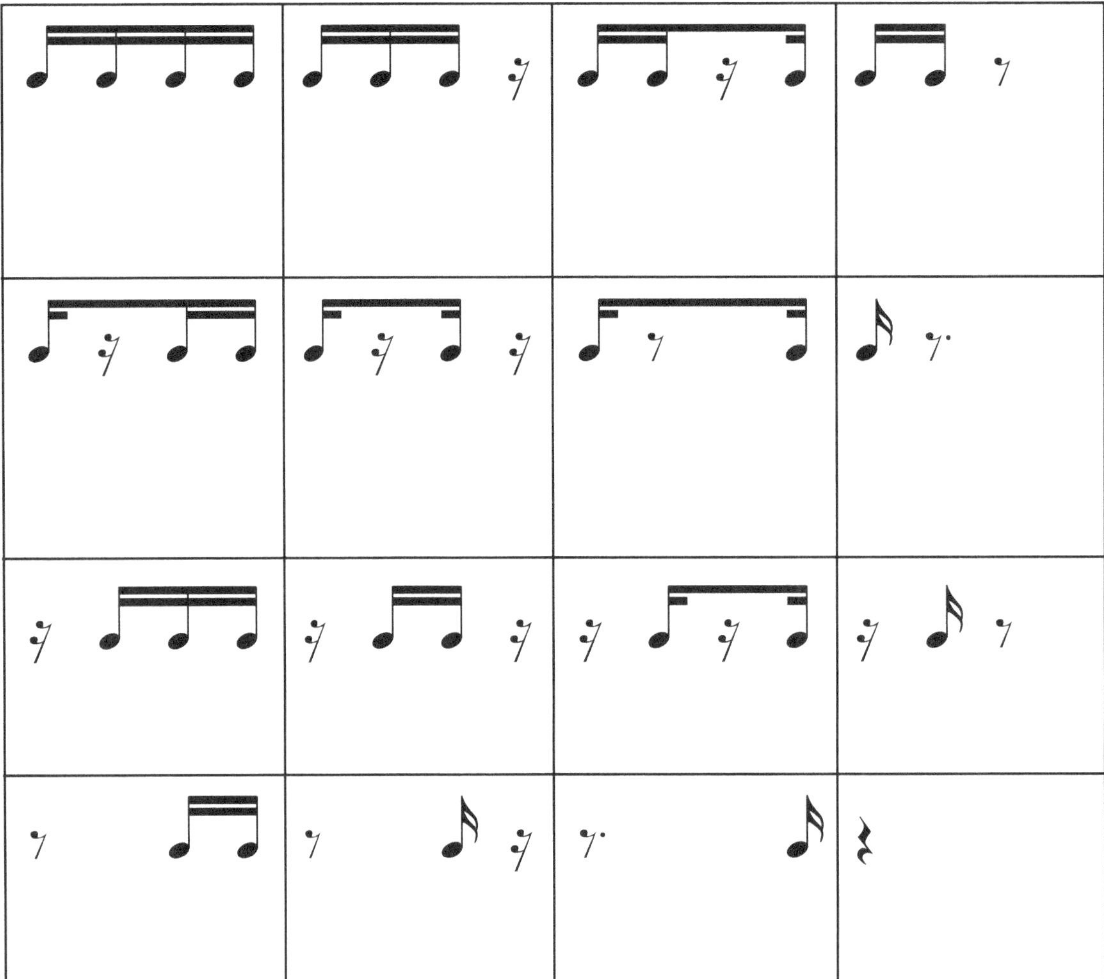

The table contains every possible way to fill **one beat** with sixteenth notes and rests. It is exactly similar to the rhythmic vocabulary lists for quarter notes and eighth notes. This time I'll guide you to write all the equivalent rhythms that you're likely to see in common practice. Memorize the sound of each so you can play them from memory instead of counting out each note.

Beams are used instead of flags to make beat groups easy to see, and I've already combined neighboring sixteenth rests into larger rests where possible.

Exercise 79.

1. Find the table cells where any sixteenth note is followed by a rest. Write these measures out again using an eighth note in those places. Make sure the one-beat groups are beamed and add up to four units.

2. It's uncommon to see a note cutoff that is on a precise offbeat, so for cells 4 and 12, add a dot to your eighth note and erase your sixteenth rest.

3. In cell 7, add a version using a dotted eighth note instead of a sixteenth note followed by rests. Cell 8 is equal, attack-wise, to a quarter note. Write that version in.

The rhythmic versions with fewer sixteenth rests are easier to read. In common practice these versions are often used preferentially, with the note cutoffs implied for styles like funk, or directed by articulation marks such as the *staccato* dots in this example. Technically, a staccato mark tells you to play a note for half its written duration, but often staccato dotted and tied notes are also meant to be clipped off to a sixteenth note too, so that almost no rests are used at all, as in measure 4 here.

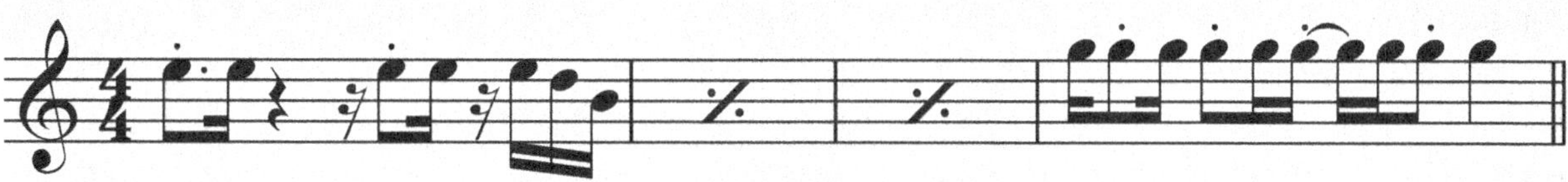

Exercise 80.

Write the correction notation for the given attacks. Use the pitches given in the tab.

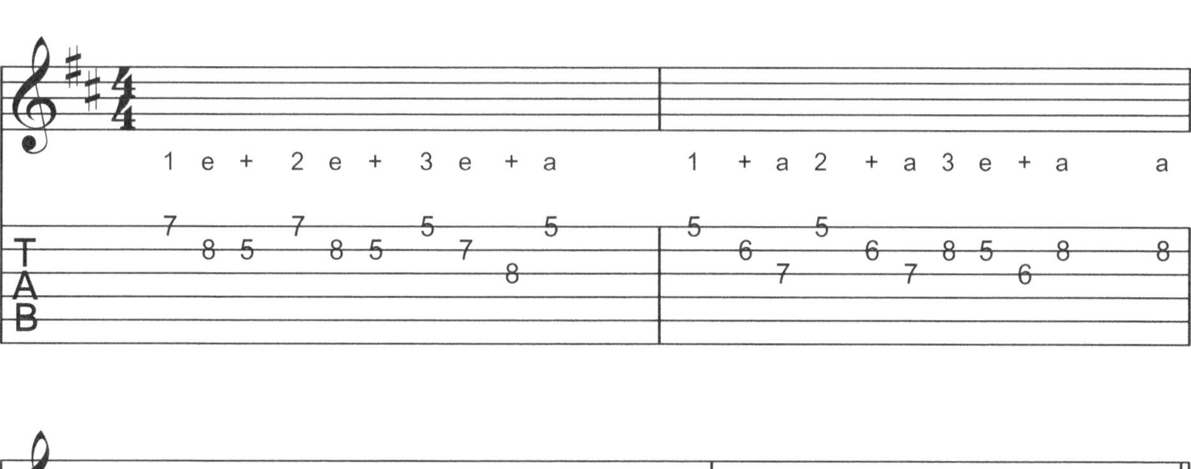

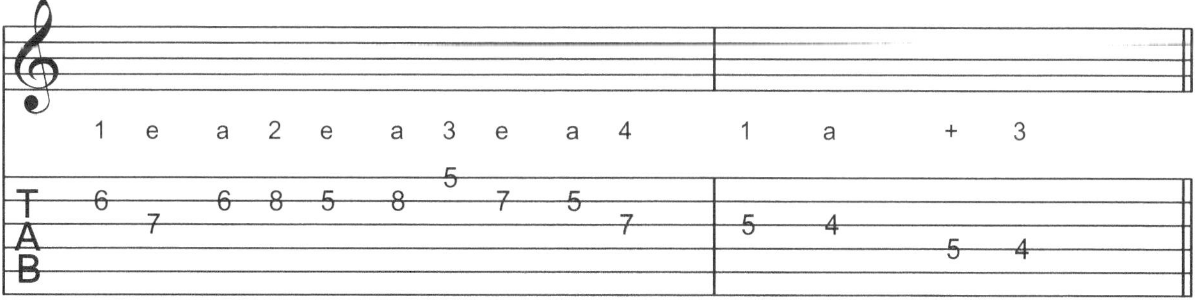

**Practice**

1. Practice the sixteenth-note vocabulary list, reading the measures from left to right. Then read them in reverse order: read the final measure, then the second-to-last, and so on. Then try skipping around, for example reading down the first column and up the second. Be sure to practice the equivalent-attack versions too.

When reading sixteenth notes, take in one or two beats at a glance. Once you know a rhythm, like a written word, you want to see it, identify it accurately, and play it without really thinking about each mark on the page. As soon as you know what you'll be playing, look ahead at the next measure, or, if you're already so far ahead you risk overloading your memory, look straight ahead instead of looking at your instrument. Try looking away, then back at the page to see if you can easily find your place again.

2. Draw one random four-measure rhythm example per day this week, using quarter, eighth, and sixteenth notes and rests. Include some dotted quarters and eighths, and a few ties, making sure you have exactly four beat's worth of correctly written notation in each measure.

Make it easy to read, keeping the notes on A on the second space of the staff. Play your examples, counting aloud and tapping your foot with the metronome.

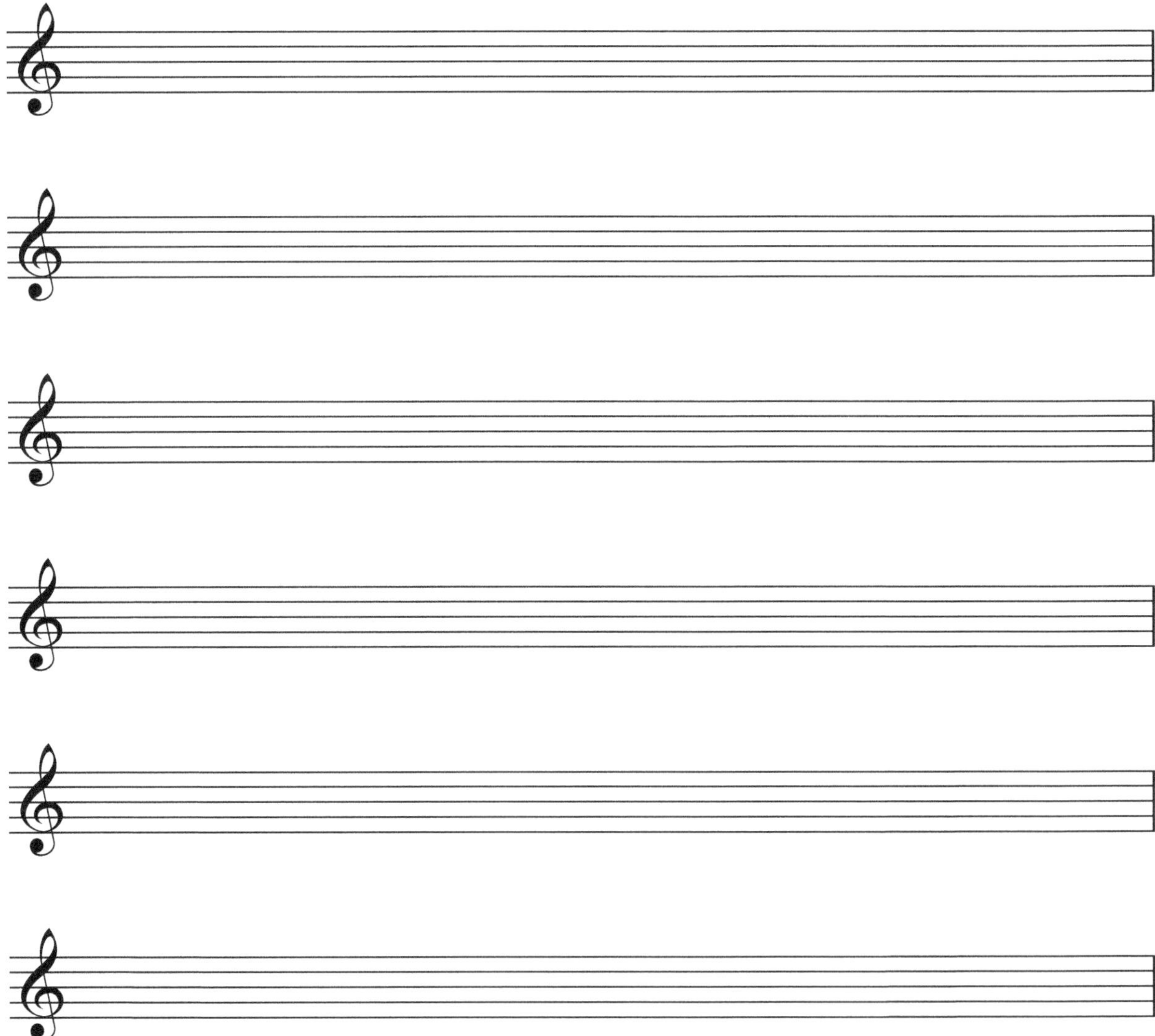

# Chapter 12: Chords

A *chord* is when more than one note is played at the same time. Chords have consistent characteristics on the staff that we can learn to recognize. These consistent staff shapes sometimes translate into differing shapes on the fretboard because of the guitar's physical limits and slightly-irregular tuning.

Chord shapes have many permutations to memorize and fingering challenges to overcome. You can expect to spend years working on playing and reading chords. Also, instead of drilling you with 3-4 more chapters covering the notes on the entire fretboard, I'm leaving some of that work up to you (and I'm trusting you to go do it) so we can forge ahead and see how the knowledge is going to be applied.

## Double Stops

Any two tones played at once are a type of chord called a *double stop*. The first double stops we'll learn come from the **harmonized scale** in diatonic 3rds in the key of C major or A minor.

Because it's impossible to play two simultaneous pitches on the same string, some of the double stops must be played outside a single fretting-hand position, as in this example. When reading notes consecutively, we'd play E and G both on the 2nd string. We can't do that with a chord, so we have to shift up or down.

Though there are many ways to finger double stops, first focus on minimizing position shifts so you don't have to take your eyes off the paper. To do that—and to cultivate good technique—try to play notes on higher frets with the 3rd and 4th fingers; there's a typical fingering marked on the example. Feel the frets beneath your fingertips as you read.

Rehearse the shapes, then play with the metronome. The double stop B–D may also be played at the 4th and 3rd frets on strings 3 and 2. The double stop E-G may also be played on the top two strings at frets 5 and 3.

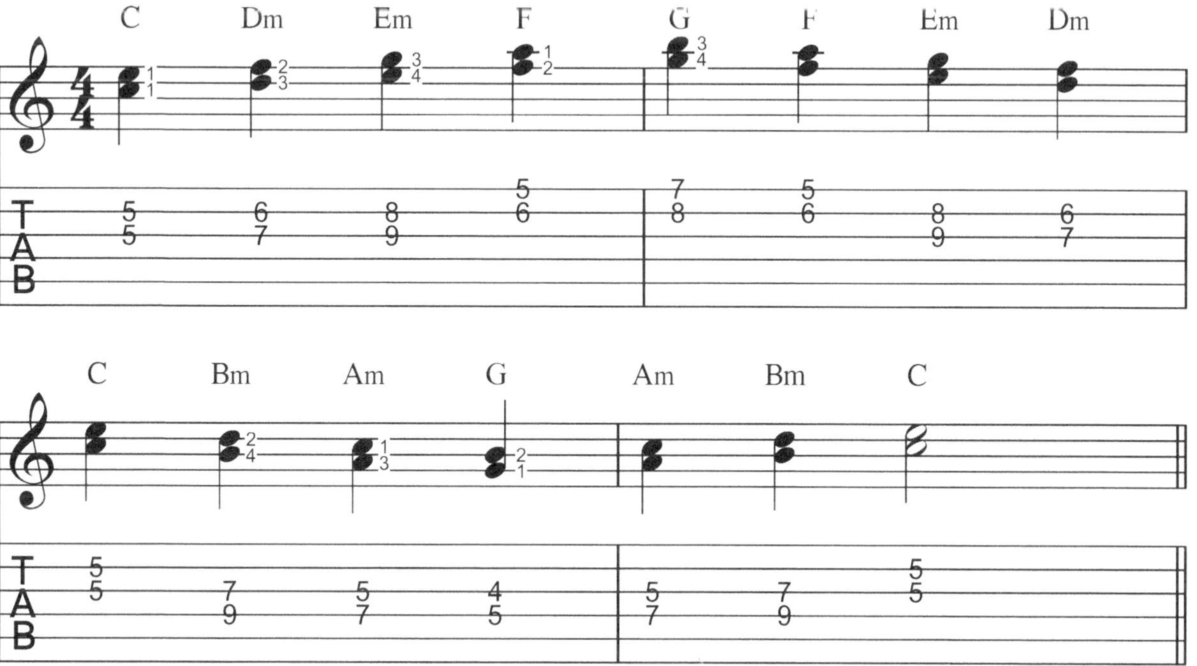

On the other hand, if you want more smoothness (and speed), and you have time to rehearse, play the same example entirely on strings 2 and 3. When two double stops in a row are both minor 3rds (steps 2 and 3) or both major 3rds (4 and 5) , you can keep the same fingering and slide it up or down by two frets. Carefully strum just the two desired notes (using downstrokes of the pick since they are quarter notes), or try *hybrid picking*, using the pick for the low note and plucking the higher one with your middle finger.

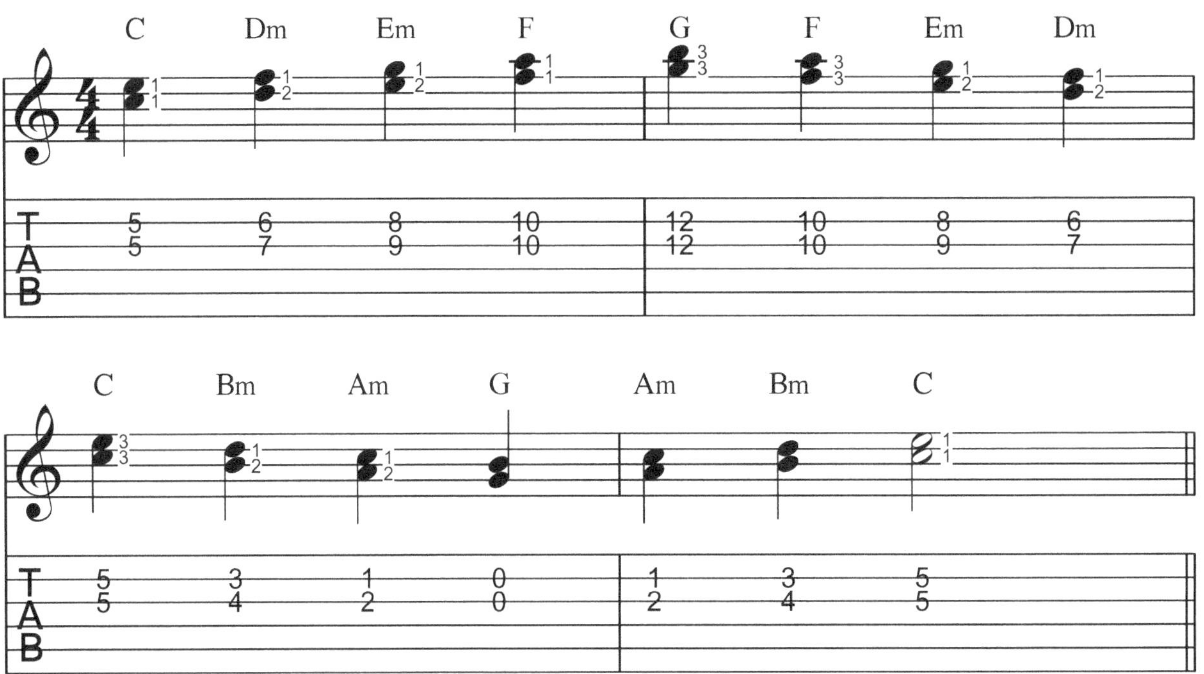

Again, it sounds good this way, but you can end up in an unfamiliar position for reading later notes.

Exercise 81.
Staying diatonic to the C major scale, stack a 3rd above the note given on the staff. Then add the note to the frame to complete the double-stop diagram. Make sure your frame is playable as a chord.

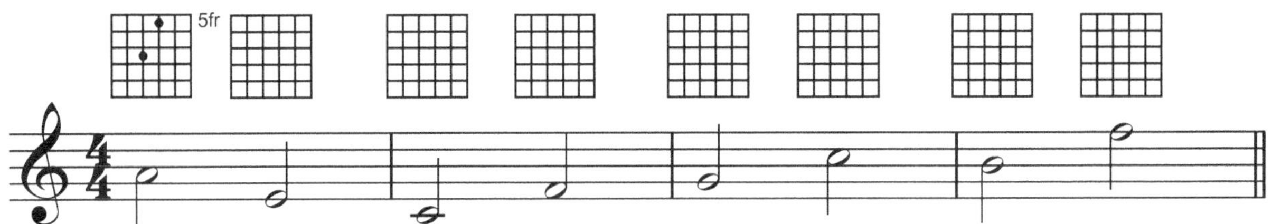

Exercise 82.
Staying within the C major scale, write a diatonic 3rd **below** the note given on the staff. Then draw a playable double stop in the frame.

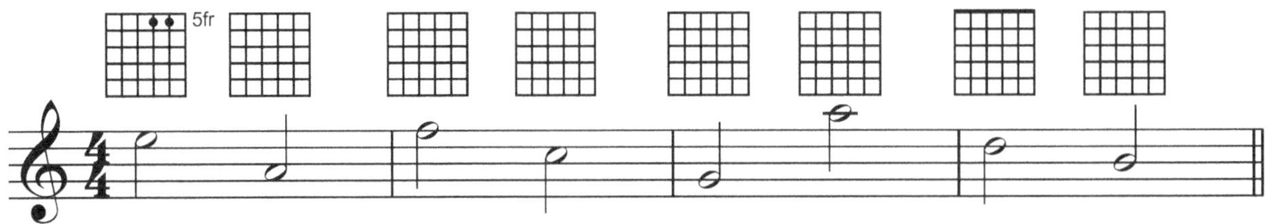

## Harmonized 3rds in G or E minor

By adding one sharp to the key signature, we get two double stops that are different from those in C, found on steps 5 and 7 of the G major scale. The new double stops are D major and F♯ minor.

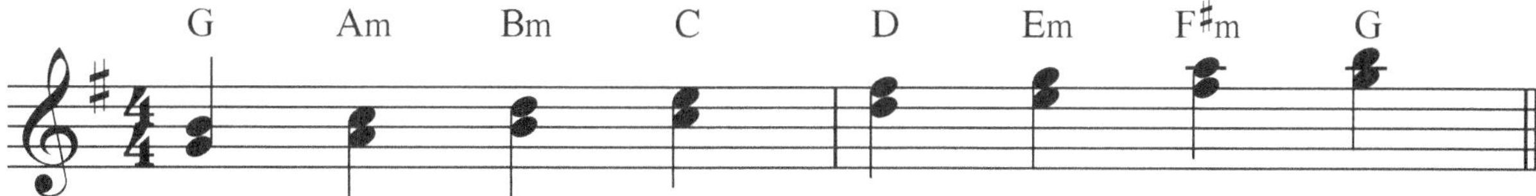

Exercise 83.

Here is the key signature and complete pattern-5 scale for G major in 5th position. This time you're going to provide the tablature, but do not touch your guitar at all. Visualize it instead. Add diatonic 3rds above the notes on the staff, then tab out the two-string shapes that are created, staying as close to 5th position as possible. Label each 3rd by name and quality—**major** or **minor**.

Exercise 84.

Now work out the harmonized 3rds in G using only the 2nd and 3rd strings, as we did with the C major scale. Complete the double-stops on the staff, name them, and write them in tablature.

## A New Key Signature: One Flat

The key of F major has one flat. Three B♭s occur in our 5th-position reading. F roots are on strings 2 and 5, so we're looking at a pattern-1 major scale shape, shown with an F major chord in 5th position. The scale shows all the notes we can reach in F without shifting position. Review the locations of the roots, then the B♭ notes on strings 6, 4, and 1. No position shifting is required to play this scale pattern.

## F root shape,  major chord and scale

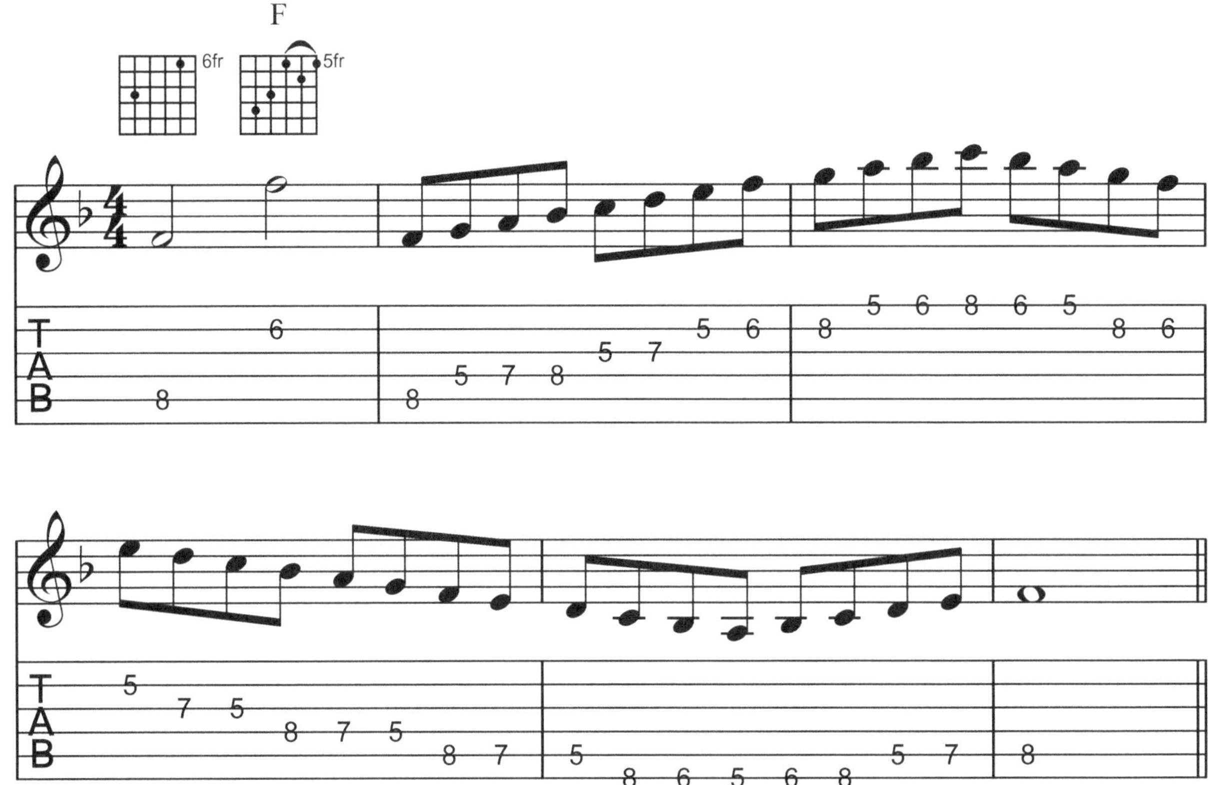


The one-flat signature is shared by the key of D minor. Here are the pattern-2 roots and a D minor chord. The scale fingering is the same as for F major, but this time we start and stop on D.

## D root shape, minor chord and scale

Exercise 85.

Name the notes and write the tab below, then slowly work up the piece with a metronome.

Exercise 86.

Translate these 3rds in F major from tablature into notation with the rhythm implied by the count. (There is a tie across the bar line.) Then cover up the tab and play.

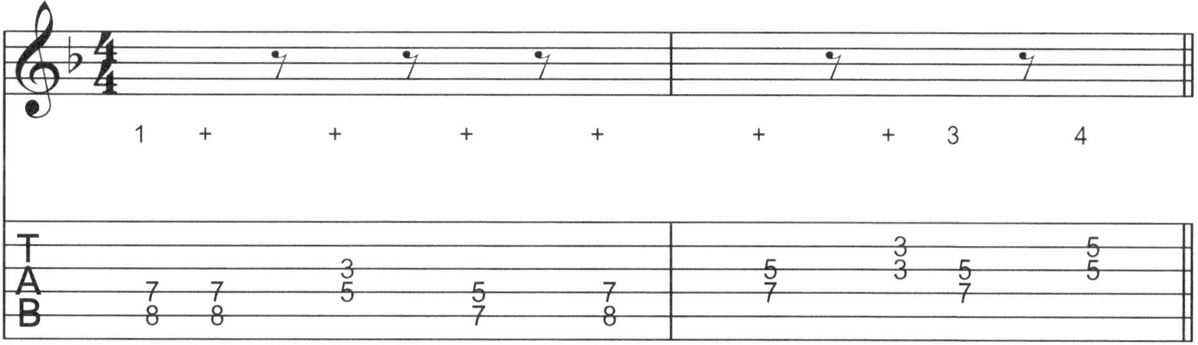


## Major-Key Triads

It's easy to get confused by the onslaught of numbers (for scale steps, intervals, strings, frets, fingers, scale patterns, ad nauseam), so Roman numerals are used to name the chords in a key. They're still pronounced the same way—a iii is still a "three."

By stacking another note atop the double stops (*dyads*), we get the seven diatonic triads in a key. A *triad* is a three-note chord with a root, 3rd, and 5th, called its *chord tones*. Chord tones are numbered from the root of each chord. For example, the I (one) chord has chord tones 1, 3, and 5, which are also degrees 1, 3, and 5 of the diatonic scale. The ii chord consists of degrees 2, 4, and 6 of the diatonic scale, but the notes are also numbered 1 (root), 3, and 5 in relation to the chord itself.

The harmonized major scale produces triads of these qualities: Major–minor–minor–Major–Major–minor–diminished. Memorize the quality of the triad on each degree, shown here in the key of C. The vii chord has a minor 3rd and diminished 5th, producing a diminished triad, which is sometimes designated with a little circle.

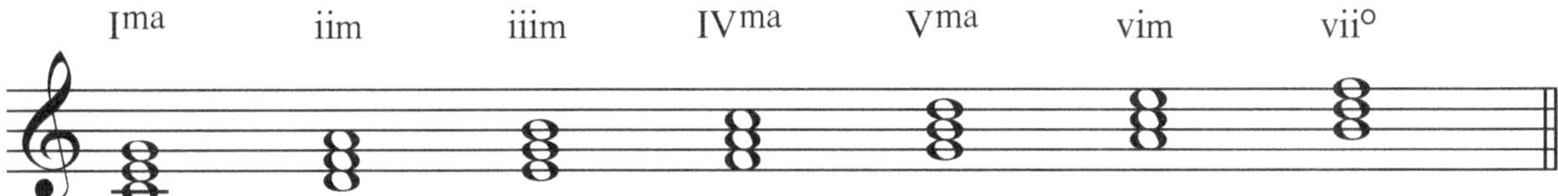

Cover up the solutions below and answer.

1. What quality is the V triad?
2. What quality is the vi triad?
3. Which triads are major?
4. What quality is the iii chord?
5. What quality is the vii triad?
6. Which triads are minor?
7. What are the root, 3rd, and 5th of the **ii chord** in the key of C?
8. What is the 3rd of the **IV chord** in the key of C?
9. What is the 3rd of the **V chord** in the key of C?
10. What is the 5th of the **IV chord** in the key of C?

Solutions

1. Major          2. minor          3. I, IV, and V   4. minor          5. diminished
6. ii, iii, and vi     7. D, F, and A   8. A              9. B              10. C

As with double stops, playing the triads requires us to move out of position a bit. These diatonic triads in C are written as near to 5th position as possible.

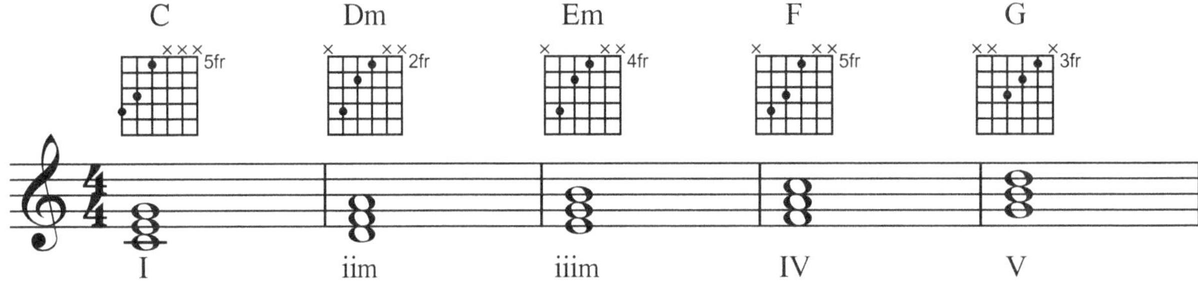

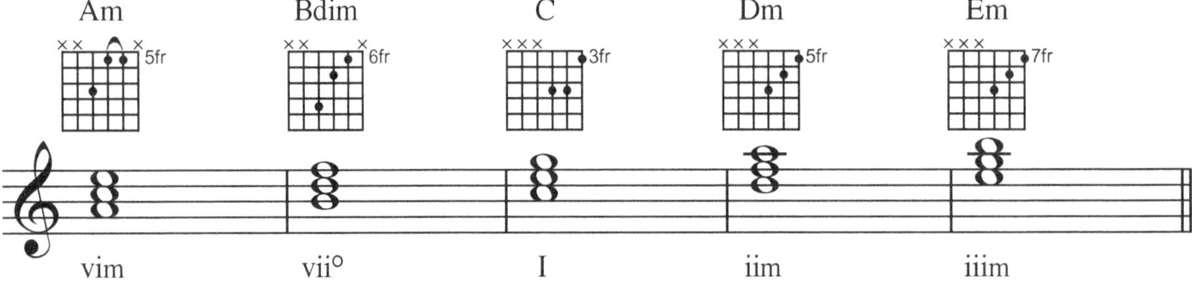

The chords we are studying are said to be in *root position* because each has its root as its lowest pitch.

Unless they're affected by accidentals, three notes on adjacent lines or spaces always spell a triad that is diatonic to the key signature. Practice fretboard shapes for the diatonic triads within a key, using two or three neighboring scale patterns, and you won't have to read each pitch when you see three noteheads in a stack. Just read the root, and play the triad with the correct quality: major for I, IV, or V, minor for ii, iii, or vi, and diminished for vii.

Exercise 87.
Label the chords with correct names, then play.

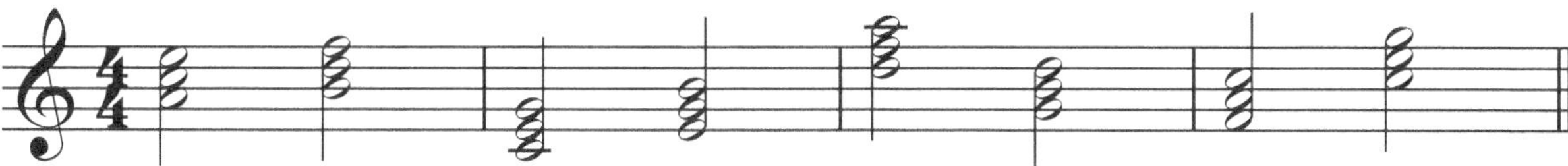

Exercise 88.
Name and draw the diatonic triads in the key of G major on the chord frames. Play with the metronome.

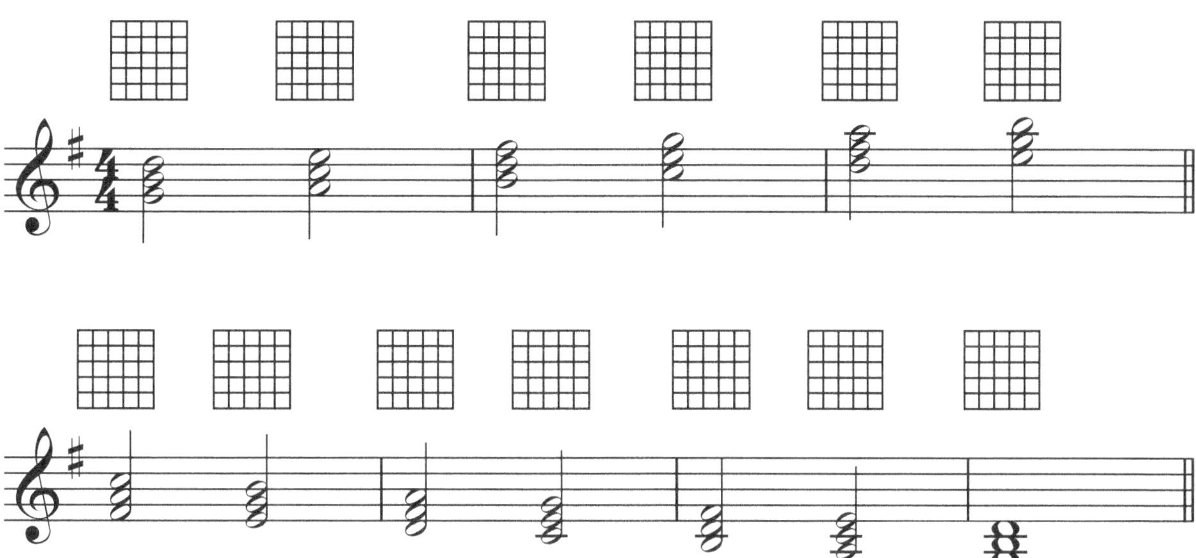

Exercise 89.

Write these diatonic triads in the key of F major in half notes on the staff. Play with the metronome.

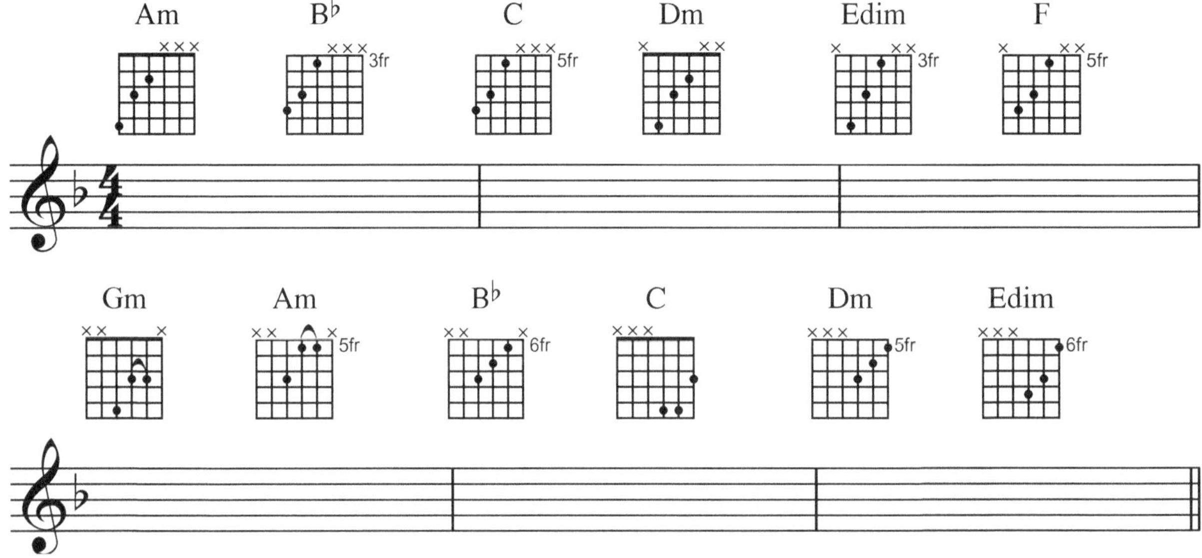


Exercise 90.

On staff paper, write out and label the diatonic triads in all major keys up to 6 flats and up to 6 sharps. You should have thirteen sets with seven triads in each. Spread the project out over a week.

Cover up the solutions below and give complete answers: number and quality.

1. What is the V triad in the key of D?
2. What is the vi chord in the key of F?
3. What is the ii triad in D?
4. What is the iii chord in B♭?
5. What number chord starts on F in A♭ major? What is its quality?
6. What is the vii triad in A major?
7. What number triad starts on B in E major? What is its quality?
8. What is the I chord in the key of C?
9. What number chord starts on A♭ in E♭ major? What is its quality?
10. What is the iii chord in B major?

Solutions
1. A major.
2. D minor.
3. E minor.
4. D minor.
5. vi minor.
6. G♯ diminished.
7. V major.
8. C major.
9. IV major.
10. D♯ minor.

Exercise 91.
Analyze these chords, label with correct names, and play with the metronome.

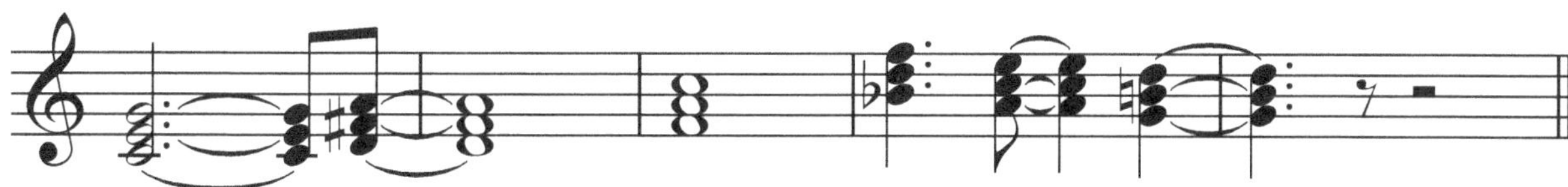

## Arpeggiated Triads

Unlike for chords, you don't have to shift out of position by more than a fret to play the diatonic arpeggios in a key. Look for three consecutive notes on lines or spaces, then identify the triad the notes would create if played simultaneously.

As with the two-note diatonic intervals, we can practice triad arpeggios ascending or descending, with alternating up-and-down movement, and sequenced in other ways.

## Inversions

The order of notes in a chord is called its *voicing*. A composer may specify an *inverted* voicing in order to get a desired bass note below a chord.

An inverted chord has a note other than its root in the bass (the bottom note). A root-position chord is by definition not inverted. The root is its lowest note. In a *first-inversion* triad, the 3rd is the lowest note. A triad in first inversion appears on the staff as a 4th stacked atop a 3rd. Inversions may be specified with *slash chord* symbols. The chord name is on the left; the bass note comes after the slash. Verbally state the name like this: "C over E."

Play these diatonic triads in first inversion in the key of C.

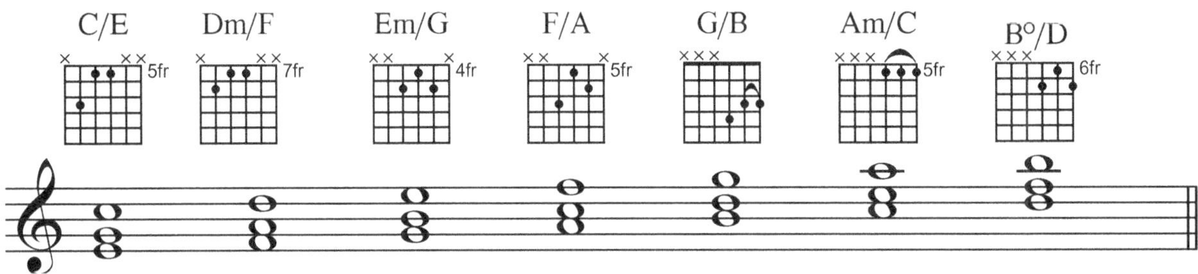


Exercise 92.

Write out these first-inversion diatonic triads in the key of G.

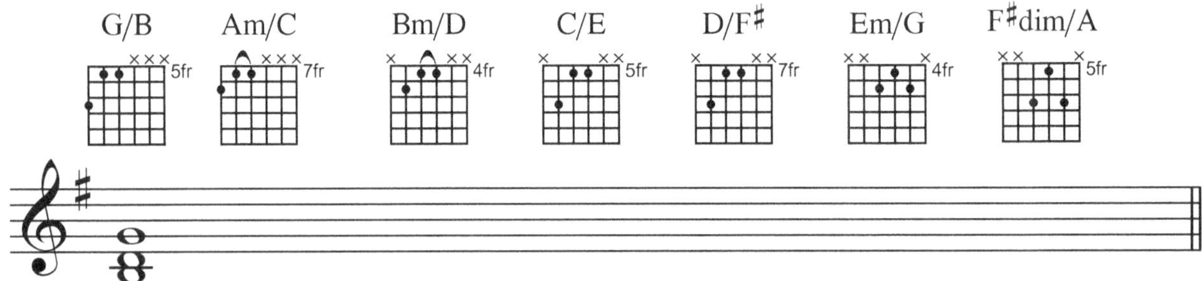


Exercise 93.

Name and draw these first-inversion diatonic triads in F major on the fretboard as close to 5th position as possible.

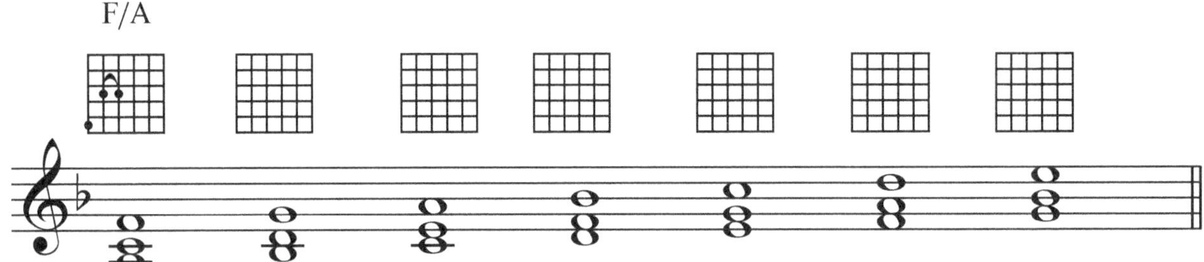


Exercise 94.

The given exercises only included inverted triads in one octave. Write out higher ones within your range of readable notes on separate staff paper, and find them on your instrument.

A triad in *second inversion* has its 5th as the lowest note, and is a 3rd over a 4th on the staff. Play these second-inversion triads in the key of C.

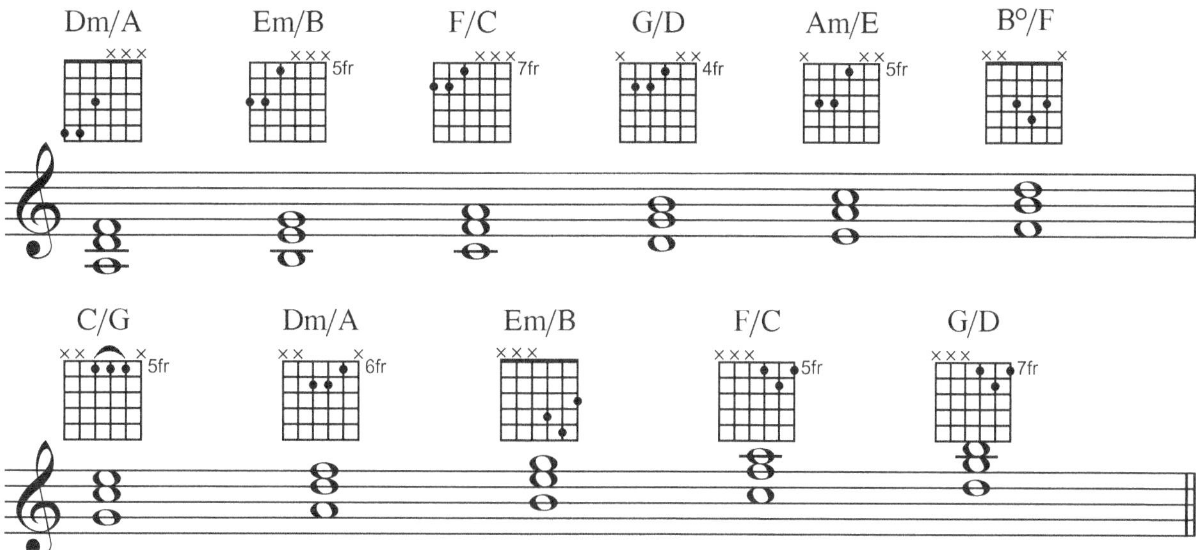


## Exercise 95.

Write out these second-inversion diatonic triads in the key of G.

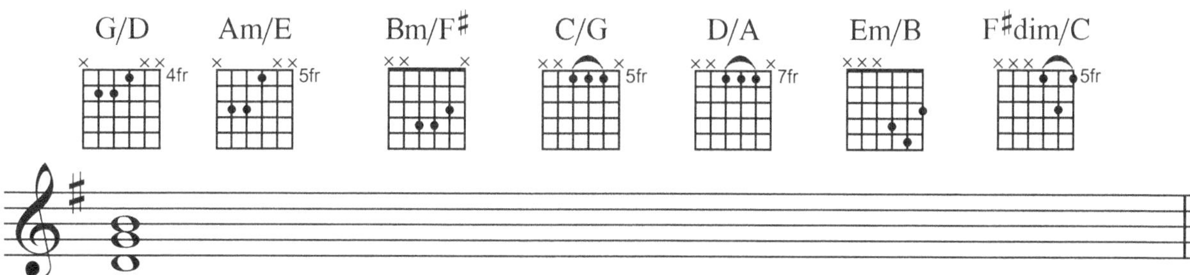


## Exercise 96.

Name and draw these second-inversion diatonic triads in F major on the fretboard as close to 5th position as possible.

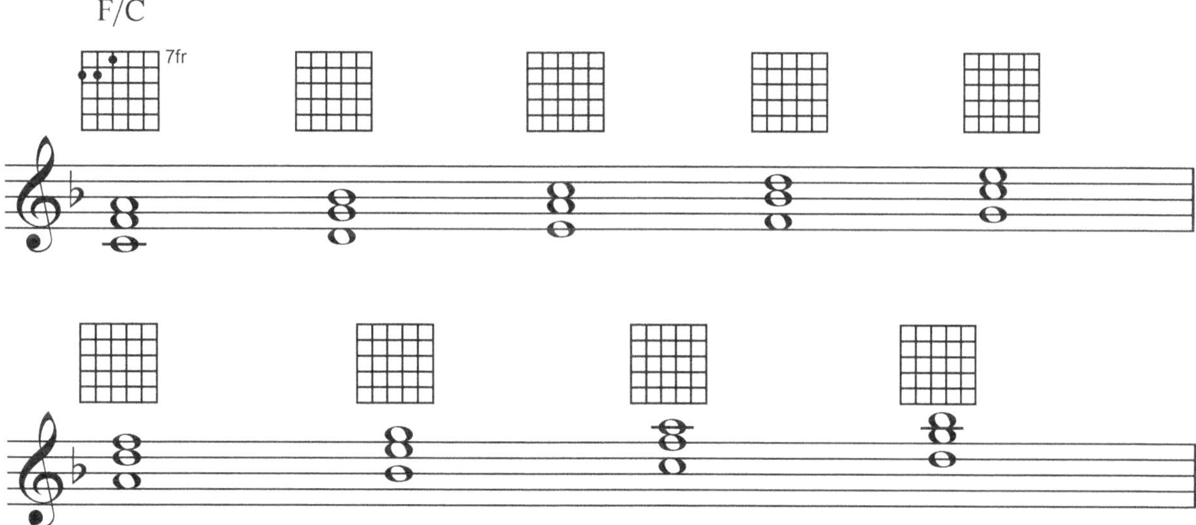

Written melodies frequently include arpeggiated chord inversions. Look for the same patterns on the staff: a 3rd above a 4th is a second-inversion triad voiced 5–1–3, whether it is *harmonic* (simultaneous notes) or melodic (arpeggiated notes). A 4th above a 3rd is a first-inversion triad, voiced 3–5–1.

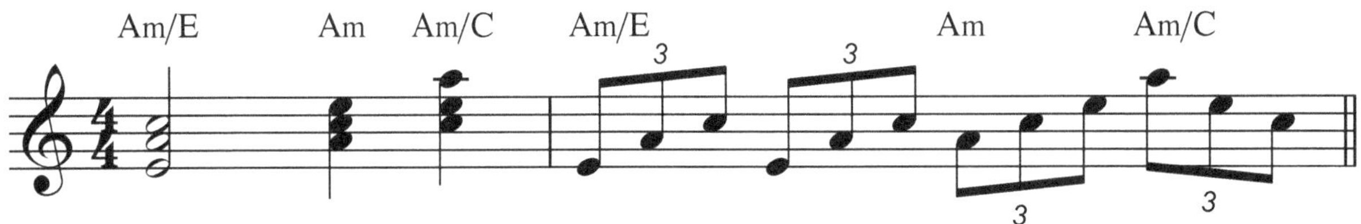


Exercise 97.

In this example, find the triad arpeggios and label each with its chord name. Recite the names aloud as you prepare to play.

## Practice

1. Write out harmonized 3rds on the staff in the keys of D and B♭. Play them first moving up and down the 2nd and 3rd strings, then remaining in 5th position as much as possible.

2. Draw a set of frames for diatonic 3rds on each set of two strings (6-5,  5-4, 4-3, etc.) to help you learn the shapes in any key.

3. Play 1st- and 2nd-inversion diatonic triads in the keys of C, G, and F, in chords and as arpeggios, in time with a slowly-ticking metronome.

# Chapter 13: Harmony

You can further boost your reading speed, comprehension, and rate of memorization if you identify common chord progressions, and melodic notes as being related to those chord progressions. The study of harmonic concepts will help other aspects of your playing beyond reading.

The first and probably easiest chord move to recognize is V–I in a major key. Commonly, a V chord (G in this example) will be followed by the I, or tonic chord. In the V–I chord progression, the root moves down by a perfect 5th or up by a perfect 4th.

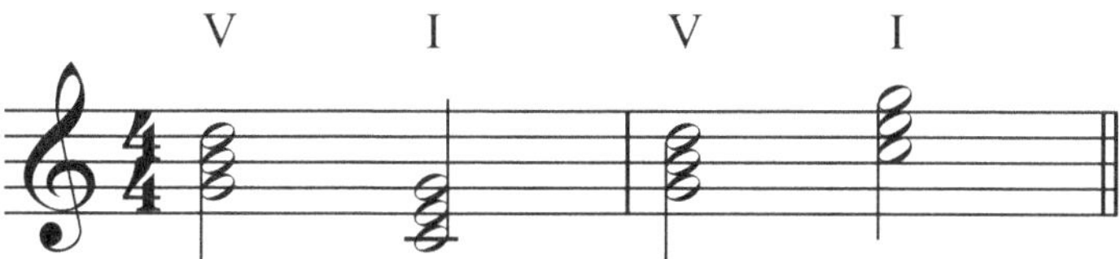

Exercise 98.
Using root-position triads, write V-I progressions in G, D, and A (the first three sharp keys), and then in F, B♭, and E♭ (the first three flat keys). Name the chords.

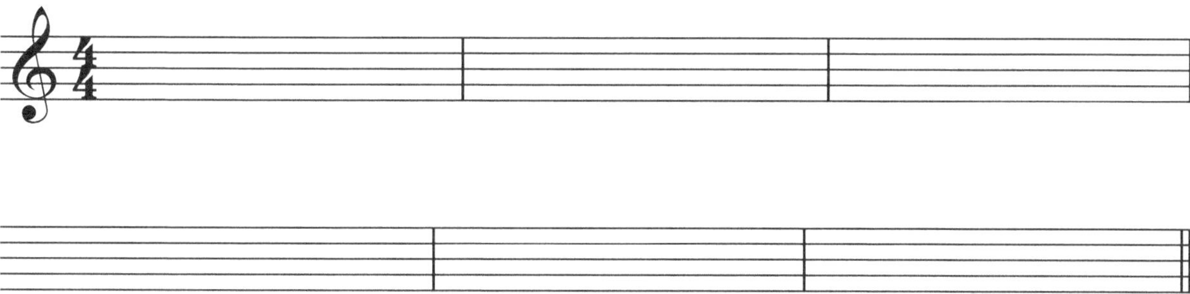

The same root movement is often used to cycle through the other chords within a key. For example, the V chord may be preceded by the ii chord. From ii to V is up a 4th or down a 5th.

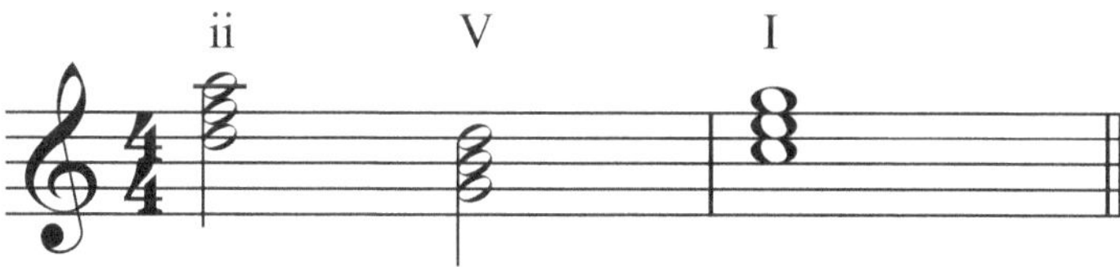

Exercise 99.
Using root-position triads, write ii–V–I progressions in G, D, F, and B♭.

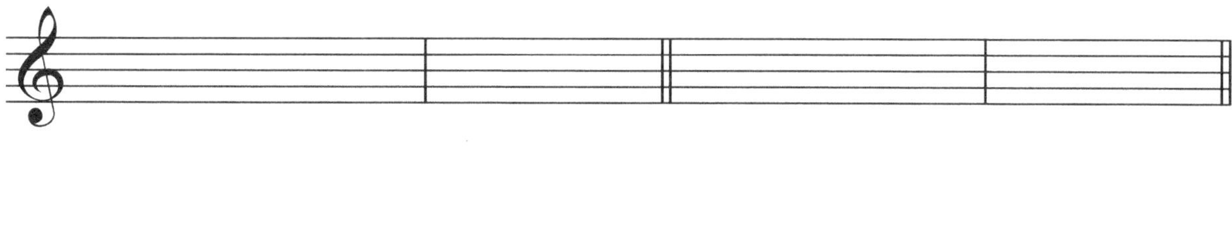

Continuing the cycle-of-5ths root movement, the ii may be preceded by the vi, and the vi may be preceded by the iii.

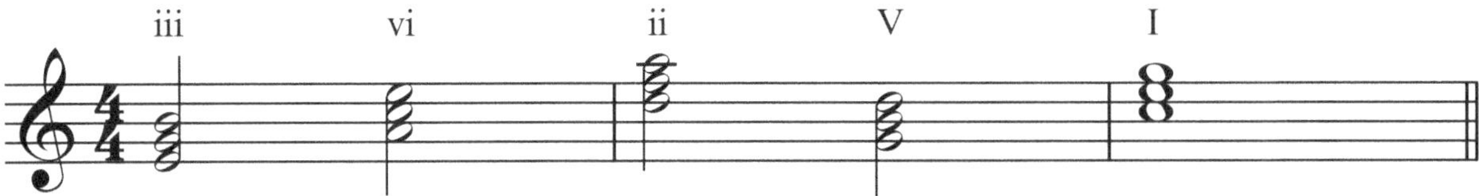



Exercise 100.

Write iii–vi–ii–V–I progressions in G and in F with the same chord durations as the above example. Use accidentals or key signatures. Work through the triad shapes and play with the metronome.

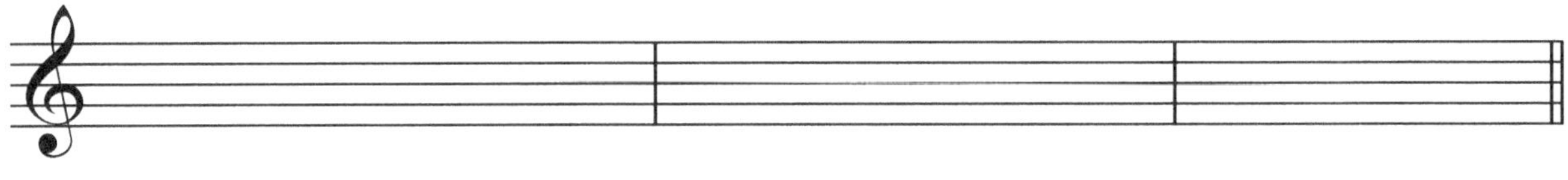

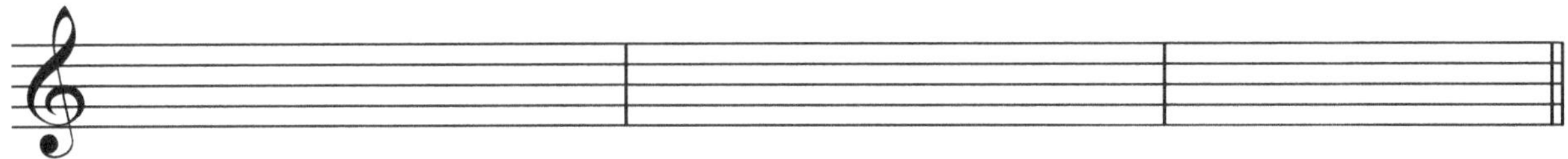

I–IV is another example of root movement down a 5th/up a 4th that you'll see thousands of times. When you're on the I, expect it to be followed by IV if the tune is a blues or country song.

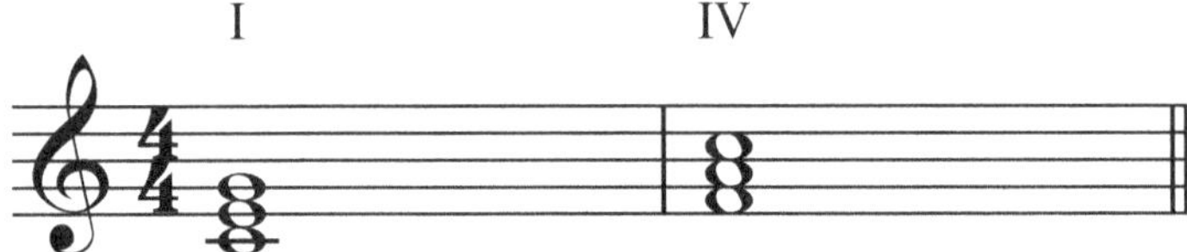



Cover the solutions below and answer these questions.
1. What is the diatonic IV chord in the key of G?
2. What is the diatonic V chord in the key of A$\flat$?
3. What is the diatonic iii chord in the key of D?
4. What is the diatonic IV chord in the key of F?
5. What is the diatonic V chord in the key of C?
6. What is the diatonic vi chord in the key of A?
7. What is the diatonic ii chord in the key of B$\flat$?
8. What is the diatonic IV chord in the key of E?
9. What is the diatonic vii chord in the key of B?
10. What is the diatonic V chord in the key of E$\flat$?

| 1. C | 2. E$\flat$ | 3. F#m | 4. B$\flat$ | 5. G |
|------|------|------|------|------|
| 6. F#m | 7. Cm | 8. A | 9. A#dim | 10. B$\flat$ |

## Voice Leading

*Voice leading* is where, instead of blocky root-position chords, inversions are used so that the individual notes move by the smallest possible distance as the chords change.

Here is the iii–vi–ii–V–I progression again. The root of Em is also the 5th of Am, so it can stay there for both chords. The G note moves up to A, and the B moves up just a half step to C. The same principle is applied throughout the progression. In each chord move at least one note stays the same. Play this example carefully.

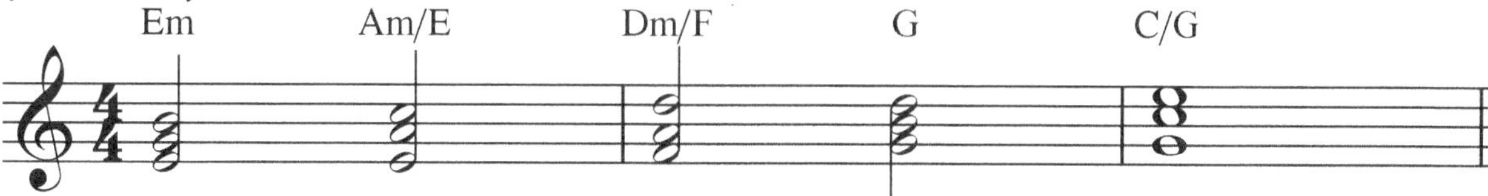


Exercise 101.

Write the iii–vi–ii–V–I progression in the key of C using the closest possible voice leading, this time starting with Em in first inversion.

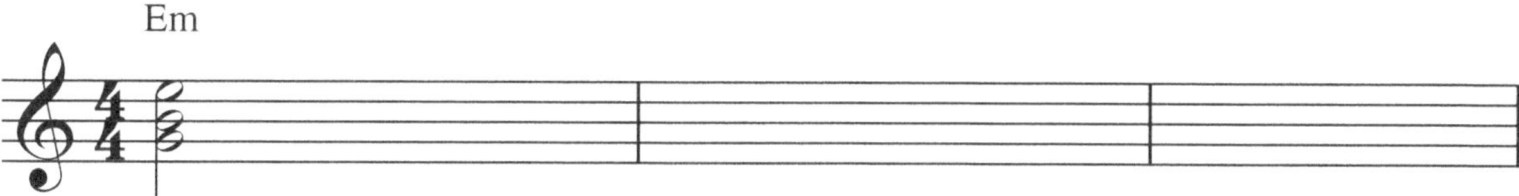


## Leading Tones

Though the V chord in a minor key is diatonically a minor triad, when a V–Im move happens, very often the 3rd of the V chord will be raised by a half step, creating a feeling of tension that makes the resolution stronger when the tonic minor chord arrives. Compare the diatonic move of Em–Am with the move E–Am. The G♯ note moves by a half step to A.

Exercise 102.

Write V–I progressions in the keys of E minor, B minor, D minor, and G minor, using a major triad for the V chord.

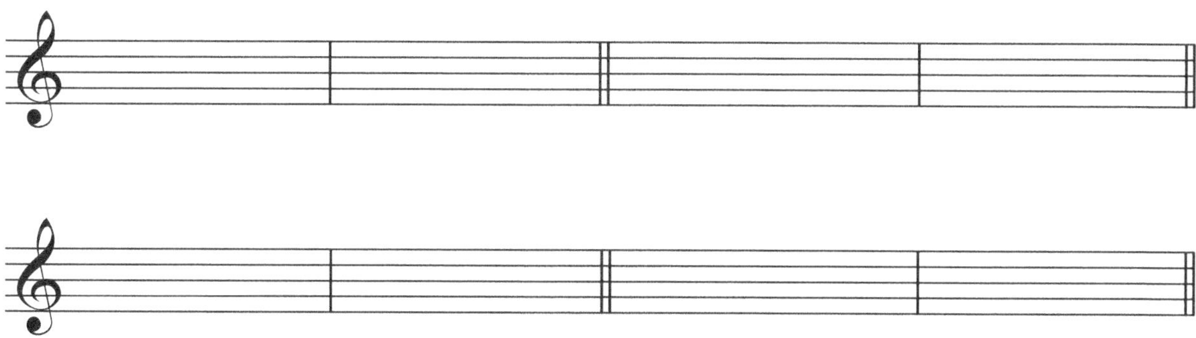

This new note is a raised or major 7th in the overall minor key. It is also called a *leading tone*, because it leads your ear toward the root of the upcoming I chord. The same sound happens melodically, which means that the familiar *natural* minor scale now has a major 7th degree and is called a *harmonic* minor scale.

A Harmonic Minor Scale

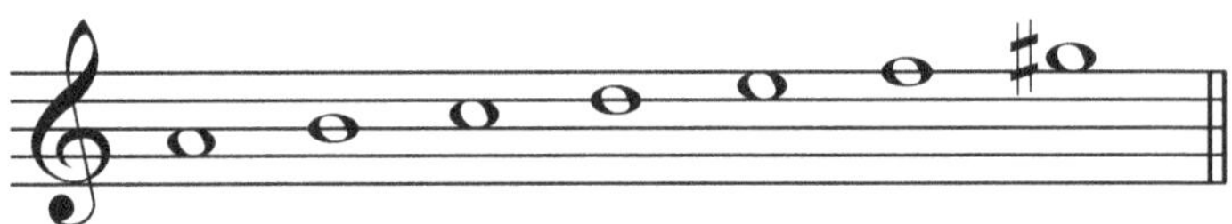

The new tone occurs most often on the V chord in a minor key. The root of the scale will usually not fall on a downbeat with the V chord. Listen to the chords then play the notes in this example.

Exercise 103.

Without placing key signatures at the beginning of the line, write harmonic minor scales on the staff using the I–V–V–V–I progression like the one above, in the keys of Em, Dm, Gm, and Cm.

Besides the V in a minor key, any minor chord that descends by a 5th may have its 3rd raised to increase the sense of resolution when its respective I arrives. When this is done, a sort of temporary or false key center is produced; the target or would-be I chord is said to be *tonicized*. The preceding chord is called the "V of" the upcoming chord: V/iii, V/vi, and so on. These short key-center sounds only last for a few beats and are not true key changes, but we should learn to recognize them, even when the chord names are not written out.

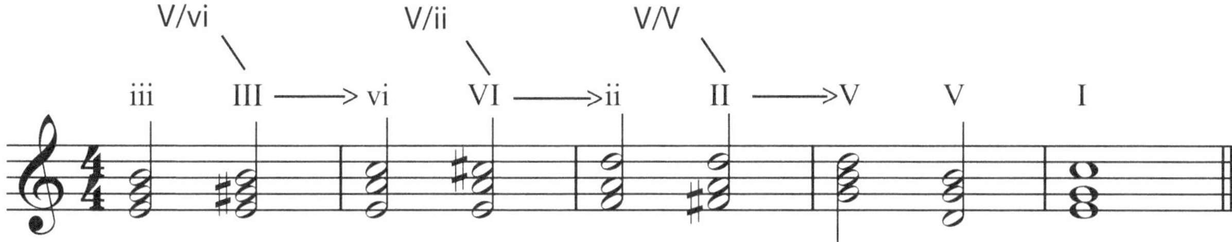


Exercise 104.
  Name the triads in this arpeggiated exercise. Work out the shapes and play with the metronome.

Now we know how to recognize what may be the most common accidentals: 1) when reading in a major key, a diatonic minor chord has its 3rd raised and 2) in a minor key, a sharp raises the 7th, or a natural sign cancels a flat on the 7th that was previously dictated by the key signature, changing the vm to V. Both are a form of leading tone.

## Seventh Chords

By stacking another note atop the triads (1–3–5), we get 7th chords (1–3–5–7). Here are the 7th chords in the key of C major. The triad qualities stay the same with the addition of the new note, but by staying diatonic we get major 7ths on I and IV, and minor 7ths added to all the others.

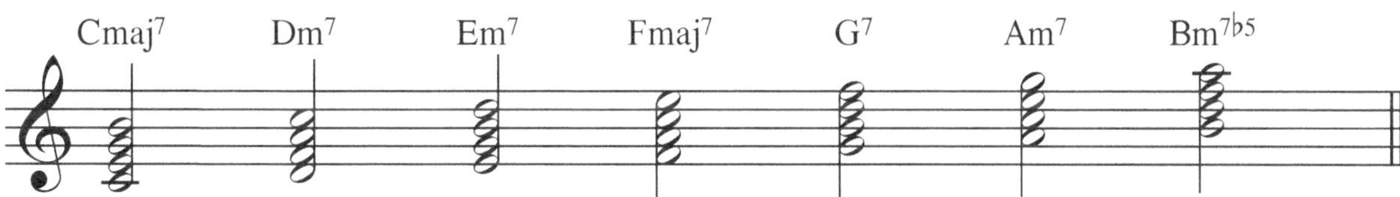

Cover up the solutions below and answer:

1. Which chords are maj7 in quality?
2. Which chords have a minor 3rd and a minor 7th?
3. Which chord has a minor 3rd, diminished 5th, and minor 7th?
4. Which chord has a major 3rd but a minor 7th?
5. What is the quality of the four-note IV chord in a major key?

1. Imaj7, IVmaj7
2. iim7, iiim7, vim7, viim7♭5
3. viim7♭5
4. V7
5. maj7

You could play those *close-voiced* (all stacked 3rds when in root position) 7th chords by starting in open position, keeping each root on the 5th string, and moving up the fretboard, but it's not necessary to make those stretches right away. To make 7th-chord voicings easier to play you can raise the 3rd by an octave. This is a common interval shape to see on the staff in guitar music: a 5th, a 3rd, and a 4th stacked together are a stock *open-voiced* 7th chord with the root on the bottom.

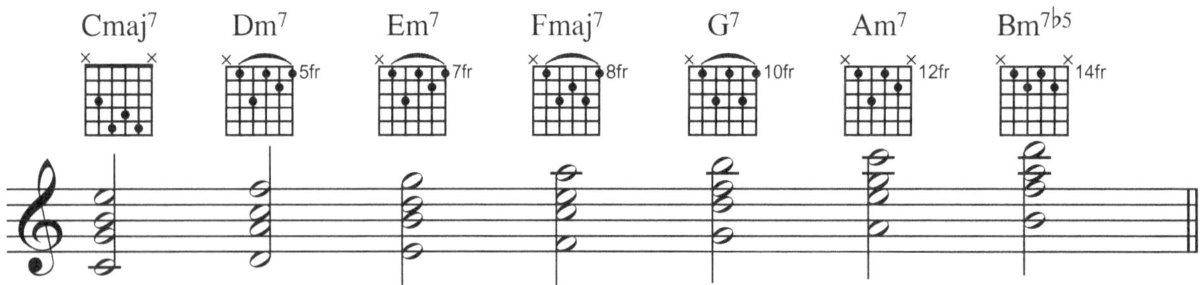


Depending on the style of music, a 7th chord may be substituted for any triad on the same root. We're paying special attention here to the V7 chord, the effect it produces, and how that effect is applied in other places in a progression, producing accidentals in the music that we can learn to recognize.

With a minor 7th included in the V chord (G–F is a minor 7th interval), we have a new chord type, the *dominant 7th*. The type is signified by the number 7 alone following the chord name. Using this chord adds to the tension-release effect of the V–I move. While its 3rd resolves up to the root of the I chord, the 7th moves down to its nearest destination, the 3rd of the I. In a minor V-I there are already two half-step resolutions, but we can use a 7th chord there too. The half-step resolution is the driving force behind most Western (classically-influenced) music.

Exercise 105.

Write V7-I progressions in Bm, Em, Cm, and Gm. Start with any inversions you like, but keep smooth voice leading.

As with major triads, a dominant chord may usually be substituted for any chord whose root is moving by an ascending 4th or descending 5th. Each chord in the iii–vi–ii–V cycle may be changed into a dominant chord for the purpose of increasing the momentum toward the next chord throughout the progression. The III7, VI7, and II7 are called *secondary dominants*.

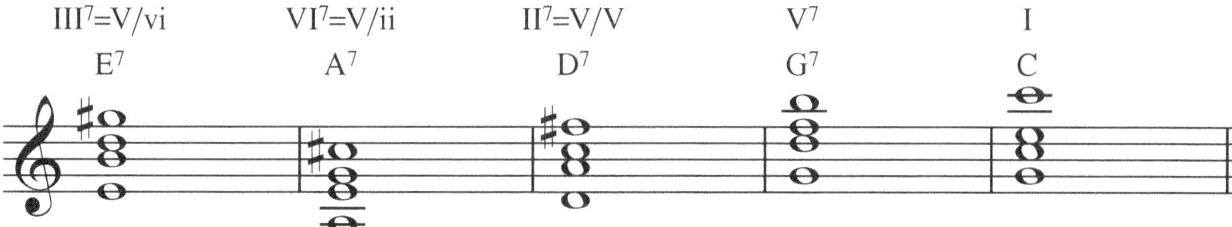


Once this custom was established, players and composers often decided to also make the I chord dominant instead of its diatonic major 7th quality. I7 is another secondary dominant: the V of IV (in the key of C, the IV is F. The V of that F is C7).  There is also a VII7, the V/iii.

The IV chord is also made into a dominant 7th, though it doesn't create exactly the same leading-tone effect. Finally, dominant chords that were once used to create tension are now thrown in without resolution to the expected chord, just because people have grown used to and now like hearing them, producing lots of blues, jazz, rock, pop, and country progressions. We won't analyze all the harmonic functions of dominant chords here. We do want to recognize, however, that they are often the source of accidentals in music. If we know what chords are being implied, we can read more easily.

Another source of accidentals is a little easier to understand and read. *Passing tones* may be added between diatonic steps of a scale, producing jazzy *chromatic* licks and melody lines.

Exercise 106.

Note the "shuffle feel" indication over this example. Play all eighth-note attacks as if they were shuffle rhythms. Think New Orleans-style blues as you run through it a few times and you'll get the feel. The challenge is to figure out the chords, using the accidentals and your ear. Mark each measure with a chord name (there is one measure with chord changes on beats 1 and 3); mark any passing tones with a "p."

## Practice

1. Work out harmonic minor scales by raising the 7th of the minor scale patterns you already know.

2. Draw frame or horizontal neck diagrams and practice diatonic 7th arpeggios with the metronome, using all five possible root shapes. This should take several months to master, but it'll drastically improve your playing in the long run.

3. Write out 12-bar blues progressions in different keys, then write out your own solos like the one above to follow the chords. There are many variations on the progression. Probably the most common one is shown here, with each symbol representing one measure. All the chords are dominant 7ths.

| I | IV | I | I |
|---|----|---|---|
| IV | IV | I | I |
| V | IV | I | V |

# Chapter 14: Octave Transposition

There are many topics we could keep adding to this book: more chords, scales, and arpeggios, more fretboard positions, more time signatures, modal music, exotic rhythms, and so on, until it's as thick as the L.A. phone book. But this is meant to be a workbook to teach you the system of music notation, and you've probably done enough written exercises for that basic understanding by now. It's time for you to start honing your skills by writing and reading some music that is of personal interest (or other profit) to you.

Before I release you into the wild, however, there's one more thing to know that would come as quite a shock if you met it unprepared on a job. So far we've been reading notation strictly as if it were written with the guitar in mind by the composer, but in real life you're going to encounter a lot of music that was written generically for any instrument that can play a melody.

The guitar is actually one of the *octave-transposing* instruments. The notes we play when reading music written just for the guitar sound an octave **lower** than other instruments would play them. For example, the C on the first ledger line below the staff, *middle C*, would sound an octave higher when read by a pianist or singer. When reading music originally intended for these **non-transposing** instruments, we could play the C on the 3rd string instead of the 6th.

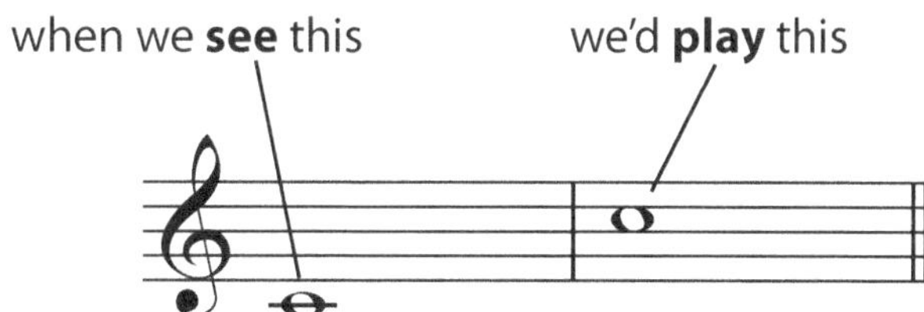


You should assume that any piano/vocal lead sheets or treble-clef parts for wind, brass, or string instruments should be played an octave higher than written, so that they sound in the intended register. If you don't make this transposition, you may risk having your melody buried by the band. You might even have to transpose parts that were written for guitar, because composers may forget or ignore the fact that it customarily sounds an octave lower than written.

Exercise 107.

For this melody, first write the letter names of all the pitches. Then write the notes on the tab staff **an octave higher** in 5th position. Visualize the fretboard locations, then cover the tab and play the octave-higher notes while reading the original melody line and naming the pitches aloud. Work it up to a reasonable tempo so you can hear the melody.

Exercise 108.

Translate the tab notes onto the staff as they'd be written for a non-transposing instrument, an octave **lower** than usual for guitar. Any rests are provided. Refer to the written beat numbers and write the appropriate eighth notes and quarter notes with dots and/or ties.

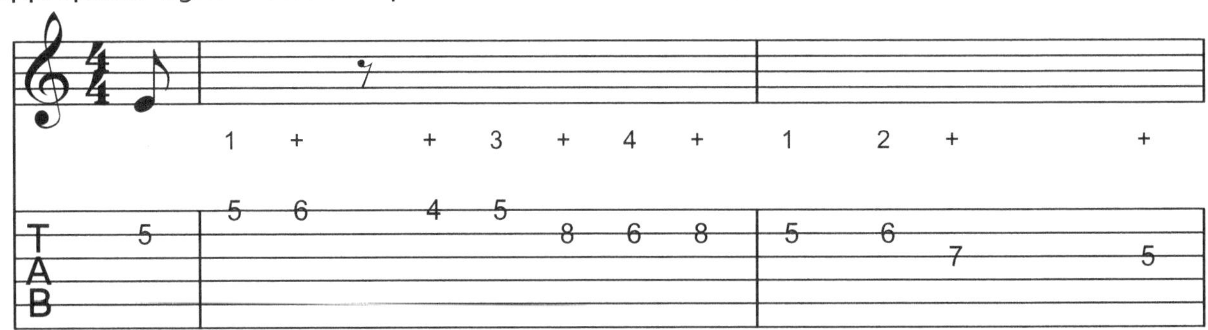

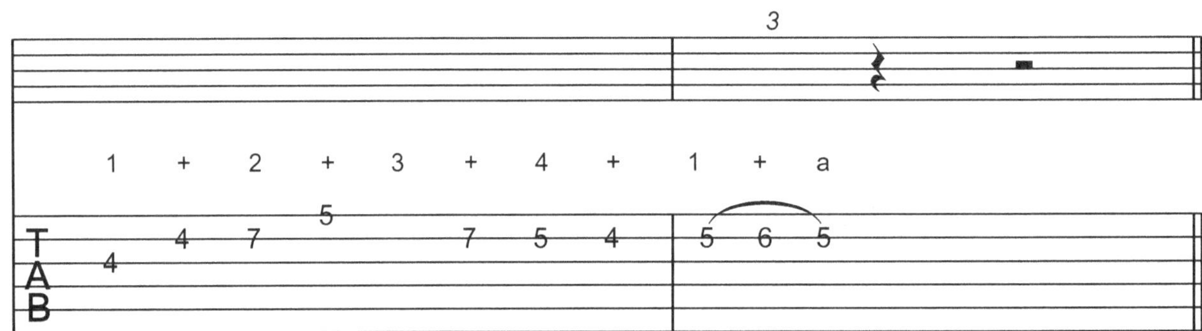

Though we won't make any transpositions that are more difficult than this in the book, there is also a lot of music out there that is transposed by intervals **other than an octave** to make it easier for certain instruments to read; for example, B♭ or E♭ trumpets, saxophones, and clarinets.

Of course you may read any music you can get your hands on "as is" if you are playing alone. But remember that when playing with others, if you are reading a B♭ trumpet chart, for example, you'd have to play all the notes a whole step lower than written to sound in tune with the rest of the band. The chord symbols over the notation may or may not be transposed also, depending on whether they were written for the rhythm section or to facilitate a trumpet solo.

The main things to take from this discussion are that when buying pop or jazz standards you should choose books designated for C instruments, and play the melodies an octave up.

## Twelfth Position

Taking melodies an octave higher will often require you to move beyond 5th-position reading. Though you should, when you're ready, start to work on reading in open, 3rd, 7th, and 9th positions so you can play things in the best-sounding places and with the easiest fingerings you can find, let's go to 12th position now so we can get more of those high notes. One nice thing about 12th-position reading is that the notes, scales, and chords are the same as those in open position, with the natural half steps in the same spots, so this will be some preparation for tackling that area.

Here are 12th-position natural pitches on the top five strings, in a frame and shown on the staff as they'd be written for guitar. If you learned your scales, you'll recognize this as a pattern-2 A minor or a

114

pattern-1 C major scale, without the 6th-string notes. We're going to stay off that 6th string for now.

Until we get to the last four ledger-line notes, the pitches on the staff are ones we already know by name, but we have to learn alternate fretboard locations that go with them. This makes the guitar a challenging instrument to read on, but you can do it without too much trouble if you know your scale patterns and the alphabet. Use them to get started. In the long run, you want to see a pitch and choose one of the possible places to play it without having to think about its name.

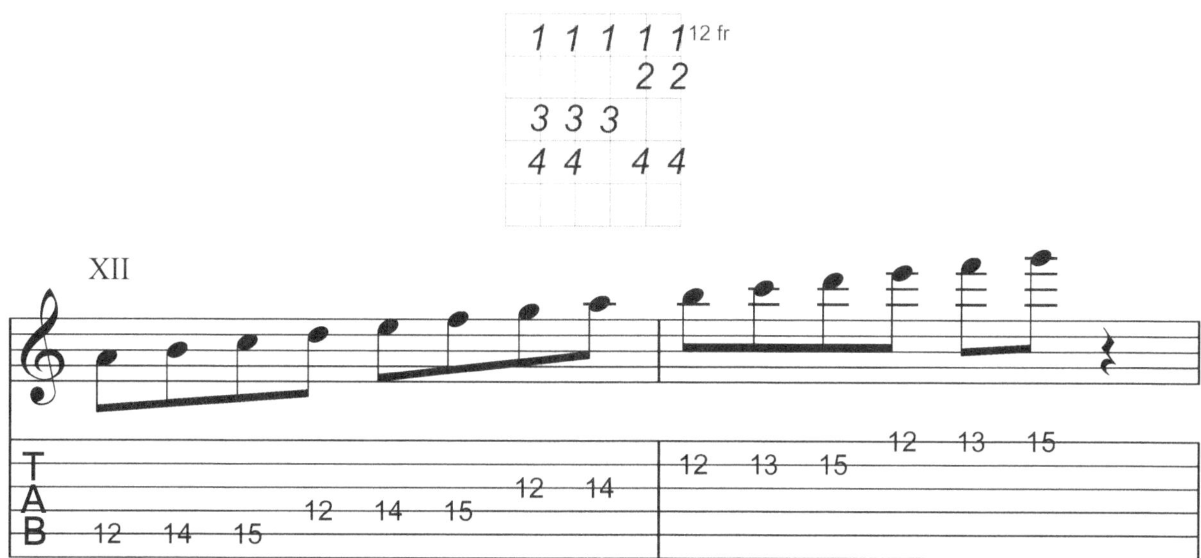

Just like for previous new notes, use verbalization and visualization to learn these new locations. Name each pitch aloud along with its string and fret number, and its place on the staff, as you play while looking at—and then away from—the diagram and the staff. Count all the way up to the fourth ledger line above the staff for the high G at the 15th fret.

To help name notes on ledger lines, remember the spaces inside the staff: they spell **FACE.** The same thing happens on the lines starting from the top of the staff and then into ledger-land. Anything you can think of like this that helps you learn them is great.

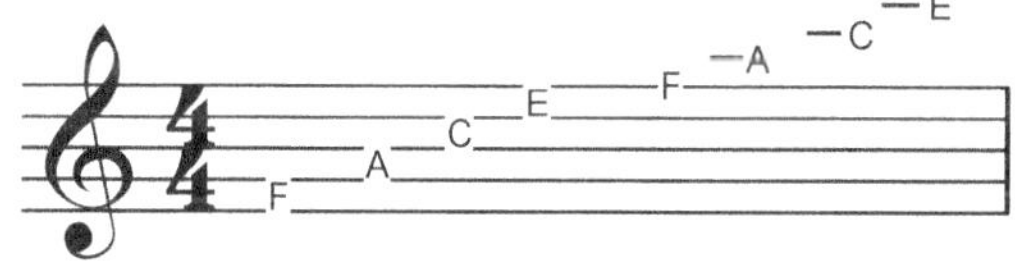

Going even higher, the **E**very **G**ood **B**oy **D**oes **F**ine series that applies to the staff lines starts over on the 3rd ledger line, so you can imagine another staff starting there. Though there is no limit to how high they can go, I hope you never have to read more than five or six ledger lines above a staff. We'll soon see an easier way to write high notes.

Exercise 109.

Translate this into tab at 12th position. Visualize where you'll play it, then count out the rhythm. Then cover up the tab and go for it.

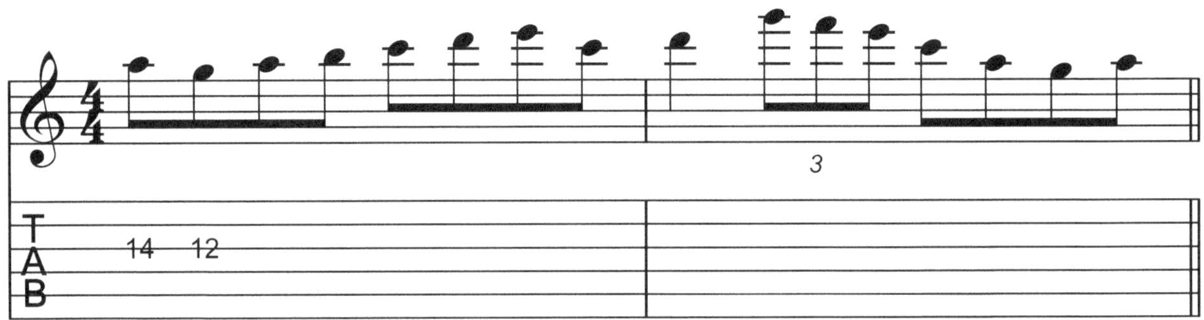

Exercise 110.

Translate the tablature into notation. Every pitch you'll write is an eighth note here. Keep your ledger lines spread evenly as if they were staff lines. This is a lick for a solo in A minor. Work it up to speed slowly so you can hear how it should sound.

Now here are the same 12th-position notes we've been using, but this time they appear on the staff as if they were originally written for a non-transposing instrument. I've just added a position mark as a reminder. Quickly recite the names and fretboard locations again, but with the alternate staff positions; for example, "A on the 12th fret of the 5th string, 2nd ledger line below the staff."

Of course, even though we're transposing these notes up by an octave, we could still play most of them in our familiar 5th-position reading area, starting with the A on the 7th fret of string 5. We'd just have to do some potentially-awkward position-shifting to get the last four notes. It's usually better to read an entire phrase in one position if you can, and perform any shifts during rests.

## 8va

Short for the Italian word *ottava* (*all' ottava alta—at the high octave*), an **8va** (just say "eight V-A") over the music **explicitly** tells you to play the notes an octave higher than written. The *8va* may be followed by a dotted line bracketing a group of notes. Notes after the bracket are read in the original octave. You should use the *8va* symbol to avoid excessively-high ledger lines. While you're learning the concept, take your time and try to get inside the music in the example—learn it and play it convincingly. This is part of the same solo as the previous example, with the chords provided so you can hear how the lick works over the chord changes.

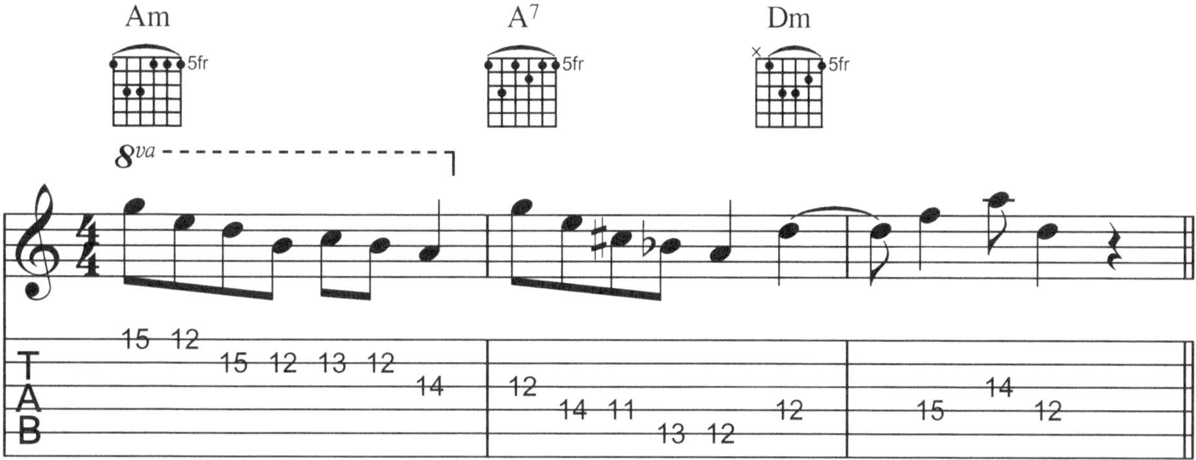


If the *8va* passage is longer than a few measures, the dotted line may be omitted. The *8va* instruction is understood to continue until the end of the piece or until you see the word **loco** (*place*, as in "go back to playing in the original place"), as shown in the next example.

Remember that the word *loco*, thought it means *place,* only dictates in which octave the notes on the staff should be played. It does not refer to a position change on the instrument, though that may sometimes be necessary. In this example we can still reach all the lower notes by playing in 12th position. When preparing to read, visualize the possible positions for notes and phrases, paying special attention to the highest and lowest pitches, and decide on the easiest place for performing the passage.

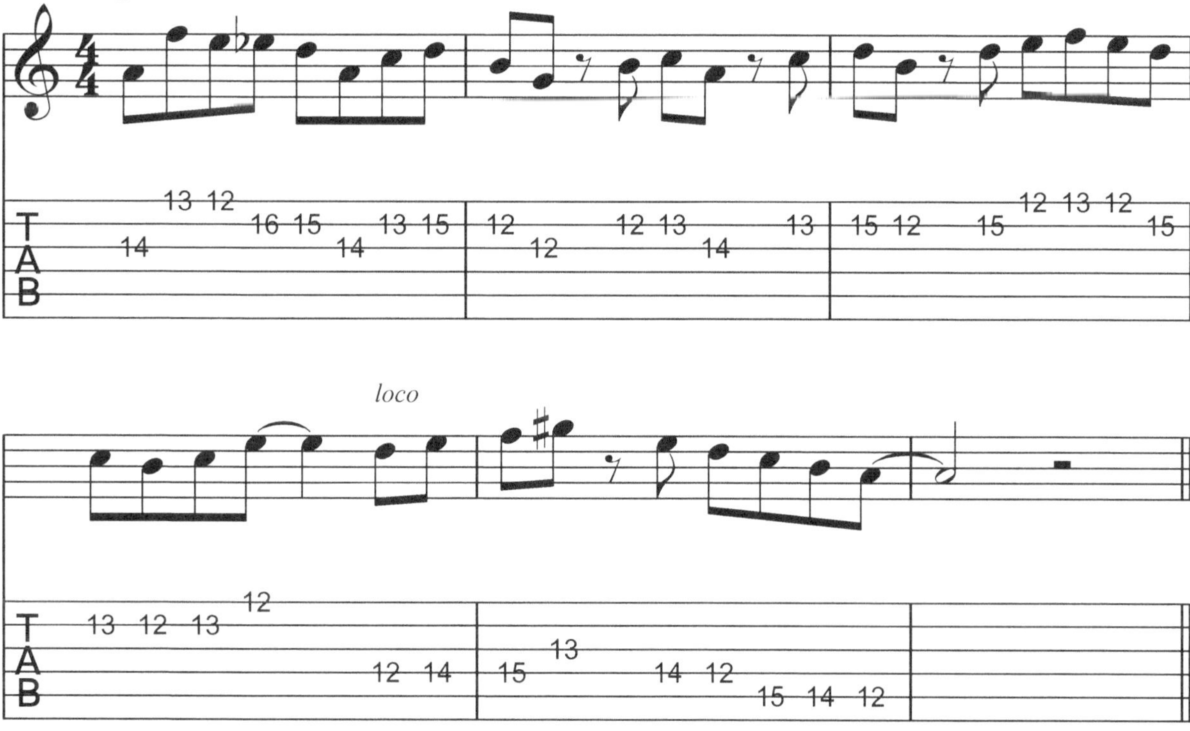

Exercise 111.

First play this example and decide where you'd like to make position shifts. Write position marks using Roman numerals at the places you shift. Then recopy the notation onto the blank staff, making it easier to read by using *8va* only when the pitches stay mostly above the 2nd ledger line above the staff. Do not change all of it; just the high notes.

## *15ma* and *8vb*

Once in a while you may see *15ma* (*quindicesima*, 15 steps or two octaves higher) written to make very high notes easier to read. *8vb* (*all' ottava bassa*) may be placed **below** the staff with its bracket pointing up to show that a passage is to be played an octave **lower** than written. *8vb* is not really necessary for standard-tuned guitar parts, because they don't go more than three ledger lines below the staff, but you should know about it for special cases like drop-tuned parts.

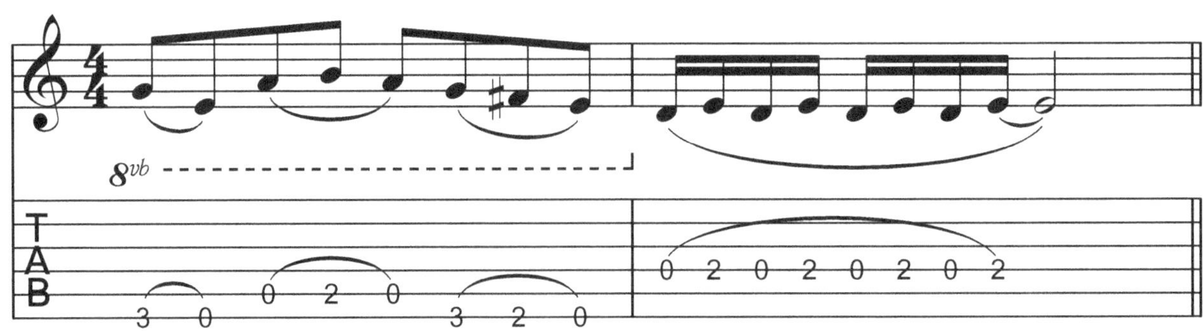


118

**Practice**

1. Continue the fretboard memorization process by reciting aloud everything about the 12th-position notes as you did with those in 5th position: letter names, strings, frets, fingers, and their locations on the staff when reading either in place on ledger lines or *8va*.

2. Get some books of standard tunes, like *The Ultimate Fake Book*, *The Real Book*, and *The New Real Book*, and start reading new melodies that require octave transposition every day. Play them both as written and an octave up.

3. Write out some melodic music every day, even if it is only a few measures. It can be anything: familiar sounds like Christmas carols, TV themes and commercials, pop songs from the radio, or your own compositions. The goal is to read and write enough that eventually you see the notation in your head when you hear music, and to hear music in your head whenever you see notes on a page. Keep going, and it'll happen.

**Afterword**

If you have made it to the end of this book and completed all the exercises, congratulations! You haven't been exposed to every aspect of reading there is (that should take a lifetime), but you have a foundation for understanding larger chords, more-complex rhythms, higher or lower melodies, and are ready to start reading and writing some real music.

# Solutions to Exercises

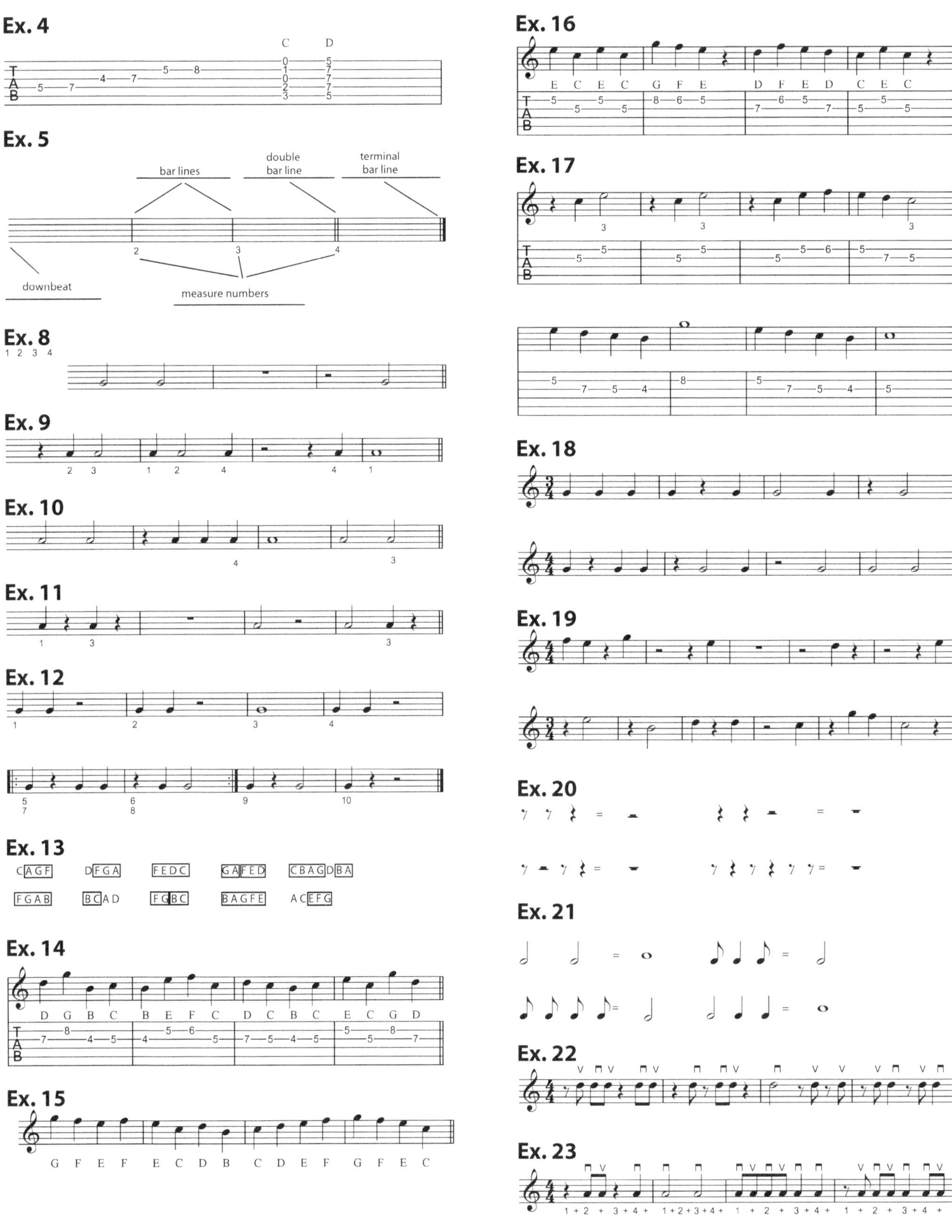

120

**Ex. 24**

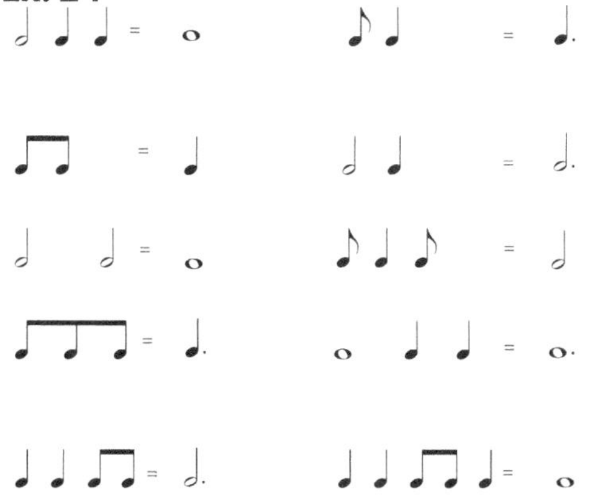

**Ex. 25**

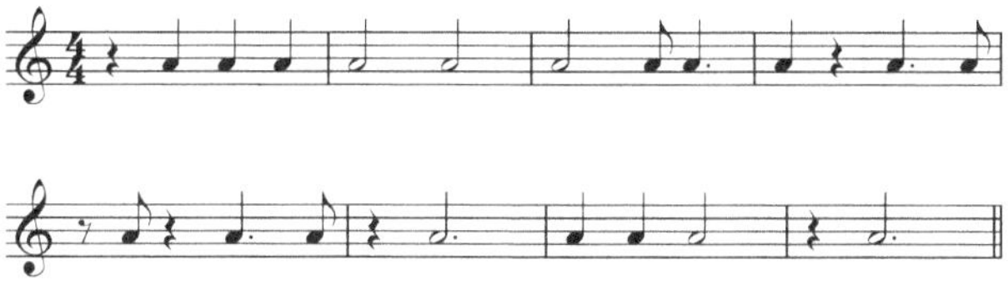

**Ex. 26**

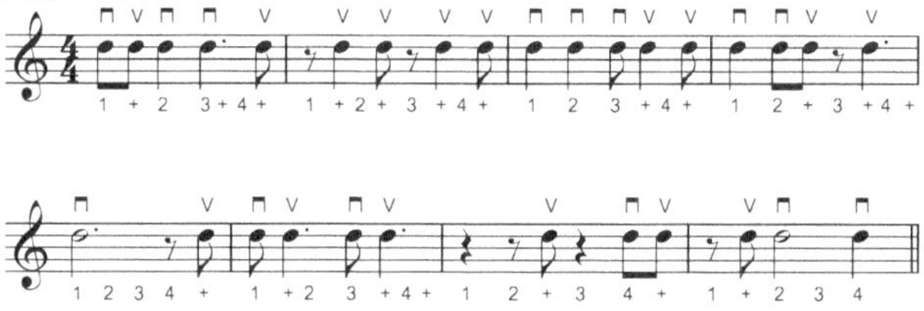

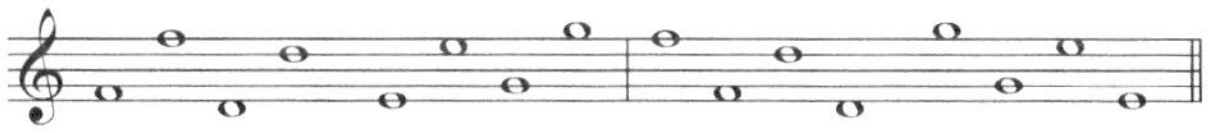

**Ex. 27 Eighth-Note Vocabulary**

**Ex. 28**

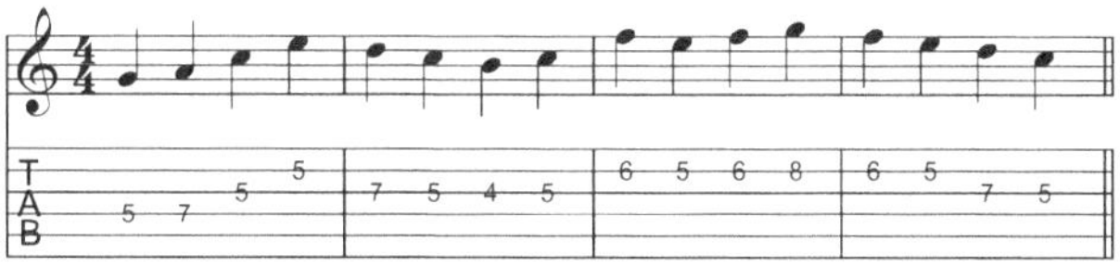

**Ex. 29**

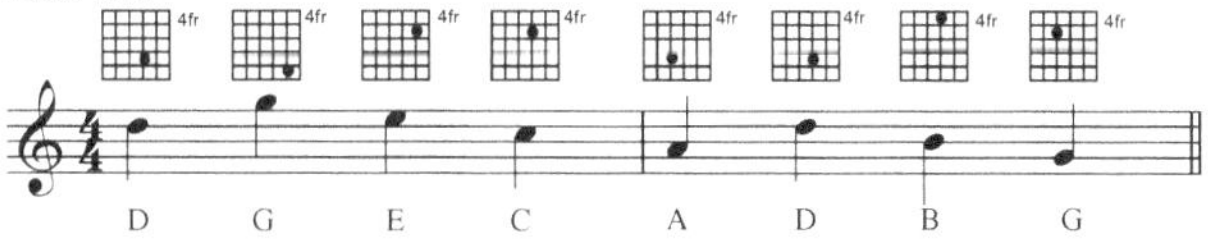

**Ex. 30**

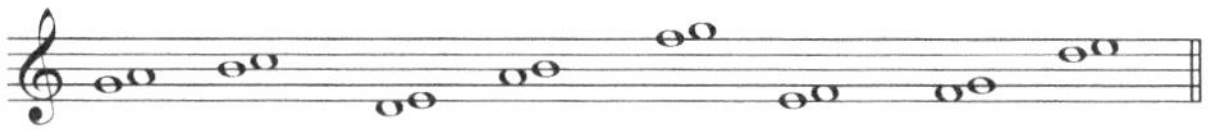

**Ex. 31**

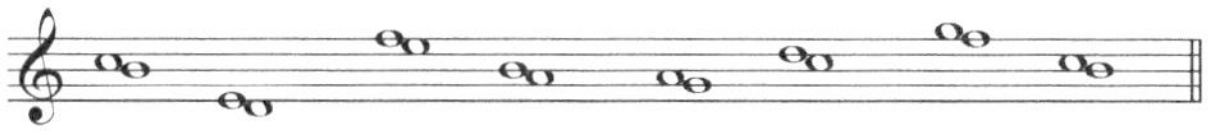

**Ex. 32**

**Ex. 33**

**Ex. 34**

**Ex. 35**

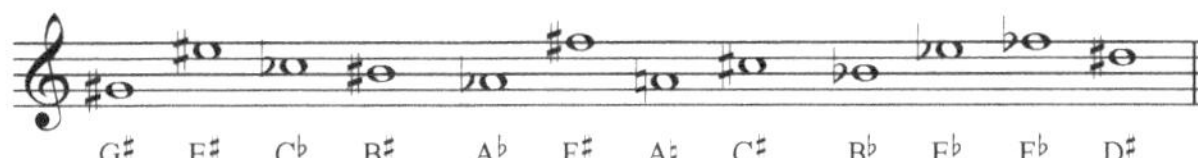


**Ex. 36**

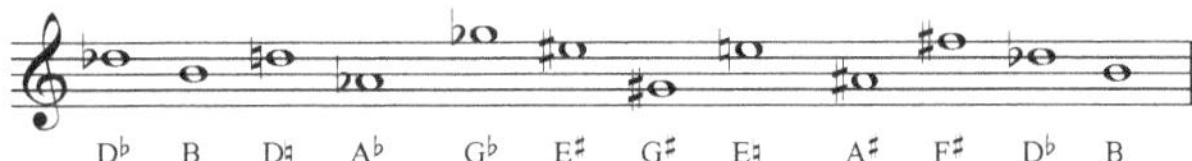


**Ex. 37**

**Ex. 38**

**Ex. 39**

**Ex. 40**

**Ex. 41**

**Ex. 42**

**Ex. 44**

**Ex. 45**

**Ex. 46**

**Ex. 47**

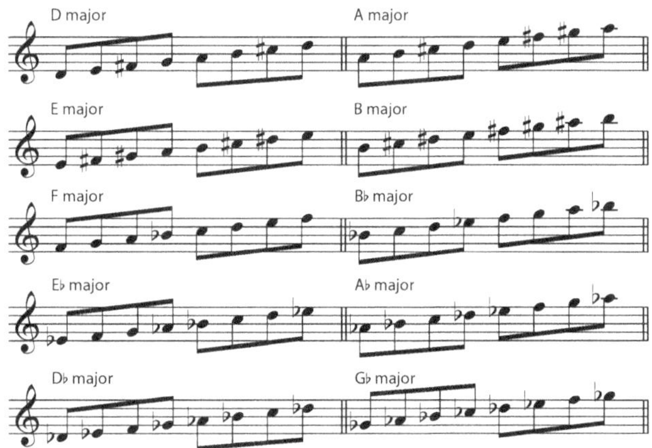


**Ex. 48**

**Ex. 49**

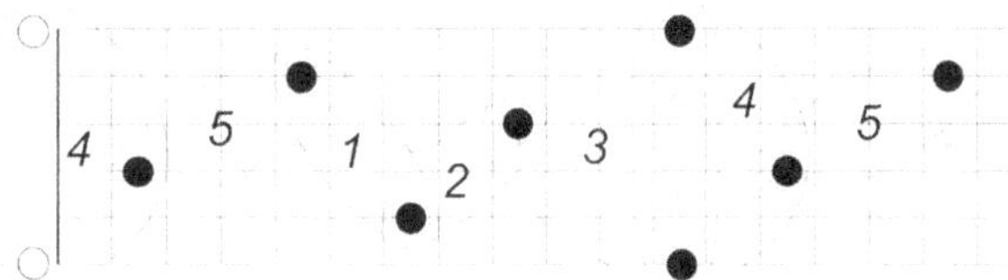

## Ex. 52

## Ex. 53

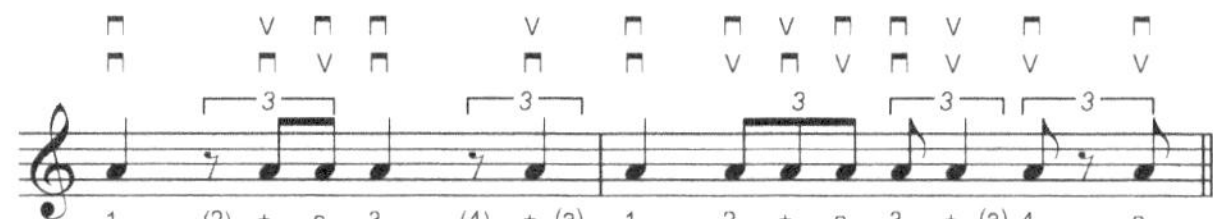

## Ex. 54

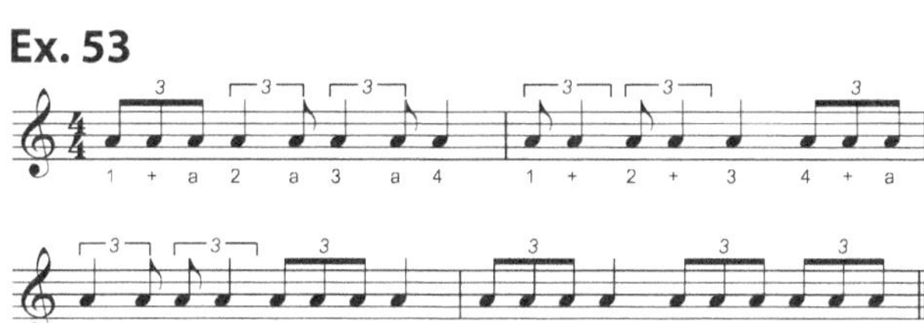

## Ex. 55

## Ex. 56

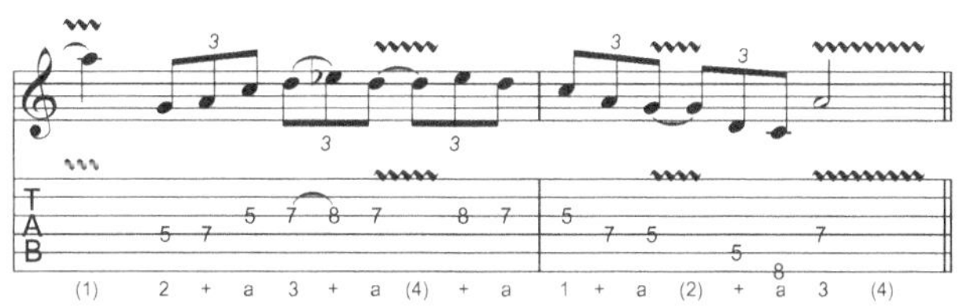

## Ex. 57

## Ex. 58

## Ex. 59

## Ex. 60

## Ex. 61, 62, Diatonic 3rds

## Ex. 63

## Ex. 64, Diatonic 4ths

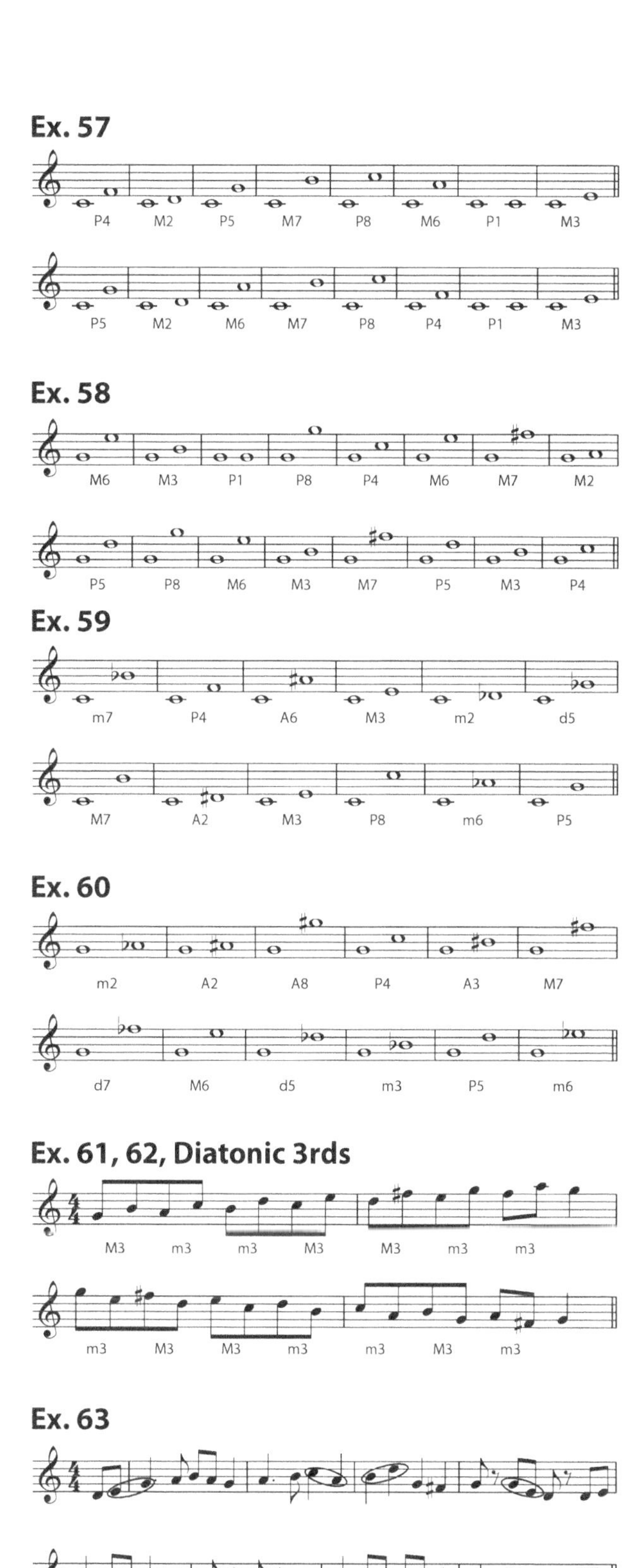

## Ex. 65, Diatonic 5ths

## Ex. 66, Diatonic 6ths

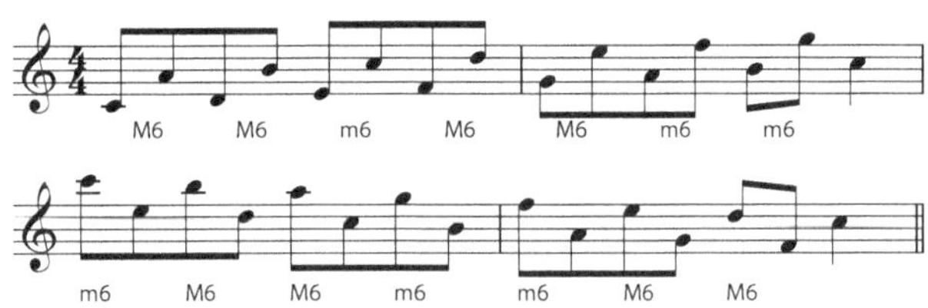


## Ex. 67

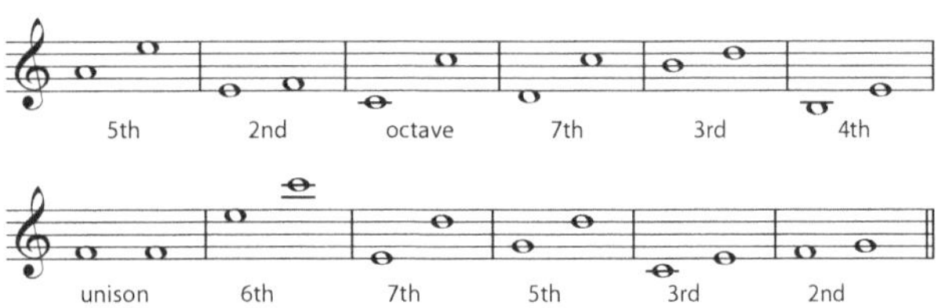


## Ex. 68

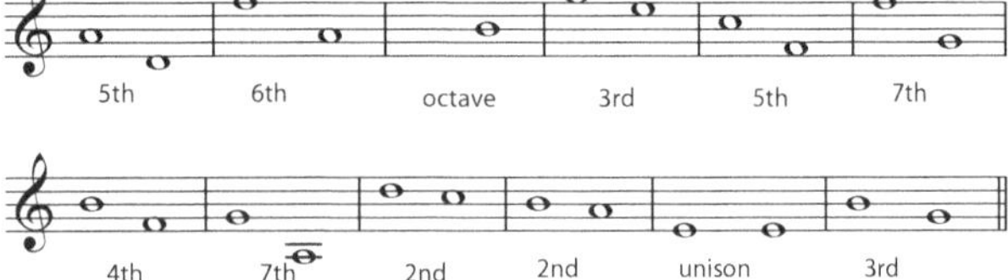


## Ex. 73

## Ex. 74

## Ex. 75

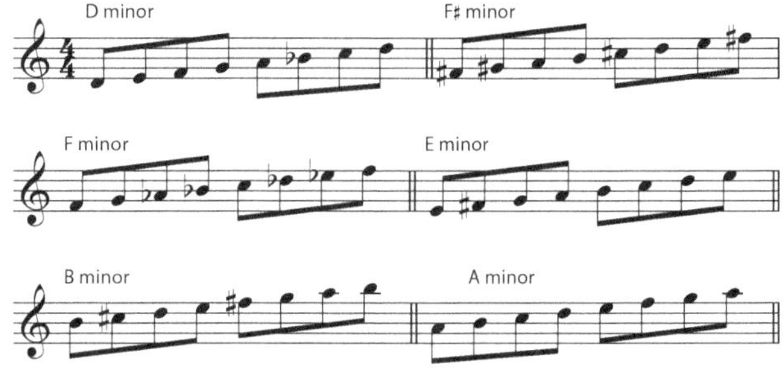


## Ex. 76

## Ex. 77

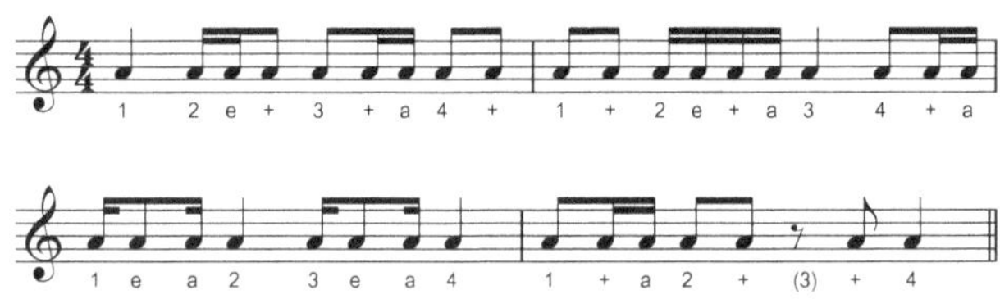


## Ex. 78

# Ex. 79 Sixteenth-Note Vocabulary

## Ex. 80

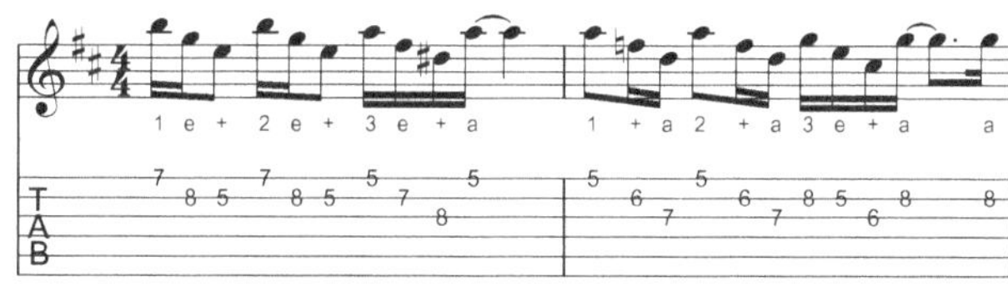

## Ex. 81

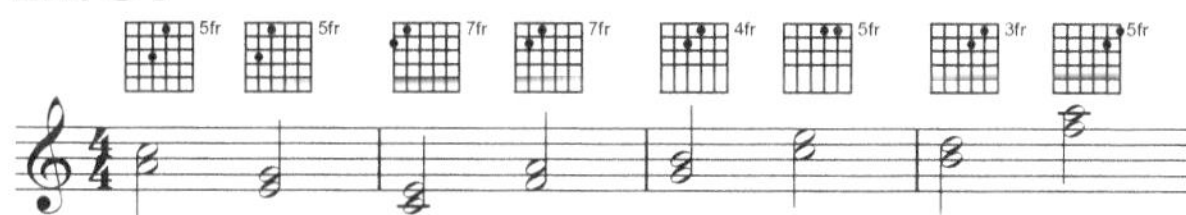

## Ex. 82

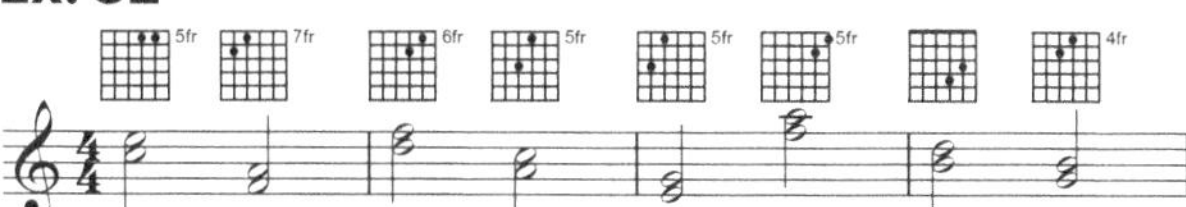

## Ex. 83

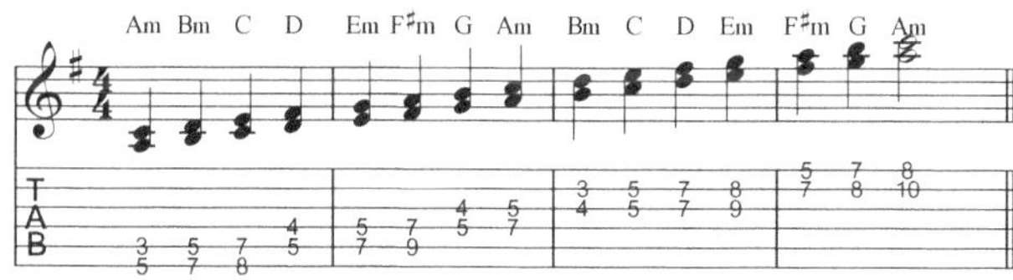

## Ex. 84

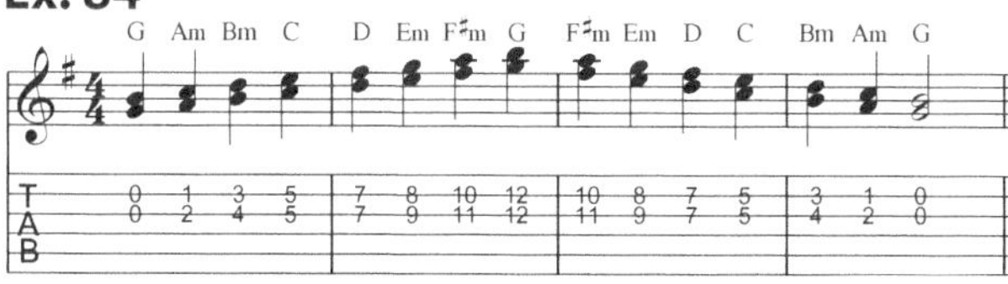

## Ex. 85

## Ex. 86

## Ex. 87

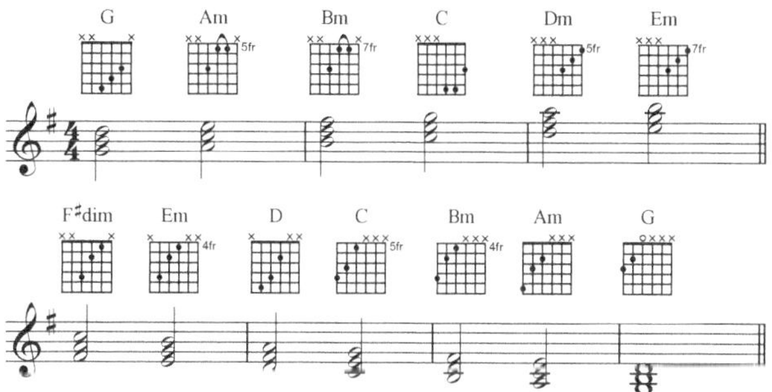

## Ex. 88

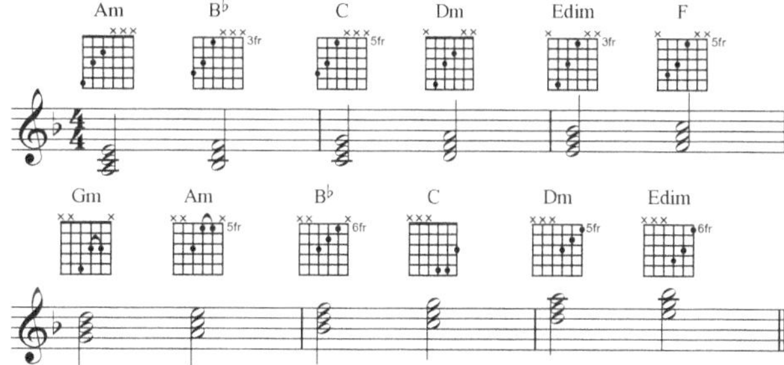

## Ex. 89

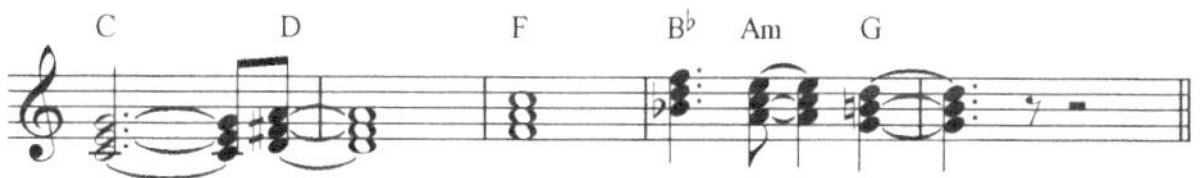

## Ex. 91

Ex. 90

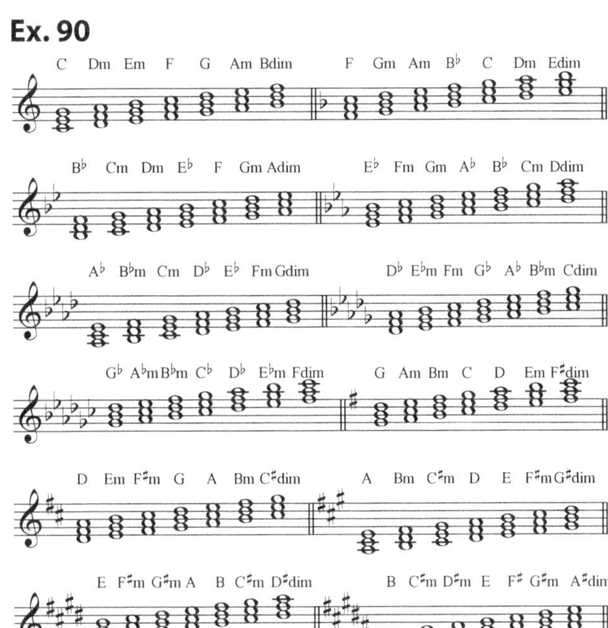
C Dm Em F G Am Bdim    F Gm Am B♭ C Dm Edim
B♭ Cm Dm E♭ F Gm Adim    E♭ Fm Gm A♭ B♭ Cm Ddim
A♭ B♭m Cm D♭ E♭ Fm Gdim    D♭ E♭m Fm G♭ A♭ B♭m Cdim
G♭ A♭m B♭m C♭ D♭ E♭m Fdim    G Am Bm C D Em F♯dim
D Em F♯m G A Bm C♯dim    A Bm C♯m D E F♯m G♯dim
E F♯m G♯m A B C♯m D♯dim    B C♯m D♯m E F♯ G♯m A♯dim
F♯ G♯m A♯m B C♯ D♯m E♯dim

Ex. 92

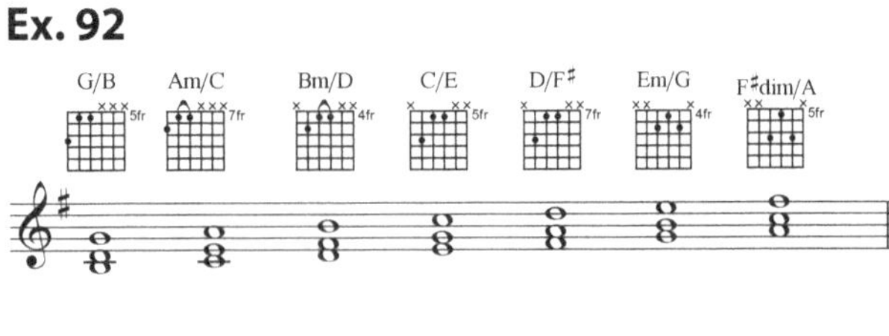
G/B  Am/C  Bm/D  C/E  D/F♯  Em/G  F♯dim/A

Ex. 93

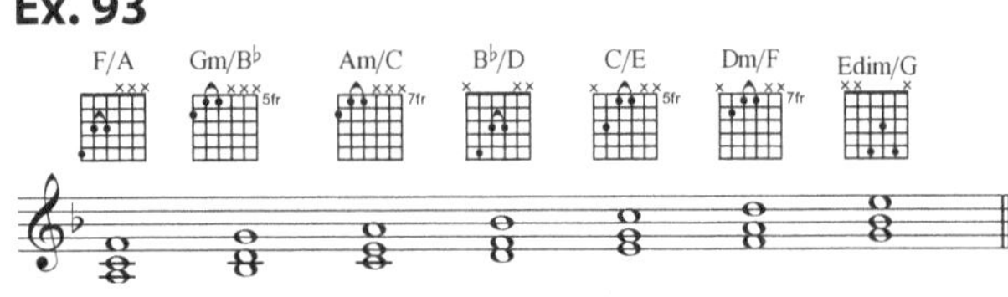
F/A  Gm/B♭  Am/C  B♭/D  C/E  Dm/F  Edim/G

Ex. 94

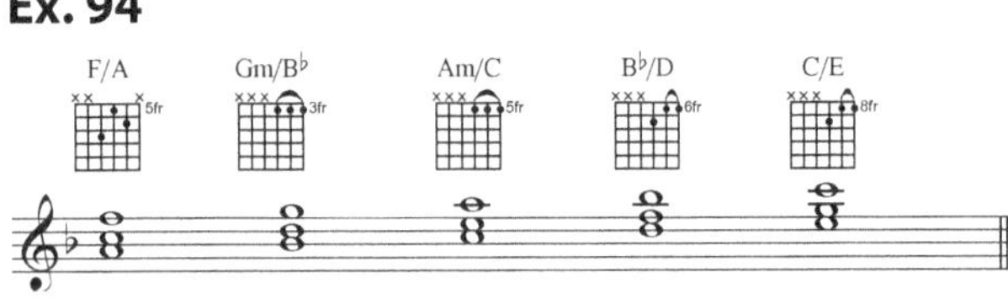
F/A  Gm/B♭  Am/C  B♭/D  C/E

Ex. 95

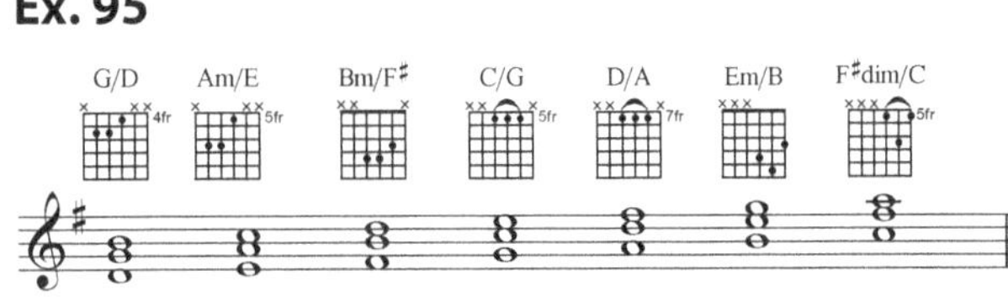
G/D  Am/E  Bm/F♯  C/G  D/A  Em/B  F♯dim/C

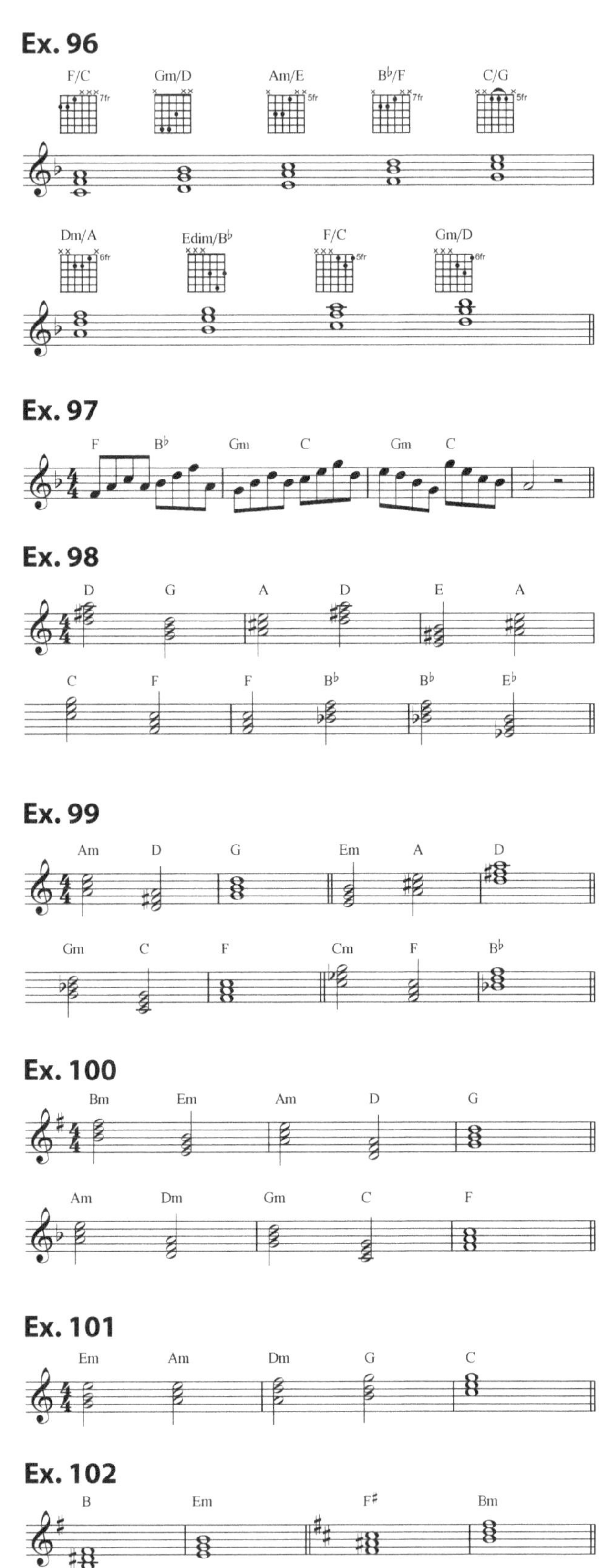
Ex. 96
F/C  Gm/D  Am/E  B♭/F  C/G
Dm/A  Edim/B♭  F/C  Gm/D

Ex. 97
F  B♭  Gm  C  Gm  C

Ex. 98
D  G  A  D  E  A
C  F  F  B♭  B♭  E♭

Ex. 99
Am  D  G  Em  A  D
Gm  C  F  Cm  F  B♭

Ex. 100
Bm  Em  Am  D  G
Am  Dm  Gm  C  F

Ex. 101
Em  Am  Dm  G  C

Ex. 102
B  Em  F♯  Bm
A  Dm  D  Gm

# Ex. 103

# Ex. 104

# Ex. 105

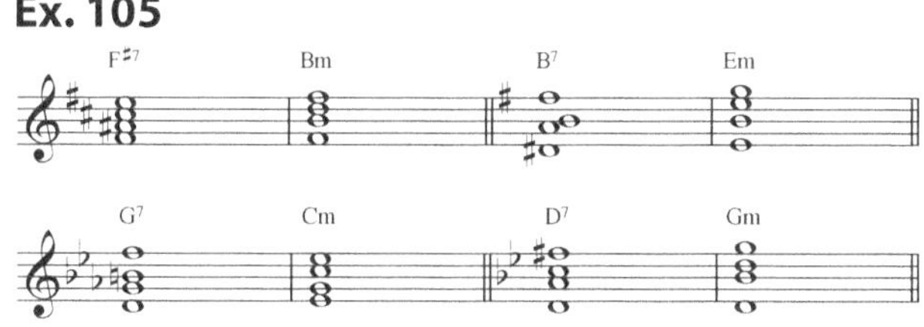

# Ex. 106

# Ex. 107

# Ex. 108

# Ex. 109

# Ex. 110

# Ex. 111

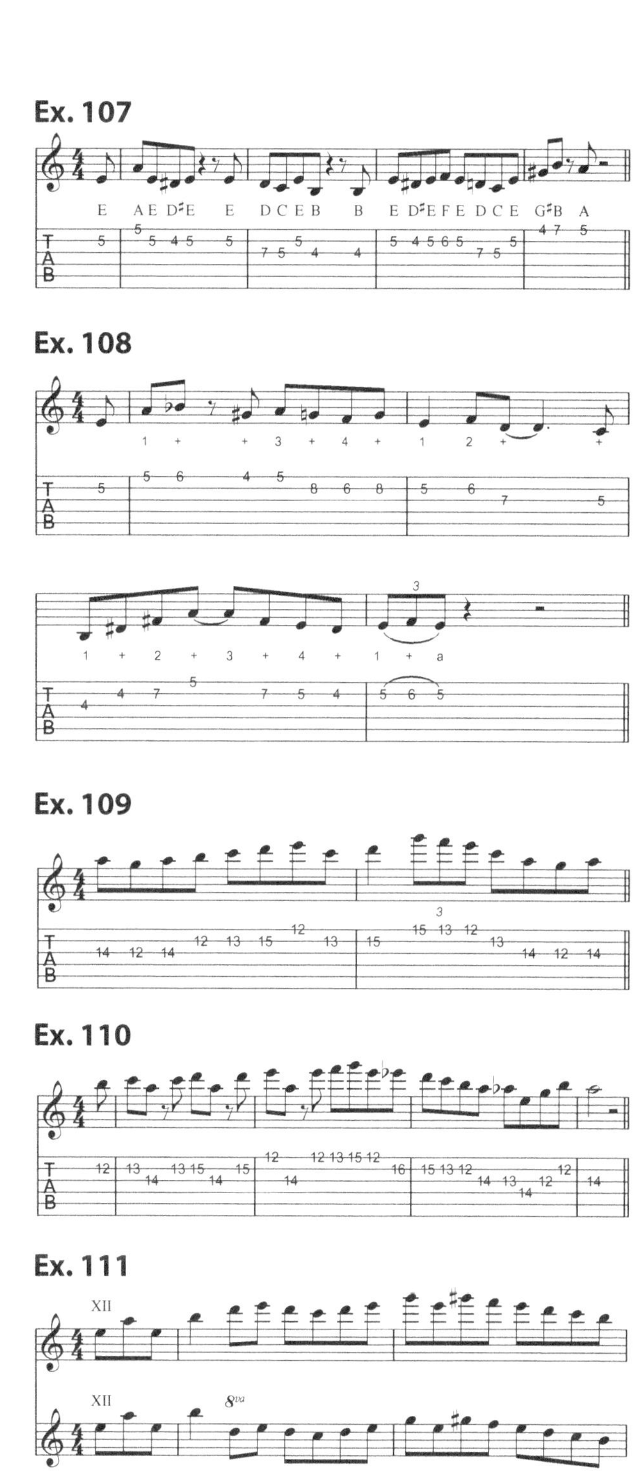